Growing Older, Getting Better

Ellen Shub

Growing Older, Getting Better

A Handbook for Women in the Second Half of Life

Jane Porcino

Addison-Wesley Publishing Company
Reading, Massachusetts • Menlo Park, California • London
Amsterdam • Don Mills, Ontario • Sydney

Many of the names accompanying the quotations are fictitious; the ages, however, are accurate.

Drawings by Kenneth J. Wilson, except for the drawings on page 257 which are used courtesy of The American Cancer Society.

Library of Congress Cataloging in Publication Data

Porcino, Jane.
    Growing older, getting better.

    Bibliography: p.
    Includes index.
    1. Middle aged women. 2. Middle aged women—Family relationships. 3. Middle aged women—Education. 4. Middle aged women—Diseases. 5. Middle aged women—Mental health. I. Title.
HQ1154.P647 1983   305.2'44   82-24438
ISBN 0-201-05593-7
ISBN 0-201-05592-9 (pbk.)

ABCDEFGHIJ-DO-89876543

Dedication

I dedicate this book to my husband, Chet, whose loving and loyal support has been steadfast, and to my seven unique and wonderful children: Joseph, Mary, Ann, John, Paul, Jeanne, and Vicky.

This book is especially dedicated to my firstborn, Joseph, who died recently at age 30 after a short, valiant fight with cancer. Joe respected and supported my work for older women, and it is a great personal sadness that he is not able to celebrate with me the publication of my first book.

Acknowledgments

I am grateful to the hundreds of women across the country who have shared portions of their lives with me through long letters and hours of conversation in the warmth of their homes.

Special thanks go to my daughter Ann, who advised and encouraged my efforts during the first tremulous weeks of writing, and to my daughter Jeanne, who read and offered advice as the book was nearing completion.

My sisters, Virginia Jacobs and Ann Dibble, and my friend Richard Grossman encouraged and supported me when I needed it most.

I am also deeply grateful to the six people on my doctoral committee who critically read and reread the manuscript over a two-year period: Leo McLaughlin, Beth Hess, Audrey Faulkner, Ellen McCall, Kendall Smith, and Roy Fairfield.

Several other people offered suggestions on individual sections of the book: Barbara Gross, Elaine Friedman, Peggy Bruhn, Antoinette Bosco, Gladys Engel, Carmella Heedles, Helen Murdoch, Marilyn Dahl, Judith Steinhart, Kathy Goggin, Rita Arditti, La Verne Gurley, JoAnn Sage, Barbara Rubin, Rosalie Marinelli, Rose Walton, Lois Stein, Dana Van Buskirk, Anna Manigault, Janet Ashton-Glossock, Dee Dee Jamison, Clemmie Barrie, Jane Nodstrum, and Stephanie Covington.

The health sections of the book were carefully reviewed by Malkah T. Notman, M.D., of Harvard Medical School and Tufts New England Medical Center, and Michael Dolamore, M.B.B.S., of Colchester, England.

And finally I offer thanks to my editors, Doe Coover and Cyrisse Jaffee, my agent, Lynn Davis, and to all the other friends, relatives, and colleagues who offered continuing love and support.

Jane Porcino

Contents

Foreword by Maggie Kuhn   xiii
Introduction   1

Part I. Women in Transition   5
Introduction   7

Chapter 1. Family Matters   13
Long-Lasting Marriages   13
Postparenting Years   17
The Grandmother Role   21
Resources   25

Chapter 2. Going It Alone   27
Lifelong Singlehood   28
Divorce and Separation   31
Widowhood: An Ending and a New
    Beginning   42
Resources   54

Chapter 3. New Beginnings   59
   Remarriage after Forty   59
   Motherhood after Forty   63
   Reentry to School   67
   Resources   79

Chapter 4. Women in Crisis   83
   Aging Parents   83
   A Disabled Spouse   87
   Domestic Violence   92
   Resources   95

Chapter 5. Lifestyles in Transition   99
   Remaining in Your Own Home   100
   Sharing a Home: A Nontraditional
     Lifestyle   103
   Traditional Housing Options   106
   Resources   111

Chapter 6. Financial Independence   115
   Women in the Work Force   115
   Resources   135

Chapter 7. Thriving, Not Merely Surviving   139
   Maintaining Mental Health   139
   Being Our Age and Learning to Like It   151
   Resources   155

Part II. Our Changing Bodies   159
   Introduction   161

Chapter 8. Menopause: A Turning Point   167
   Signals of Menopause   168

Hysterectomy   177
Resources   182

Chapter 9. Sexuality and Intimacy as We Age   185
Resources   196

Chapter 10. Fitness after Forty   199
You're Never Too Old to Exercise   199
Eating May Be Hazardous to Your Health   206
Resources   223

Chapter 11. Osteoporosis   227
Resources   231

Chapter 12. Common Afflictions of Older
Women   237
Cardiovascular Disease   237
Coronary Heart Disease   238
Hypertension   242
Stroke   244
Rheumatic Disease   248
Lupus Erythematous   249
Cancer   253
Breast Cancer   254
Other Types of Cancer   265
Lung Cancer   265
Colon and Rectal Cancer   267
Uterine Cancers   268
Skin Cancer   270
Diabetes   273
Resources   280

Chapter 13. Other Health Concerns   289
Urinary Incontinence   289

Hearing Changes   293
Vision Capacity of Women over Forty   299
Skin   305
Hair   309
Dental Health and Dental Problems   312
Resources   316

Chapter 14. Women and Addiction   319
Alcoholism   319
Drug Use and Abuse   328
Resources   336

Chapter 15. The Economics of Good Health   339
Medicare   340
Medicaid   341
Medi-Gap   342
Four Million Women Have No Health
    Insurance   343
Resources   344

Conclusion   347
Older Women—A Bibliography   353
Index   357

Foreword

Jane Porcino has written a unique and useful handbook for the encouragement and empowerment of women in midlife and late life. *Growing Older, Getting Better* is a reference and a resource, a handbook to share with other women (and men) who are aging.

In this new age of liberalism and change, women have opportunities and challenges beyond the dreams and imaginations of our mothers and sisters of earlier decades. New ways of thinking and ordering our lives are described in the pages that follow and deserve to be considered with an open mind.

The changes needed in society and in ourselves will not be easy to make or instantaneous in coming. Many women have lived so long in the small private worlds of their homes and families, their plight worsened by isolation from each other and by the lack of supportive relationships so essential to well-being.

Older women from all walks of life must take an active part in changing and redesigning our lives. We are not wrinkled babies. We are a new breed of older women. There are more of us alive today than at any other time in history. We are better educated and healthier. Together we have to fight the combined impact of ageism and sexism in our society, and through this book Jane Porcino encourages women to join together in this struggle.

As an old feminist, I would like to see women coming together to establish a new kind of selfhood—not only for ourselves but also for our lovers, husbands, fathers, and brothers.

I'm glad I've reached seniority. I feel free to speak out and act in ways I wasn't able to when I was younger. I've outlived a great deal of my opposition. I don't dye my hair, can't afford a face-lift, and regard my wrinkles as badges of distinction—I've worked hard for them. It's really wonderful to be able to tap into the incredible energy of the young while making use of the knowledge and experience that comes after living a long, full life.

Old age is not a disease. It is strength and survivorship, a triumph over all kinds of vicissitudes. In our old age we become more free to innovate; we're free to burst out and be creative. At 76, I've made a resolution to do something outrageous at least once a week. We're getting older, and we may as well enjoy it. Old age is the time to take risks and initiate social changes.

Jane Porcino does *not* feel that the problems older women now face are inevitable. She provides us with the information we need to achieve maximum good health, whether we're 40, 60, 80, or 100, and to thrive in our lives, not merely survive.

Women have an enormous potential to live out the second half of their lives with dignity and zest. This book gives us essential information as we take responsibility for our own wellness and well-being.

Jane Porcino is a Gray Panther writing for all of us who will age, if we're lucky. I am excited by her contribution.

Maggie Kuhn
National Convener, Gray Panthers

Ellen Shub

Introduction

Perhaps once a century, there's a sort of act of faith, and there's an enormous heave forward in one country . . . an act of imagination of what's possible for the whole world . . . each time the dream gets stronger . . . we need to keep the dream alive . . . we are the boulder-pushers.

Doris Lessing

The history of this book goes back more than ten years. In my forty-eighth year I suddenly felt, for the first time in my life, that I no longer had a specific role to fulfill—or a certain future to look foward to. I lost my sense of direction, my self-image plunged, and I went into a state of panic and deep depression. When I reached out for help there was none to be found. My friends, many of whom were slightly younger, didn't want to discuss the problems of midlife, those changes that signaled aging. My gynecologist patted me on the head as if I were a little child, told me it was all "just part of menopause," and increased my estrogen dosage. I didn't know much about menopause, and my attempts to find out more about it were frustrating. My gynecologist had few answers; a library search turned up nothing. I felt absolutely alone.

Since that time my personal renaissance as an active older woman has been the result in large part of loving support from my husband and seven children, who helped me when I needed it and encouraged me to move on with my life in new ways. But it was a consciousness-raising group that made my initial reemergence and the realization of those "new ways" possible.

We were eight women who met weekly for almost a year. We helped each other talk out feelings about our lives and growing older; we learned to trust ourselves and each other as we discovered new choices and options. We gathered strength and confidence from sharing and began to discard our sense of isolation and confusion. This network of caring enabled me, at age 50, to apply for admission to a graduate school of social work. In one of my early papers I wrote: "I do indeed want to grow and change in my own life. And I want to learn new skills to help other women make the second half of their lives more dignified and zestful." Within a society that has generally ignored the issues of aging and the concerns of older women, this has been my challenge and struggle these past ten years.

The day after graduation from graduate school a friend and I treated ourselves to a rare trip without our families. We flew to the National Organization for Women meeting in Houston, where the first national task force of women over 40 was meeting. There we were introduced to Tish Sommers, who has been an activist for older women, and to about fifty other exciting women in midlife and later life from all over the country. Together we drew up an older women's manifesto, which the entire N.O.W. delegation stood up to applaud.

Strengthened and energized, we returned to Long Island to form our own regional women's task force. For four years we met monthly with a core group of twenty women aged 40 to 64. Another hundred women joined us for meetings of particular interest. We were married, single, divorced, widowed, childless, grandmothers, professionals, and homemakers. We shared deep personal feelings and experiences on a wide range of topics, from menopause and sex after 40 to finances and future dreams. Because there was so little printed information available to us, we taped our meetings with the intention of collectively writing a book. Although our group never had the opportunity to pull it all together, this book is the result of that dream.

I began to develop a curriculum about aging and went

on to teach gerontology (the study of aging people) at the State University of New York at Stony Brook. Here, one of my courses is "Older Women in America: Problems and Potential." At age 55 I decided to get my doctorate degree at Union Graduate School and began the process of collecting information and writing this book. My work also led to the formation of the National Action Forum for Midlife and Older Women in 1977. Approximately seventy-five women and men of all ages enthusiastically responded to handwritten signs saying "Unite for Older Women" posted all around the Hilton Hotel in San Francisco, where the 30th Annual Scientific Meeting of the National Gerontological Society was being held. National leaders in gerontology formed a board of directors and goals were set: to form a national support network of those concerned about older women's issues, to increase public awareness of the status and needs of women over 40, to serve as an informal clearinghouse for information, and to publish a news letter called "Forum." Today the newsletter, newly named "Hot Flash," reaches five thousand persons in every state and nine foreign countries. My filing cabinets are now bulging with material on all aspects of growing older as a female. Much of this material consists of the thousands of letters I have received from women and the hundreds of interviews I conducted during the past ten years. These women's voices are heard throughout this book. They are role models of courage, change, and power.

Eda LeShan has written, "Nothing in life comes easy—nothing is truly free. Everything we do has a price of some kind. . . . We should live and work and love as fully as possible without expecting to avoid pain and unhappiness." As older women we have learned this. Yet we also continue to learn how to experience the moment, to take personal control over our health and happiness, and, in the process, to make exciting changes in the fabric of our lives. We have begun to join forces to fight the ageism and sexism that limit and oppress us in society.

I have a genuine belief that the world will change for older women—and that older women will change their world. The women's movement provided that "enormous heave forward" toward new possibilities for all of us. Today our talents and capabilities have the opportunity to flower. If we, women of *all* ages, can harness our collective strength, we will become "boulder-pushers" together and will move forward in force. I delight in what women are revealing, becoming, accomplishing.

Ellen Shub

Part I

Women in Transition

Introduction

It happened when my oldest left for college and my youngest entered high school. All of a sudden it hit me: I'm almost out of a job, and now what? I've had twenty years with my parents while growing up, twenty years with my own family, raising them, and now the next twenty years could be for me to go out into the world and see what I can do for myself.

Mary, age 43

This transition time of my life is marked not only by the end of a half-century of living, but by the end of a lifestyle that character-ized most of those years. I have raised six children, mostly alone. I've been immersed in the mother/breadwinner roles, with every-thing I did—from earning money to leisure—being done against the background of the needs of my children. Now I'm down to living with one older teenage child, who will soon leave. I've changed jobs and we've moved out of our big house into an apartment. I know I project to others an aura of ease because I've a good job, I'm in good health, and the bulk of my mother-

ing work is behind me. And yet, I'm suddenly at a loss about where my life is going! For the first time ever I find myself wandering from room to room asking, Is this going to be it? Will it be enough for me to go to work and fill in the time between with sewing, concerts, and jogging—for the next twenty or thirty years? I know I'm in a time of transition, being somewhere between vaguely and acutely disrupted; I know the old ways I've lived are no longer adequate and the new stage of life has not yet emerged. It's a painful yet challenging place to be.

Marsha, age 49

In the second half of our lives most of us experience major life changes, particularly in our work and personal lives. We are in a time of transition requiring us to reevaluate and readjust our values and lifestyles; the old ways of living no longer apply and we're not sure what the new ways will be. A transition may be a role addition (going back to school, reentering the labor market, becoming a grandmother, remarrying) or it may be a role loss (being widowed or divorced, having children leave home, retiring).

Whether we choose our own transitions or they are forced on us by life circumstances, each new adaptation to change involves some degree of stress. Not all of these transitions, however, are times of crisis. Many of us have learned to use these times to develop new strengths and potentials.

Transitions are necessary for women to move from one phase of their lives to another. A human relations program sponsored by the University of California at Berkeley calls these years the *RE years*—a time to revitalize, renew, review, reassess, reflect, revise, reenter, and reaffirm our values and our roles.

As our marital status changes (and it does for more than half of all women in midlife and late life), as our children leave home and our parents require increasing support, we may find ourselves asking some unsettling questions:

♦ Who needs me?

♦ What is the meaning of life now?

♦ What is my role now that childrearing is over?

♦ Will I be alone?

♦ Who will take care of me if I'm sick?

8

♦ Will I be hired even if I go back to school to learn new skills?

♦ Is this all there is to life?

Today our transitions are made more difficult because we have few role models. At the beginning of this century not many women lived to experience menopause; their roles as wife and mother lasted for as long as they lived, to about age 48. Today we live a quarter of a century longer, to age 75 or 85—some eight years longer than most of the men around us. We are indeed in uncharted territory. It takes a lot of self-energy for women to plan the necessary transitions in their lives. We're not used to pursuing our own needs; all too often women in midlife continue to use their energies for nurturing others rather than for seeking self-reliance. As one woman said recently, "Now is the time for me to do me." The years after age 40 are the time to redefine our own self-image and our roles.

How can we successfully prepare to meet our own needs as we experience both the expected and the unexpected changes that will occur in the second half of life?

The process begins with developing a strong sense of self. Only we are responsible for our own lives. One important step toward self-reliance is to practice being alone and enjoying

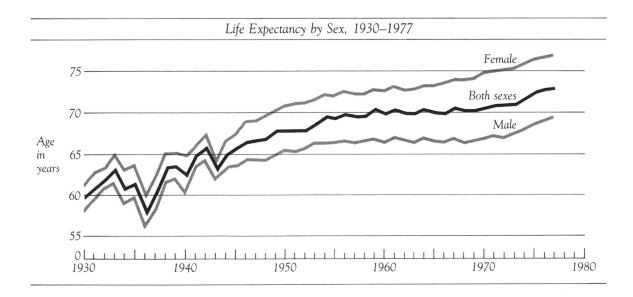

Life Expectancy by Sex, 1930–1977

your own company. Take a day, or a week, to do whatever you like to do in solitude. Anne Morrow Lindbergh describes this self-reliance beautifully in her book *Gift from the Sea*:

Perhaps one can at last in middle age be completely one-self. . . . What a liberation that would be . . . for is it not possible that middle age can be looked upon as a period of second flowering, second growth? A woman must come of age by herself. This is the essence of "coming of age"—to learn to stand alone. She must learn not to depend on an-other . . . she must find her true center alone . . . she must become whole.

Women in transition should actively seek the support of other women who are going through similar experiences. There is a new sharing among all women—married, single, divorced, widowed—initiated by the women's movement during the last ten or fifteen years. This sharing began among young women, but older women are beginning to adopt the idea. Support groups, for ex-ample, provide a safe place for women to discuss their common concerns, share their dreams, explore their options, and support each other in taking the risks necessary for creative change and growth.

Many of us are experiencing a painful transition and are seeking support through individual and group counseling. If you are considering therapy, search out a trained and knowledgeable therapist who is sensitive to adult development and to the specific needs of women. Your local women's center or NOW chapter is a good source of referral. Even if we don't find a need for formal counseling or group support, it helps enormously to talk honestly about these issues with friends who are experiencing the same problems, the same transitions.

Many of us look to literature for support. May Sarton, Flora Scott-Maxwell, Doris Lessing, Elizabeth Janeway, and Anaïs Nin have written about their own aging transitions, and their books can be very helpful.

A major transition for many women over 40 is the end of their marriage, through widowhood, divorce, or separation. This means not only the loss of one's significant other, but the loss of one's social role in a coupled society. Women must shift abruptly into the new and unexplored role of singlehood, which often necessitates developing a whole new group of friends and adjusting to a drastically reduced income.

It is important to remember that while transition periods may be difficult at first, even those we don't choose can force us to continue to grow and improve the quality of our lives. Although each step forward is a step into the unfamiliar and involves change and loss, the risk of movement is essential for growth. If women are too frightened by transitional changes to make positive moves, they may spend the second half of their lives merely surviving when they could be thriving.

This section will help you identify the many changes you might experience as you age—changes related to divorce and widowhood as well as to education and career. It presents resources to assist you in reevaluating and readjusting your goals so that the second half of your life becomes a time to enjoy independence, courage, and new growth.

Ellen Shub

Chapter One

Family Matters

Long-Lasting Marriages

> *We began our marriage thirty-one years ago with the firm intent of achieving a "oneness" in union. Well, we've evolved in all these years. An anniversary card my husband gave me last year says it well: "When we are together, we are one. When we are apart, each of us remains whole. Let this be our dream—our goal." I think we are both healthier and happier with our new goal.*
>
> Monica, age 59

As life expectancy increases, there are more and more long-term marriages, with older couples remaining together into their seventies and eighties. And yet, to remain happy in marriages lasting decades longer than ever before in history requires conscious transitional action: each partner needs to continue to grow and develop as an independent person as both continue to strengthen their mutual goals and love. A unique lifetime continuity is present when couples who truly love, respect, and like each other stay married for fifty years or more, they share a lifetime of memories, joys, and crises, with a very special continuity. Research has shown that those who remain married are usually younger-looking, healthier, and more stable financially than others their age. This is true even for marriages that are not filled with affection and romance.

Satisfying, long-lasting marriages are usually based more on friendship than romance, although both can be present. As William Auden said: "A combination of sexual desire and affection, based upon mutual interests, values and shared experiences, is the securest basis for a happy marriage."

Not all long-term marriages are successful. An interesting study reveals that even unhappily married couples often stay together long enough to reach their golden anniversary. Thirty-five couples, married for fifty years or more, were studied at California State University and the University of Tel Aviv. Sixty percent of the couples remained together not so much as an expression of love and happiness but because they did not believe in divorce. They had achieved more of a friendly alliance that allowed their marriages to provide enough satisfaction for them to remain together.

The other 40 percent of couples in the study, who were happily married, attributed their satisfaction to shared decision making, feelings of equality within the marriage, the ability of both partners to talk and express feelings and to bring large and small conflicts into the open, a commitment to the value of marriage, persistence in working on ways to improve the marriage, speaking respectfully about their partners to others, skilled compromising, and sharing the problems and joys of daily life.

We've been married for almost twenty-five years and have raised not only our own four children, but seven others who lived with us for long periods of time. I didn't even begin college till I was 36, bringing my new baby to classes with me. I've been encouraged and supported by my wonderful husband to keep going, and last year I received my Ph.D. in adult education and administration. I couldn't have handled all this without his constant support, caring, and loving. Who would have believed that as the fourth child of ten, in a North Carolina sharecropper's family, I would be teaching at a college, with my own four children in college, . . . and about to celebrate twenty-five years of struggle and love.

Suzanne, age 48

Husbands and wives who celebrate their golden wedding anniversaries provide each other with companionship, financial security, and a basis for healthier and longer lives. Relationships are built from early romantic beginnings through problem-solving years involving children, careers, family, and friends, to the later years, when the couple is alone again. Marriages must grow and change so that each partner can meet the ordinary and extraordinary daily needs of the other, which shift and change with the years.

An important period of renewal and renegotiation within marriage is the middle years. Often, the marriage contract of early years no longer works in a new and radically changing world. The middle years are the time of lowest marital satisfaction, especially for women. Each person has grown and changed and has developed different needs. This becomes more apparent as children leave home and as each partner begins to examine his or her past and future. Partners may have ceased meeting the other's needs for companionship and intimacy for a variety of reasons. It is the time when many men experience a midlife crisis, which often means leaving a long-term marriage to prove their virility with a younger woman. Couples are in a transitional stage in their relationship, as they face the loss of youth, separation from children, aging parents, the physical signs of aging, and the possibility of death.

Couples live longer than ever before, and so there are few role models and almost no books on how to maintain a satisfying long-term relationship.

It's up to us to pave the way for those who follow us. We know that it is important for each spouse to participate even more actively in the later years of the relationship. Marriage counselors advise couples to rethink and relearn ways to encourage each other's individual growth. Moments of togetherness and sharing need to be balanced by moments of privacy and individual activity in which each partner can pursue his or her interests independently. The challenge is to work out a balance between dependability and innovation, to keep the marriage fresh and thriving.

When you love someone you do not love them all the time,
in exactly the same way, from moment to moment. It is an
impossibility . . . and yet this is exactly what most of us
demand. We have so little faith in the ebb and flow of life,

of love, of relationships. . . . The only continuity possible,
in life, as in love, is in growth—in fluidity—and in freedom.

Anne Morrow Lindbergh *Gift from the Sea*

One midlife event that often causes crisis in marriages
is when children leave home. Many people are concerned about
whether their marriages will endure when their mutual investment
in childrearing is completed. It is important to plan ahead for this
change and to anticipate what it will feel like to be alone together,
without the children. How will you handle this time of new free-
doms and leisure—and the potential for increased intimacy?

> *For fifteen years we were never alone. We ate, slept, and
> breathed children—365 days a year. Finally, we had an opportu-
> nity to take a two-week trip without them. Would you believe we
> each worried about our capability to enjoy time together? What a
> relief it was to have a fun-filled fourteen days! And we vowed
> never to let another year go by without that "investment" in our
> long-term relationship.*
>
> Maura, age 46

As more and more women reenter school or renew a
career after their childrearing days are over, their new lifestyle or
newfound identity often has a profound effect on their marriages
and family life.

> *When I became a professional woman in my fifties, the changes
> this entailed caused the equilibrium of our marriage to shift.
> Work responsibilities needed to be shared within the home as I
> assumed some of the financial burden. There were at least two
> years of turmoil and confusion. We had to work very hard to
> define new ways to relate to each other, and my husband began
> a new period of growth and learning. With the help of good
> marital counseling we weathered the storm and deliberately chose
> each other again, renewing our commitment to our marriage and
> love.*
>
> Gwen, age 59

A relationship needs to be flexible to adjust and expand
to new experiences of midlife and later life. Often it is very painful

to reevaluate oneself and one's marriage; obviously, some couples find that their paths are too divergent or that they are unable or unwilling to let go of old habits and demands and aren't able to stay together even after twenty-five or forty years of marriage.

The changes in sexuality that occur as many couples mature together can be even more satisfying for women in the second half of life. There is more time to devote to each other without the earlier strains of finances and pressures from career and family. As couples let themselves enjoy the special kinds of comfortable intimacy that later years can bring, they may find their relationships even improve. Although modern marriage is a difficult and demanding partnership, it can be a process of creativity making our later years our best years.

Postparenting Years

> *I liked my four children as babies. I liked them as teenagers. But I must say I like them much better since they're older and have left home. Now I like them as people—as "old" friends with whom I've shared many years of experiences. We can, and do, choose to do things together which we enjoy. We have contact and companionship without daily responsibilities.*
>
> Anita, age 68

One of the most dramatic family changes we have witnessed in the twentieth century is the number of years remaining to a couple after their last child has left home. This period of years is expanding as people live longer and have smaller families and as children leave home in their teenage years. Today, on the average, the last child in the family is launched into the world when a woman is 47. She has a possible thirty-seven more years to live, two-fifths of her life ahead of her. If she is married, she can expect that twenty or thirty of those years will be shared with her spouse. If she is a single mother, this transition away from active motherhood has unique joys and concerns.

In the early stages of postparenting, adult children remain fairly dependent on their parents. In the later years, as the children establish their own homes and become self-supporting, a more equal relationship is usually formed between them and their parents.

Parents should try to prepare for the postparenting years by learning new ways to connect not only with each other, but also with their young adult children. This is a time to develop both autonomy and relatedness.

My husband and I find ourselves alone at home, for the first time in twenty-eight years . . . and are experiencing readjustments in many phases of our lives. We are eating together at whatever time is most convenient. Nine o'clock dinners are not unusual. Another change is that we no longer have sons around to help with the yard work. Our love life has also changed. We have more time to enjoy one another and are more sensitive to each other's needs. Had anyone told me thirty-two years ago that I would be more fulfilled and would enjoy my sexuality more at this age, I would never have believed them. I still find great joy in making my husband happy. Fulfilling his needs and desires when making love was always utmost in my life—but now there is that added dimension that I too am an important person whose desires need to be filled. From being just a loving, giving person I've become a loving, giving, and living person. At the end of a busy, hectic week, one evening of each weekend we have a special at-home "date," with snacks, wine, and a simple but elegant dinner—listening to our old albums and relaxing. These three or four shared intimate hours seem to set the mood for the whole week.

Tish, age 57

The moment of truth in many marriages comes after the children leave home. Studies of marital satisfaction indicate that happiness is at a high level early in a marriage before children are born and later when childrearing is completed.

Parenthood is often stressful to the couple relationship. It's not easy to remain active lovers and companions while preoccupied with raising children. Some couples survive the struggles of parenting only to discover that they have little left in common when their children leave home. They have forgotten how to communicate with each other and each may be in a different phase of life. The woman may be entering the world outside the home at the same time that her husband is thinking of retirement from the work world.

I'm just ten years into my teaching career and I love it. Now that the children are gone, my husband wants both of us to retire—sell our house and move to Florida. He wants me free to play and travel with him. I'm not ready yet, and probably won't be for ten more years. It's a real crisis in our marriage.

Paula, age 58

Not every woman enters the postparenting years knowing how to let go of her children gracefully. For some women, the launching of the first (and later the last) child is an emotionally traumatic time. This is especially true if a woman's major identity has been motherhood and her life has evolved around her children's lives.

I cried all the way home when we left our oldest at an upstate college. He looked so frightened and bewildered, and yet my feelings were mixed. I was proud of his growing spirit of independence and at the same time worried about his ability to adjust to a new environment. Would he change for the worse? All the way home my husband and I reviewed this oldest son's entire life— from birth on—and all the precious moments. The feeling of loss and loneliness was never again as great, as each succeeding child left the nest. Perhaps it's necessary to momentarily mourn each transitional life stage.

Brenda, age 59

Women often feel bereft or depressed when their children leave home, and it's important that they recognize and accept the grief and anxiety of this transitional period and try to move on with their own growth and development, as well as the needs of the family remaining at home. Some women find the support of a therapist helps them sort out the conflicting emotions of this time.

Increasing numbers of adult children are *not* leaving home "on schedule." Such a situation postpones the postparenting years and frequently causes stress in a marriage. Even when children do leave home, they may seem to adhere to a "revolving door" policy. They come back for short or long periods to the home they grew up in and to the place they can count on for nurturing. They return during vacation, after college, between jobs, or later, after a divorce (sometimes with grandchildren). Some couples find they just get used to being alone when one or more of their children return. Many children demand that their rooms be left intact and continue to store their personal belongings in their parents' house—one foot out of the home and one foot in! Often parents continue to provide financial and emotional support for adult children long after the children have left home. This can cause parents to feel resentful and to experience conflict about the best course of action without turning an adult child away. Parents want the time and money to reestablish their own relationship, to pursue new projects or careers after years of providing for children, and yet some parents may feel that denying help to their children is selfish.

Women who have used their early middle years to launch themselves into new careers have an easier time turning their full attention away from their children. They are better able to focus on their own needs and, if married, their relationship with their spouse.

For many decades women dreaded the launching of their adult children and the resulting "empty nest syndrome." They believed the myth that when parenting stops, life becomes empty and meaningless. This is not usually the case, however, and an overwhelming majority of women greet these postparenting years with relief and even joy. They feel a new sense of freedom, often for the first time in their lives.

For many couples the latter part of the postparenting years, when they are finally alone, is like a second honeymoon. There is time to concentrate on each other with new attention and energy. Women report feelings of peacefulness and mellowness. They can use the time to travel, to learn new skills, and to make new friends. Some couples sell their larger "child-size" home and move into a nearby city apartment or to a favorite summer home. This may be the time of life to reunite with old friends whose company you enjoy, to disengage from some friends chosen during the childraising years, and to make new friends of all ages.

Researchers have found that during the later postparenting years female and male personality traits begin to merge. Women become more assertive and less dependent, while men become more nurturing. The previous rigid sex roles can be dropped and a more complementary relationship formed.

Now that the children are gone, the friendship aspect of our relationship has surfaced. We each feel fortunate to have one special friend to always count on.

Dot, age 66

The Postparenting Years Alone

For women alone, the empty nest syndrome may be a more potent threat. Single mothers may initially feel a deep loneliness during the postparenting years compared to married women who have their spouses to share the empty nest. Having had to put 200 percent of their energy into supporting their children, financially and emotionally, single mothers may experience a longer and more difficult transition.

I am pleased that my children are the neat young adults that they are. I salute them, and I salute myself. We had one hell of an experience together and we love one another deeply. But, my God, how I wish there wasn't that empty side of my bed!

Marie, age 53

Some single mothers find the postparenting years a source of renewal and an opportunity for exploration.

After thirty years of faithfully fulfilling the role of motherhood, I have become an ex-mother. It's not that I love my children any less, but now it seems more mutual. I'm happy that they are finally independent. Now we can help each other, as loving people do, but I am no longer an indispensable suppport for them and I don't feel responsible for their decisions. I have loved well—and now, as a single woman, I am ready for new responsibilities and new adventures.

June, age 60

The Grandmother Role

My grandchildren mean everything to me. They are my links to the past and to the future. I like being able to choose when we spend time together—and to use that time in a relaxed, fun-filled, accepting manner. These four children, for whom I have few responsibilities, add light to my life.

Mary Louise, age 62

Today, with our longer life expectancy, we are more likely to experience not only grandmotherhood, but great-grandmotherhood. The average women is 46 when her first grandchild is born and 80 percent of us are grandmothers by our mid-fifties. A relationship with a grandchild may last as long as thirty years.

As women marry earlier and have fewer, more closely spaced children, grandparenting has become a middle-age, not just an old-age, phenomenon. We are likely to have small grandchildren in our late forties and fifties when we are involved in busy work and social lives. The contemporary, handsome, well-dressed, sensuous grandmother is a far cry from the stereotypical picture of granny in the kitchen baking cookies.

As grandmothers, we can act as important role models, as mediators, nurturers, mentors, and teachers. We can help our grandchildren have a sense of security and roots. Our love for them can be unconditional, since it has no behavioral strings attached.

We can choose how active we want our grandparenting to be. Only 10 percent of grandparents live with their adult children. Older women who chose this lifestyle are usually widows who enjoy caring for their grandchildren. Their presence often allows the younger parents to work and the children to return home from school to someone who loves them and will listen to their daily tales.

Many grandparents live near at least one adult child. It is not unusual, particularly among working-class families, for an adult daughter to choose to live near her mother. Many older women then take active roles in their grandchildren's daily lives and in the care of their own children's households. This is particularly true when the adult child is a single parent. For some grandmothers this is a positive chance; for others, this type of grandmothering is a burden. Some women who have just completed their own childrearing resent the frequent requests of their adult children for advice, physical resources, and baby-sitting services. Indeed, many older people move far away to have more privacy, a life that is less demanding, and more time to expand their own interests. Recently, however, there has been a reverse migration for many older people back to living close to adult children and their families.

Some women enjoy playing an occasional grandmother role. They decide when they will see their grandchildren, and they use those times to build a relationship based on play and leisure activities. This can revitalize the lives of both grandmothers and grandchildren.

Having grandchildren is the best of all possible worlds. I don't have any responsibility for them—I just do all the fun stuff. It's very exciting when they are old enough to respond to you, and it's sensational when Andrew hugs me. I love seeing what a great mother my daughter is, and I have the satisfaction of knowing that if I hadn't been a good mother to her, she wouldn't know so well what to do.

Mary Beth, age 49

After some 600 interviews with both grandchildren and grandparents, Dr. Arthur Kornhaber concluded that the bond between grandparent and grandchild is second only to the relationship between parent and child. He found, however, that children today, in an era of great mobility, see much less of grandparents than children in earlier eras did, and he calls today's children "grand-orphans." He found that:

- Only 5 percent of grandparents have ready access to their grandchildren, spending time with them at least twice each week.
- 80 percent see their grandchildren only occasionally (from once a week to once a year).
- 45 percent live more than one hundred miles from their grandchildren.
- 15 percent never see or hear from their grandchildren.

Children, grandchildren, and grandparents in Kornhaber's study discussed the loneliness they feel because of the lack of a vital connection between the generations.

Women who want to remain close to their grandchildren despite a physical distance might try establishing a regular exchange of photographs, cassette tapes, and phone calls. Send postcards when you travel, and frequent small gifts—remembering those important birthdays and holidays. As grandchildren grow older, arrange for each child to visit you individually and include visiting them individually and include visiting them in your vacation plans. One single woman in her seventies takes a different teenage grandchild traveling with her on month-long summer vacation trips. These trips intimately connect the two generations and provide a closer link between the families.

Nongrandmotherhood

A growing number of married couples are choosing not to have children, to have only one child, or to have their children late in life. For older women who have expected and looked forward to being grandmothers, this may be a source of considerable distress. Women who had valued highly their own motherhood role may feel confused, betrayed, deprived, and angry at such decisions by their adult children. They would benefit from trying very hard, and perhaps seeking professional help, to learn how to cope with their strong emotions without harming their basic relationship with their children.

Women have solved this problem of delayed grand-motherhood or nongrandmotherhood in a variety of creative ways. Some move into living situations with mixed age groups. Here they willingly exchange baby-sitting services for services they need, such as shopping. Others become surrogate grandmothers by volunteering several hours a day or week in local elementary schools, offering the one-to-one attention some children need to blossom in today's overcrowded classrooms. Often they share their personal history (what it was like to live during the Depression, to live through World War I, and so on), bringing to life the lessons in the classroom. Still others have found a solution in becoming foster grandparents in local hospitals or mental institutions. They provide three or four hours of daily tender loving care to needy infants and children who are chronically ill. Often they report enormous personal rewards from this volunteer work.

Grandparents Anonymous

In an age in which one out of every three first marriages ends in divorce, one problem that is seldom discussed but is important to an increasing number of older women is the visitation rights of grandparents. Divorce has robbed many of us of our role as grandmother, especially as parents of sons (since child custody goes to the mother in roughly nine out of ten cases). If a mother who has custody severs the ties to her former in-laws, grandparents may be denied access to their grandchildren and have no legal recourse. This is the cause of a great deal of anger and pain.

Do grandparents have any rights in the eyes of the law? Many states (New York, California, and Arkansas among them) have enacted grandparent rights statutes, owing in part to a small but growing number of politically active grandparents who are pressing for their legal visitation rights. These statutes leave the courts free to decide what is in the child's best interests. Courts are looking with more and more favor on grandparents' petitions for visitation. They do this to preserve the special kind of love and affection only grandparents can give. Indeed, the love of a grandmother often fills an emotional void created in the lives of children whose parents are separated or divorced.

A new self-help group called Grandparents Anonymous, with more than a thousand members, has been established in Sylvan Lake, Michigan. Group members share frustrations and experiences and are pressing for grandparent rights legislation within Michigan. They have succeeded in prompting Michigan to declare its first Grandparent-Grandchild Day. This type of support-action could easily be followed in other states.

Resources: Grandparenting

Publications

Cohler, Bertram. *Mothers, Grandmothers and Daughters.* New York: Wiley, 1981.

Dodson, Fitzhugh, and Paula Reuben. *How to Grandparent.* New York: Harper & Row, 1981.

Kornhaber, Arthur, and Kenneth Woodward. *Grandparents/Grandchildren: The Vital Connection.* New York: Doubleday, 1981.

Hilda Bijur

Chapter Two

Going It Alone

Many women over 40, almost half of us, live alone, either by choice or by virtue of events in our lives that thrust us into a life of "single bliss." All of us should be developing the capacity to live indepent, self-governing lives, with or without marriage. Despite what they have in common, women without husbands are not a homogeneous group. There is frequently an unacknowledged difference between widows and divorcees. In a divorce, it is still possible to see and hear the other person. Although the mourning may be less intense, and of a shorter duration, anger can be more intense and last for years. Older divorcees tend to "tear down" their partners, whereas older widows may idealize them. A divorcee often has a shattered ego, needing reassurance that she still has the capacity to sustain new relationships. She frequently feels at fault, like a failure. Widows are less ego-damaged by their experience. In their search for new social roles, widows are most often greeted with compassion and kindness, while divorcees too often are the subjects of disdain, although this seems to be changing. Also changing is the recognition by women (and society) that the single life is an honorable and meaningful option. We are developing powerful new role models to guide us, women who have proudly acknowledged their single status and who are "going it alone" and thriving.

Lifelong Singlehood

I try to impress upon my friends that my way of life is out of choice and it's my own free will to remain unmarried. I've hardly found a handful of married women who have managed to retain their individual identity. It was for me a matter of priority—whether I settled down as a wife and mother or continued to study and learn, travel to other countries of the world, and make friends with the "family of nations." My friends keep asking me if I'm not worried about my security and fulfillment. I ask them if this is guaranteed in marriage. It is not marriage as such that I have been against, but I have yet to find the kind of person and the kind of marriage I would feel comfortable with.

Lillian, age 46

Approximately one out of every twenty people reaches middle age without having married. As the following statements show, the unmarried lifestyle is a conscious choice for many women but for others it just happens.

I knew from my early twenties that I would need to focus all my resources and energies on developing a career in science. There was no time for marriage in my chosen life.

Although I assumed I would someday be married, I've not yet met a man I love enough to spend the rest of my life with.

I'd observed my parents' unhappy marriage. My mother was always pregnant, never had control over money, and felt personally unfulfilled. I decided early that I'd not be a "servant" to any man.

I've always had a sexual preference for women.

For twenty years I was caretaker to my ailing mother. I never was free to consider marriage.

I want, above all else in my life, to be psychologically and socially free. I've managed my own home and money for some forty-three years now—never accounting to anyone else for my time or actions. I wouldn't change my lifestyle for anyone.

Studies show that older single women are more likely than older married women to have achieved a high educational and career status and to be assertive and goal oriented, with a high level of self-esteem. They have learned how to live alone and how to be independent. Because they are less likely to have strong family ties, they have formed a wider variety of nonfamily relationships (clubs and friends) from whom they expect and receive a lot of support. Never-married women often form strong relationships with their sisters and brothers in their later years.

Although younger never-married women seem to lead more exciting lives then married women, this advantage reverses itself in later years when never-married women have significantly lower incomes and are more likely to be living alone. Retirement and the loss of an important work role are often more difficult for women who have never married. They may have a variety of friends, but they lack the constant presence of spouse confidants. Some women spend their lives searching for marriage.

> *I feel like a loser—reaching 55 without ever experiencing "a meaningful relationship." There is no support in our couple-oriented society for living alone. I feel like there must be something basically wrong with me. I'm too tall, not smart enough, too assertive, not attractive—something's the matter!! I must admit to a real fear of remaining alone as I grow older. Who will be there when I'm retired—and sick? Will I be the perfect candidate for a nursing home?*
>
> Gale, age 55

For those never-married women over 40 who still want to marry, the statistics are discouraging. Single women between the ages of 30 and 54 outnumber their male counterparts by a ratio of 128 to 100, and the ratio increases with every decade of age.

Most of us are extremely aware of the sexual inequities between aging men and aging women. Our society not only approves of older men marrying younger women; it even applauds men for choosing this kind of relationship (at least older men applaud each other). Older women–younger men liaisons are still considered taboo, which makes the number of men available for single older women pretty scarce.

Another unwritten law that works against women says that it is all right, and even expected, for men to marry women who are on a lower professional level than themselves and, conversely, that it is not all right for them to marry women who are professionally above them. This puts older, successful single women at a real disadvantage in forming relationships that can lead to marriage.

One woman decided she no longer wanted to live alone; she had had enough of coming home to an empty room. In her early forties she joined an intergenerational commune. Now in her seventies, she has lived in five different communal settings and feels useful, cared for, and loved. Some never-married women prefer a housing complex designed for older people where transportation, companionship, and staff are available routinely and in emergencies. Other groups of single women have pooled their resources and chosen to live collectively. (For more information and ideas on alternative living arrangements, see Chapter 5.)

Organizations specifically for single people have sprung up all over the country, particularly in large cities. One such group, the Holiday Dinner Group in New York City, caters to people between 30 and 55 who either have no family or are separated from them. Recognizing that holiday seasons can be difficult emotionally, they plan get-togethers in one another's homes on six holidays. One single woman said, "If you're not part of a family on a holiday, you feel like you're walking around with two heads on. This group is a good way to meet people and to enjoy the holidays." Other single women of all ages could adopt a similar plan in their community.

The desire for personal growth and autonomy is the strongest motivation for remaining single. Despite few legal, economic, social, and psychological supports, the never-married woman today may have as satisfying a life as a married woman with children. Indeed, some married women are envious of their single sisters' career advancement and personal independence. Studies show that more never-married women report being moderately happy in their later years than their counterparts who are widowed or divorced. The attractiveness of marriage as the only satisfying lifestyle has definitely declined as society has become more accepting of nontraditional lifestyles. The status and number of single women will continue to grow as laws and societal attitudes change.

Successful independent lifestyles, however, require strong personal resources that may diminish as a woman ages, particularly if her income decreases or if her health is poor. In the near future, more and more well-educated, successful single women will enter the second half of their lives. In addition, most of us will be unmarried in our later years (after age 75 women outnumber men two to one). The never-married woman has some distinct advantages in meeting the challenges of old age. She has learned independence and has probably developed a strong self-identity. She may become a role model for those women forced by circumstances to adjust to living alone for the first time in their later years. If the never-married woman has health, a good support system, and an adequate income, she may indeed have the happiest situation of all women alone in her old age.

Divorce and Separation

> *At age 47 I am successfully pulling out of my own unanticipated, stressful midlife difficulties and am on the way to recapturing the vital self I once had. My problems were triggered by a growing estrangement between my husband and myself, finally ending in separation when we no longer were able to live usefully together. I am now able to understand, in my bones, loss, depression, grief, and loneliness. There is a demeaned sense of self that comes with the stripping away of accustomed roles of wife and helpmate and with the loss of all the usual things that confirm that identity—daily household routine, financial security, sexual intimacy, familiar home and furnishings. I am on the up side of living, reconstructing myself in my work, which has now taken a central, rather than secondary, place in my life. I'm learning that the "I" must remain my center—that I need choices—and that interdependency with others, particularly women, is necessary.*
>
> Diana, age 47

In the early 1800s, a married couple could expect an average of twelve years together before one spouse died. Today, a married couple can expect to be together possibly forty-eight years. Is it any wonder that as our life span increases, the number of divorces grows?

There has been a steady rise in divorce in this country over the last fifty years. One-third of all first marriages end in divorce. In the late 1970s and 1980s, the largest increase of divorce has occurred in marriages of more than twenty years.

The breakup of marriages usually has a more lasting effect on women than on men and more women than men remain unmarried afterward. There are 111 divorced women for every thousand married women, compared to 72 divorced men for every thousand married men. Black urban women have the highest divorce rate: 15 percent in the high divorce years of 30 to 55, contrasted to 9 percent for white urban women.

Many couples who do not plan to remarry other mates simply separate. Separation has been called a "poor person's divorce" because it is more common among low-income people. In 1978, 3.9 million Americans separated and 8.6 million were divorced. Adding these statistics to the numbers of widowed and never-married women suggests that the future population of older women will include more nonmarried women than married ones.

"Uncoupling" is frightening and disorienting for a husband and wife. It involves a marked change in roles and, for women, a change in status. Older women report ambivalent and conflicting feelings as they contemplate leaving marriages of two, three, and four decades: hate and love, sadness and relief, mourning and rejoicing, depression and hope, feelings of failure and of excited anticipation.

The movement toward full recovery after a divorce usually takes two to four years, and it occurs in two distinct phases. The first phase is transitional: A former way of life has been disrupted and a new pattern has not yet evolved. Some practical problems, like living arrangements, may be solved quickly. Others, such as developing a new social network, may take many months. The emotional issues, however, take the longest to resolve. Divorced women undergo a grieving process during which they often feel like losers or failures. They may have strong feelings about their former mate. They fear being alone at the same time as they are afraid of new emotional involvement. Many women translate their fears into a chaotic search for new friends as well as into depression, overeating, alcoholism, and even thoughts of suicide. Women search for books and seminars on divorce, support groups of other midlife and older divorced women, encounter groups, parents without partners—seeking guideposts to help them adapt to life alone. Finally, after about eight to ten months, the healing process may be completed as divorced women begin to return order to their lives and start to function in ways that are necessarily new and different.

The second phase, recovery, follows. Divorced women gradually establish a new identity and a stable way of life. Once the transitional stage is past, most women are pleased to find they have not been shattered by the divorce. Their days have become organized and they are pursuing new goals. Small things like balancing a checkbook and managing car repairs become major victories. They begin to find satisfaction in their new roles, discovering unknown abilities in themselves as well as new interests. All too often they are poorer than before, have few opportunities for male companionship, and have little in common with their married friends. Yet most divorced women report feeling relieved to be freed from the daily burdens of an unhappy marriage; they are proud of their independence and autonomy, and many find themselves functioning as well as or better than at any other time in their lives. Most women who are over 40 married with the expectation that their role as wife would be lifelong. They helped their husbands develop careers, raised children, and participated in community affairs. If they are left by their spouse, which usually happens suddenly and unexpectedly and leaves them without emotional or financial support, they feel betrayed and bitter. They feel a personal sense of shame that they couldn't make their marriage work and sadness at the loss of a dream.

> *I am facing a divorce next month. My husband has chosen to end our thirty-two-year marriage, finding another woman to fit his new lifestyle. I am 52, mother of seven, and I desperately need guidance for a new direction in my life. . . . I hope to find a new career, despite financial obstacles and one son still to raise. I've already taken steps. My intent is to obtain a law degree (having completed my B.A. at age 49). My heart and mind are determined, but my spirit is fearful and easily shaken.*
>
> Etta, age 52

The shock of being alone is profound. And in addition to the dissolution of her relationship with her husband, the divorced woman also must face changed relationships with her children, relatives, and friends.

Children

Divorce is more complicated when children are involved. The woman usually retains custody of children, so the man becomes single but the woman becomes a single parent.

Being dumped at age 61 from a couple's world to a single's world is certainly traumatic. Being widowed is easier! You wouldn't believe the hurts, one after another. . . . A big problem is being forced to share my children's attentions with their father (especially after all the capers he performed before the divorce).

Muriel, age 61

Divorced women with teenage children need good lawyers to help them solve the multitude of problems they face. Of the seven million single women caring for children, only one-third received any child support in 1978, and the average divorced woman received $19 a week per child—27 percent of what it costs to support a child on a moderate budget. Is it any wonder that women with children often remain in unsatisfactory and even painful marriages until their children are independent? Good divorce planning for a woman with children should include an agreement that the husband will continue to support any children throughout their college years, even though in most states the maximum age for support has been lowered from 21 to 18.

Divorce, no matter how amicable, has an emotional impact on the children and the parents. Most people grow up with the notion that children should be brought up in an intact family, that children have a right to two parents living with them at all times. Many middle-aged women, however, are learning that both they and their children are healthier when a painful marriage is dissolved. They are learning to share responsibility for their children, as the women themselves grow personally independent.

My ex-spouse and I have what seems like a good arrangement for raising our three children. He picks them up on Friday night and returns them to me Sunday night. This leaves me free to build new social relationships and yet to feel in control of the daily routine of their lives.

Liz, age 45

Other divorced parents share responsibility for their children during school vacations or in the summer. A recent practice gaining in popularity is coparenting. Divorced parents who choose this type of childrearing often live near each other and have complete childcare responsibilities every other week. The children, who have not been displaced from their friends or school, thrive. Some teenage children choose to live with their father after a divorce, often because he is planning to remarry, and maintaining family normalcy (including economic security) is important for some children. Women have to fight within themselves against viewing this as a personal rejection. They can use the period following their divorce to build a completely new life, one separate from their full-time role as mother. As children grow into adulthood, they most frequently return to a mature relationship with both parents, and divorced women can look forward to that relationship.

Friends

In the early stages of a divorce a woman's old friends not only offer a shoulder to cry on but also reassurance that she is valued. All too often, however, divorce is viewed as a "communicable disease." It can stir up all the anxieties one's married friends have about their own marriages. Old friends may also feel conflicting loyalties toward both members of the divorced couple. Although one or both spouses may continue to relate to old friends, maintaining friendships is often difficult or awkward. Divorced woman may begin to have less and less in common with their married friends, and they soon begin to develop relationships with people who share their new status and interests.

Newly developed predivorce mediation counseling services, which have successfully helped many couples separate without bitterness, also encourage couples to talk out in advance how they can best relate to each other, to family, and to friends.

Economic Concerns

Most women suffer serious financial setbacks as a result of their divorce or separation. All too often they go from relative comfort to poverty. In 1978, the family income of newly divorced middle-class women fell from an average of $45,000 to $14,000 a year; the income of working-class divorced women fell from $19,000 to $7,000 a year. When a husband leaves, he takes most of the family earning power with him.

Four years ago, after a twenty-five-year marriage, my husband moved in with a female patient. I was left with a beautiful home and pool—but otherwise poor. My husband, who I put through medical school, frequently missed the $250 monthly alimony payment. I was on food stamps for ten months, and my gas and electric companies threatened to cut me off. He stopped paying the mortgage, and the bank threatened to foreclose.

Ruth, age 53

Divorced women almost always have a problem getting money from ex-husbands for court-awarded alimony or child support. In 1978, less than one percent of all divorced or separated women received alimony, and an average payment was $55 a week. Older women who have lost their financial security usually have great difficulty finding employment. When they do find jobs, their salary is usually too low to enable them to support themselves and their children in a style comparable to their predivorce lifestyle.

Loss of Health Insurance
One essential protection a woman often loses when her marriage ends is health insurance. This loss leaves the nonworking middle-aged woman vulnerable to high medical and hospital costs at a time when she can least afford them. Before she finds a job, which may offer group insurance coverage, or becomes eligible for Medicare at age 65 she often remains uncovered. While they are still married, women should check, or have their lawyer check, their husband's health plan to see if coverage is continued as part of a divorce decree and how long it lasts. Does the plan offer a conversion policy? Such a policy means you can switch to an individual policy without a physical exam. Nineteen states require conversion rights. A woman must request this right from the insurance company, and often the request is required within thirty to sixty days after the divorce is final.

Even if a woman is able to obtain an individual policy, the cost of medical insurance will be between $900 and $1,200 a year (20 percent more than a comparable group plan). Many newly divorced women cannot afford such health coverage and must face instead the possibility of staggering health-care bills if they become seriously ill.

Positive Aspects of Divorce

Karen DeCrow, in a *New York Times* article entitled "40, Single Again, and Absolutely No Regrets," summarized the positive aspects of divorce:

> The other day I celebrated turning forty. I am single again. A marvelous, delicious way to live: you eat, sleep, make love, watch television, write, talk, work, sing—when you want to. . . . Alone is supposed to mean lonely. How pleasant to travel around the world with a loving friend, but how much more we learn, see, hear, smell when we travel alone. . . . Everyone should do both—each has its value. It is only when we don't need other people, another person for social status, for economic survival—that we really delight in company.

Although most divorces are initiated by the husband, more and more women are finding the courage and support to leave unhappy and unsatisfying marriages. Although this often happens when a marriage has been painful, with an abusive or alcoholic husband, as women grow more confident and less dependent many leave their marriages because they themselves are changing and growing and their husbands are not. The two have grown apart after many years and are incompatible.

> *I changed and he didn't. He simply won't, or can't, be open to new places, new ideas, and new people. For me our marriage is like an old shoe which doesn't fit anymore. It's time to leave.*
>
> Barbara, age 50

A woman who chooses to be single again may be taking responsibility for herself for the first time in her life. Women are discovering, among other personal benefits, a new freedom, privacy, fewer responsibilities and social obligations, and fewer household chores. Many women report that being in charge of their own money (even if the amount is small) gives them a new sense of power and control. Women report several years after their divorce that they look back, often in disbelief, at the untenable situations they accepted within their marriage. Although after the divorce they faced economic problems and lack of male companionship, few are sorry they divorced, and many felt an enormous relief.

Imagine being 56 and handling my own money for the first time. My husband had always doled out money to me and I felt like a second-class citizen. This above all makes me feel in control of my life. I finally feel that I'm at the helm.

Ginny, age 56

How to Protect Yourself While Still Married

◆ Identify assets such as pension funds, insurance, royalties, and receivables.

◆ Arrange, if possible, to put all assets of the marriage into both names. Each spouse should be "joint tenant" of the family home.

◆ Make yourself knowledgeable about all financial matters that affect your life: the value of your property, the size and cost of your mortgage or rent, your husband's income and benefits.

◆ Open up your own savings account and start saving money in your own name.

◆ Retain or gain a marketable skill.

◆ If you and your husband have agreed to a divorce, read all that you can about the process (see Resources: Divorce and Separation at the end of this chapter).

◆ Find a good lawyer who will represent only you.

Choosing a Divorce Lawyer

Finding the right lawyer and knowing what to ask her or him is often not easy for women who are not used to discussing money, fees, second opinions, and their need to have sufficient time for consultation. If you don't know where to turn, you can call the lawyer referral service of the Bar Association in your county or state for the name of a lawyer who works extensively in family law. You can avoid some potential problems by following these steps:

◆ Shop around to find a lawyer you can trust, one who will communicate with you in plain English and explain all your options and their potential consequences. Evaluate lawyers for intelligence, attitudes toward women, and ability to understand the problems you face.

◆ Check with friends who have been divorced, call your local NOW office, or look for specialized feminist divorce counselors in your community who would be able to recommend a good lawyer.

◆ Organize your thoughts and set your goals before your first consultation with a lawyer, so you can articulately present the necessary information.

◆ The preliminary session is with a lawyer you have *not yet hired*. It enables you to discover whether you feel comfortable with a particular lawyer, to get an idea of how she or he would handle your case, and to discuss what fees you can expect to pay. The initial consultation may cost between $50 and $250.

♦ Lawyers can bill by the hour or charge a flat fee (usually set high), a contingency fee (paid only if you win the case), or an open retainer fee. The most sensible approach is usually the open retainer fee, under which you pay an initial sum that the lawyer estimates will cover total costs in ordinary circumstances. If the lawyer has to spend extra time, you will be asked to pay for that time based on the lawyer's hourly rate.

♦ Once you've decided on a lawyer and a fee schedule, ask your lawyer for a retainer letter that lists the services the lawyer will and will not perform, the fee, and any extra costs you will be expected to pay.

♦ Write a letter to your lawyer detailing your case, adding that you want to know what is happening at each stage and that you will document any relevant incidents, conversations, or expenses for use in the case.

♦ If you feel a second opinion is necessary, even in the middle of the proceedings, don't be afraid to ask another lawyer to review your case. (Expect to pay consultation fees for this.) If necessary, switch to another lawyer.

♦ If you cannot afford the expense of hiring a lawyer (or do not wish to do so), women's groups in your area may be able to assist you in doing your own legal paperwork. It is possible to represent yourself in court, if you wish.

No-Fault Divorce

Many states have moved away from the old legal system in which one spouse must be found guilty of adultery, cruelty, desertion, or conviction of a felony in a divorce case. Today a couple simply has to say to the court that they tried, but the marriage failed. No-fault divorce laws (operative in all but three states—Illinois, Pennsylvania, and South Dakota) declare that both spouses share the responsibility for a failed marriage. There are two key provisions of no-fault divorce: (1) Grounds for divorce are reduced to two possibilities—irreconcilable differences and incurable insanity; (2) The couple equally divides the community property. The law assumes that both contributed to the accumulation of assets as well as to the failure of the marriage.

No-fault divorce can be a disaster for older women, especially those who have remained in their homes assuming they would always be married or that at least, in a divorce, they would be awarded the home, furniture, and car. In a no-fault divorce assets must be divided equally, and although each asset is not necessarily split between the two parties, often the home is sold so that the proceeds can be divided equally. Women are no longer assured of retaining the house in a divorce settlement.

In many states under no-fault divorce, alimony (referred to as "maintenance") is limited to a specific number of years (three to five), "just enough to get the woman back on her feet." Many women, however, have sacrificed their own schooling and careers, early in their marriages, to enable their husbands to complete their education and training. It is unrealistic that, given the sexism and ageism in society, older women will be able in a few years to gain skills and find satisfying, well-paying jobs. Only a small percentage of older divorced women manage to overcome the financial odds against them.

Women have been disillusioned by the equitable-distribution law that accompanies no-fault divorce. Legal fees are much higher, accountants often need to be hired to evaluate all assets, court trials are longer, and, in the end, women often find they have received less than equal property settlements and limited maintenance payments.

Many couples decide to negotiate out-of-court settlements to avoid the costliness of a trial and the uncertainty of a court's ruling.

New Beginnings

Small mutual support groups have arisen to help older divorced women cope with the changes divorce and separation bring. These groups usually include about ten women in varying stages of the divorce experience. Such groups can help newly separated women feel less lonely, gain back their sense of self-worth and self-confidence, and develop a new identity. Groups can serve as an outlet for the normal feelings of loneliness, bewilderment, and frustration that often accompany separation and divorce.

Parents Without Partners, an active social group for divorced and separated people with children, was founded to help separated and divorced people meet new friends and develop new interests. Although it is more successful with young and middle-aged divorced women, this nationwide organization sponsors a wide range of social and self-help activities designed to introduce newly single people to one another in a relaxed social setting. Activities include theater parties, sports activities, socials, educational lectures, workshops, and family outings. More and more local churches and synagogues offer weekly or bimonthly programs for older single people. These can be helpful social networks because they are made up of people who have experienced similar life transitions.

Meeting new people often leads to dating. Although *dating* has an adolescent connotation, many newly single women must become involved again in that kind of social interaction with men. For divorced middle-aged women, dating usually begins within the first year after their marriage ends. (Older women, because of the small number of available men, have fewer opportunities for such activities.) The initial date may prove very unsettling, raising emotions of anxiety, boredom, and fear of rejection that a woman hasn't felt in many years. It may also, however, reassure a woman of her attractiveness and self-worth.

After casting away the inhibitions of a lifetime after a divorce, many older divorced women report that casual sex doesn't work well for them. Most are willing to use masturbatory methods instead and to remain celibate until the right person comes along. When that happens they find themselves responding with new and more open sexual patterns.

The search for new friends and meaningful activities can take place in several environments: volunteer social services, political campaigns, college classes, and self-improvement programs. Divorced women can meet new people as they develop their interests in music, art, theater, or sports.

> *After a painful divorce in 1966, I had to reconstruct a whole new life for myself. There was no help available at that time for older women. I found it difficult to identify with the "women's lib" movement because so many of its leaders were (and are) relatively young and bitterly aggressive. During the past thirteen years I have been obligated to try a great many new things: moving to a new state, a new job, gaining a degree, and forming a new life from the wreck of an old one. Now I don't want to try anything new. I want to cease to have to keep changing. I wouldn't have believed, however, that I was capable of so much change. I'm proud of myself.*
>
> Joyce, age 60

Divorce can be an enormous freedom for both partners imprisoned in an unhappy marriage. It may be the only way to salvage the second half of life—to make it the joyous, independent, creative period it can be.

$\mathcal{W}$idowhood: An Ending and a New Beginning

At age 57 my husband died suddenly of cardiac arrest. For the first year I walked the shopping malls rather than come home to an empty house. It soon became apparent that I was a fifth wheel in our "coupled" society, which made me feel uncomfortable enough to start declining invitations. However, despite all of this, life without my husband has had some positives. I've always loved to travel, but my husband didn't. In these five years I've traveled to Hawaii, camped my way across the country with my two adult children, and toured Italy. I also have the freedom to take some really interesting adult education courses. I'm less materialistic now, and I have a new appreciation of life and greater clarity about what is important.

Helen, age 62

Most married women live as though their marriages will last forever. They don't plan ahead for independence in their later years. Yet widowhood is a major life change faced by most older women: eleven out of twelve wives are widowed. Widowhood requires more adjustment than almost any other life event.

A Statistical Portrait of an American Widow

- The average age of widowhood is 56; 68 percent of *all* women are widows at age 75.
- The average woman can expect ten years of widowhood.
- There are five widows to every widower.
- Between the ages of 45 and 55, there are an estimated 854,000 widows; between 55 and 64, 2.1 million widows; and at ages 65 and over, 619 million widows.
- Only 4 percent of all widows are under age 45; 90 percent are 55 and older.
- The proportion of widows among nonwhite women is twice that among white women. Nonwhite women are also widowed earlier.
- An estimated 40 percent of all older widows live on or below the poverty level.
- Three-fifths of all widows live alone or with nonrelatives.

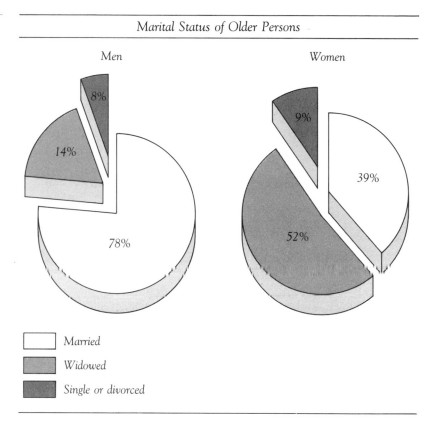

Marital Status of Older Persons

Men   Women

8%   14%   78%   9%   52%   39%

☐ Married

▨ Widowed

■ Single or divorced

Throughout life women need to plan realistically and pragmatically for the time when they must fend for themselves. They need to strive for a certain amount of independence and self-management during their marriages. Women should be continually developing themselves by education or supportive, interesting work. They should acquire social and business skills as well as an ability to spend time alone, even within marriage. All women need to learn such practical skills as writing checks, paying bills, driving cars, and basic repairs such as fixing flat tires. It is possible for a couple to plan for widowhood. Lynn Caine, in her book *Widow*, suggests that couples conduct an annual review of their finances and discuss the steps to be taken if either dies within the next year.

Barbara Moran and Mary DeGroot, each a recent widow with five children, have compiled the following checklist for wives whose husbands are still alive.

1. Make sure you and your husband have a will and your witnesses' signatures notarized on an add-on page at the end of it. This will prevent, after a death, having to locate these witnesses for affidavits.
2. Do not leave a will in the safe deposit box. Keep it at home in a safe place and file a copy with your lawyer.
3. Establish your own credit rating through gas cards, car ownership, other credit cards, etc.
4. Open a bank account with several hundred dollars or more in your own name. Joint bank accounts, over a certain amount, are frozen temporarily after the death of one of the account's consignatories.
5. Keep accurate financial records, paying bills by check where possible. Keep all cancelled checks and file income tax information separately by the year, for future reference. All records should be kept for at least seven years in case of Internal Revenue Service auditing.

It is important that women are aware of the amount of insurance coverage, accident and health insurance policies and such assets as property, savings, investment, savings bonds and checking account balances.

All properties should be in joint ownership and each partner should know what outstanding debts exist, like the mortgage and car payments. Figure out together how much money your surviving family would have to live on and exactly what benefits would be available through his pension plan, labor union, fraternal organizations, social security or the Veterans Administration.

Find a trusted financial advisor who will help both before and after a bereavement. It is wise to think out funeral plans in advance. A detailed funeral guidebook is available from Consumer Affairs, Program Department, NRTA-AARP, 1909 K Street, NW, Washington D.C. 20049.

Immediately after the funeral:

1. *Lawyer:*
   If there is an estate to settle, hire a lawyer. He/she will help you with many of the following items which you must deal with.
2. *Social Security:*
   Notify the nearest Social Security office that your husband has died. Take with you:
   a) your marriage certificate
   b) birth certificates of everyone in the family (including your deceased husband)
   c) a certified copy of the death certificate
   d) the Social Security numbers of everyone in the family.
   Social Security benefits will not start for a few months, but they are retroactive to the month you apply.
3. *Veterans Administration:*

If your husband was a veteran, notify the V.A. of his death.

4. *Insurance Companies:*
   Notify each insurance company that your husband is deceased. They will ask for:
   a) a copy of the death certificate
   b) the obituary notice
   c) an accident report, if the cause of death was an accident.

5. *Probate Court:*
   If there is an estate, your lawyer will file for probate in surrogate's court. There is a fee for filing varying from court to court. Any minor children will have a court appointed lawyer represent them in the hearing. That lawyer also receives a fee. File as soon as possible as the estate is tied up until the will has been probated.

6. *Stocks and Bonds:*
   Transfer any stock to the survivor's name. Send the certificates by registered mail to the transfer agent named on the stock certificate. Each certificate needs a cover letter and usually a certified death certificate. This may be expensive, but it is necessary.

7. *Credit Union:*
   Check to see if there are funds in a credit union. Each credit union has its own procedure for transfer to a survivor.

8. *Credit Cards:*
   Send your husband's credit cards in for transfer to your name. Send one at a time, if you have no credit rating, thus not losing all your "plastic money" at once.

9. *Real Estate:*
   If you own your own home, check to see if you have mortgage insurance.

10. *Auto Club Insurance:*
    If the car is registered in your husband's name, you must have ownership transferred. You may need to show a certified death certificate for this.

11. *Property Assessment:*
    For inheritance tax purposes, a complete assessment of goods and property will be made. You will have to pay for the appraisal; $50 is usually the minimum fee. A realtor's association can give you the name of one of their members who assesses property.

12. *Medical Insurance:*
    In certain states, you have the right to continue your family medical insurance under your husband's group coverage. This is much less expensive than obtaining private coverage. Check with your husband's employer.

13. *Records:*
    a) Make at least 6 copies of the death certificate.
    b) Keep a copy of each insurance policy and your covering letter in a separate file.
    c) Keep a separate folder or envelope for your husband's insurance transactions, legal papers, income tax, medical insurance transactions, funeral expenses, etc.

14. *Business Accounts:*
    If your husband had his own business, consult with his accountant regarding business monies and tax liabilities.

15. *Salesmen:*
    Be prepared for monument salesmen and realtors who will want to sell your house. They follow the funeral almost immediately.

Planning for the Future

Don't make any major decisions for a while—if you can help it—and then, only if you can first discuss pros and cons with an unemotionally involved third party you can trust.

The death of a spouse is the most stressful event life challenges us with. If we can help each other cope by sharing suggestions such as these, perhaps we can alleviate some of the stress and break the causal link between stress and illness which so often accompanies widowhood.

Before investing any money, such as insurance money, talk (and take notes) with your bank's trust department about safe investment. Talk with a bank officer about certificates of deposit and also get advice from an investment or stock broker. Check to see what investments are insured by the U.S. Government or other insurer.

You may also want to consider real estate or other property investments. Don't necessarily take the advice of your lawyer, or even your best friend. Investigate yourself—take lots of notes—then decide for yourself.

Don't be too anxious to invest your money in just one area. Spread it around. Do not hesitate to call for help. Your attorney, banker, accountant or financial planner will be glad to assist. But, we repeat, take lots of notes, do some research and decide for yourself. A helpful book on handling money is Sylvia Porter's *New Money Book for the 80's* which has a special section for widows.

After a Spouse's Death

The death of a spouse is *the* most stressful life event for women. Certain groups of widows are particularly vulnerable to stress:

- Those whose husbands died unexpectedly.
- Those who were very dependent on their spouse for support (or whose spouse was heavily dependent on them for social and emotional support).
- Those who did not have careers before marriage.
- Those who have always tried to be totally independent of relatives and friends; or the opposite, those whose whole life revolved around family.
- Those with teenage children. Although children can be very supportive, they need to be fed, clothed, and comforted. Their needs, joys, sorrows, and finally their separation from you take enormous energies. Many women are concerned that lack of a man around the house will have detrimental effects on their teenagers.

♦ Those whose income drops significantly as a result of the death of their husband (a widow's income can drop as much as 42 percent).

The loss in widowhood is great. Many women lose their beloved, familiar, and trusted companion; their personal and economic support; and their sense of identity. Frequently, their spouse has enhanced their sense of self by seeing them as important and unique human beings.

Women who have cared for their husbands during a long final illness have had time to explore their feelings about the dying person and have begun to disengage from him and from the relationship. Since death is not a total shock, they may experience ambivalent feelings of relief and loss. For women whose marriages have always been unsatisfying or even abusive, death of a spouse may come as a release. When death comes suddenly or violently, the initial period of bereavement is more difficult.

The Grief Process

Grief is the normal process we each must experience when we suffer a loss. It is a healing process, the only way we can detach ourselves from the person who has died. Our reaction to it may differ depending on our age, the suddenness of the death, our physical health, the number of children we have, the adequacy of our income, our ethnic background, and the number of social supports in our life.

Most grieving women show some signs of physical distress, with symptoms of insomnia, loss of appetite, fatigue, and, for some, an increased use of alcohol, cigarettes, or tranquilizers. Women report feelings of anxiety, hopelessness, anger, guilt, and remorse, expressed most often by frequent crying, depression, and inability to concentrate and to think clearly.

There are four common stages of grief: shock, numbness, disorganization, and, finally, reorganization.

Shock. The first response to death is usually shock and disbelief, followed by copious tears and deep sorrow. This stage may begin even before the spouse dies, such as at the moment when the woman first learns that her husband has only a limited time to live.

Numbness. In moments of great pain or loss our bodies adopt a strong defensive pattern that makes it easier, for a while, to handle strong emotions. A woman may experience an initial stage of numbness that begins at the moment of death and continues for several weeks or months. During this period a widow may function with unusual strength, in a mechanical yet fairly normal manner. It is as though she is anesthetized by shock, insulated for a while from the real feelings of pain. One woman described this as "a merciful numbness."

Disorganization. When the funeral is over and friends and relatives return to their own daily routines, the widow is alone with her grief. A stage of disorganization, confusion, and despair usually follows as she feels the full meaning of the loss.

Shortly after the death of their spouse, some women become preoccupied with an image of the deceased, feeling his presence and sometimes even experiencing hallucinations. Women report feelings of guilt about something they might have done to prevent their husbands' deaths, or regret that they weren't more loving. They may experience overwhelming moments of desolation and a sense of futility and injustice. During this stage, which may last a year or more, the process of mourning is unique for each individual. All women need to be encouraged to freely express their feelings as they emerge; postponing a confrontation with one's feelings can result in serious problems in the months or years ahead. It is healthy, and a sign of strength, to grieve openly. A widow may feel hurt, deserted, and angry, and she may express those feelings with tears and outbursts. The anger she feels may be directed not only at herself, the hospital or doctor, family and friends who try to help, but also at her deceased spouse, who has abandoned her. She feels overwhelmed by all the practical details of daily living and the awful aloneness of going on. Many women find themselves wishing they'd been the first to die. At the same time women may express an idealized image of the deceased. Often this is a time of temporary withdrawal from others and a rejection of all consolation. Women feel unloved and uncared for, and they feel they have no one to love and care for.

Feelings of lingering loneliness sometimes override even the feelings of loss. Loneliness is especially severe for women who are poor or in ill health or who have always lived close to home and have established only "coupled" friends, with whom they may now feel awkward or out of touch. These feelings of loneliness, which may be intense enough to make a woman feel she is "going crazy," losing touch with reality, often lead to a transient depression characterized by apathy, withdrawal, and inactivity.

Reorganization and
Recovery

Once a woman has allowed herself to experience the depth of her grief, the final stage of reorganization can begin. Most women move on to this stage, but a small number are unable or unwilling to adapt to their loss and continue to grieve throughout their lives. There is no clear time when grieving ends, but most widows describe a turning point in their lives when they are no longer centered around their dead spouse. They have finally accepted the reality that their marriage is part of their past and are able to seize control over the direction their lives will take.

Women reorganize in various ways: They get jobs, rearrange living environments, change former relationships, and seek new social contacts. The energy they used in mourning is now used to begin a new way of life. As a woman begins to feel life is worth living she grows more self-sufficient and independent and her ego grows stronger. She faces the world as a single woman, not as a widow—and her emphasis is on looking ahead and planning for her future.

Practical Problems

Financial Inadequacy
Almost every study of widowhood indicates that the economic burden is second only to loneliness. Since less than one-third of all married women of any age are financially independent, inadequate income becomes one of a widow's major problems. Widows are much worse off financially than widowers. About 40 percent of all widows live on or below the poverty level. Most have obtained income only from their husbands' earnings, and few have any pension or pattern of regular employment. Bills from a prolonged illness and from the funeral may be high. Most widows do not receive survivor benefits from their husband's pension, and social security payments (small as they are) don't begin until about three months after the widow applies for them. Life insurance policies are often inadequate, and any money a widow receives is frequently spent within the first two years. These conditions, combined with the reality that it is difficult for older women to get jobs, leave widows poor. Despite the myth of the wealthy American widow, only one-quarter of all widows report living reasonably free of financial worries. This financial insecurity is one reason women disengage from social activities such as entertaining, going to movies or restaurants, or taking trips.

Social Security

Social security is often the only financial support a widow has. But the social security "widow's gap" declares that a widow is not eligible for benefits until her youngest child's eighteenth birthday and her own age of 60 (or 50, if she is disabled). Since the average age of widowhood is 56, this leaves many widows without any source of support for several years. (The 1981 White House Conference on Aging recommended that a transition benefit of at least three years be paid to a widow of any age, allowing her to get whatever training she needs to reenter the job market.) Widows receive social security support for children until age 22, provided they are attending school and are unmarried. Many widows postpone working until after this time, so they will not have these payments reduced or cut off. Retirement age, with reduced benefits, begins at age 60, with full benefits at age 65, if one waits until then to begin receiving payments. Social security also gives a lump-sum death payment of $255 to help pay for funeral expenses.

Veterans' Benefits

Veterans are entitled to a maximum of $250 for burial expenses, plus $150 toward a private cemetery plot. The Veterans Administration also offers pensions for non-service-connected deaths for widows and children of veterans of World War I, World War II, the Korean conflict, and the Viet Nam war.

Life Insurance

A widow has the choice of receiving life insurance proceeds in a lump sum or in some other form. She can ask the insurance company for an amount to cover immediate expenses, then put the rest under an interest option with the understanding that she can withdraw any or all of it later. Such a payment plan spares a widow of making decisions under pressure.

Employer Benefits

After a widow notifies her husband's employer of her husband's death, procedures begin about company insurance policies, vested retirement plans, or investment plans. Fraternal and other organizations to which the husband belonged should be notified, as they often provide widow benefits.

Health Effects of Widowhood

Often relatives, friends, and employers, not understanding the grief process, treat a widow as "sick" and assume she is unable to make her own decisions. This may undermine the widow's attempts to put her life back in order. There can be, however, an increase in genuine health problems during the first six months after bereavement.

A study at Montefiore Medical Center in New York City disclosed that a continuous lack of the "tranquilizing influence" of human companionship leaves widows and widowers more susceptible to physical as well as emotional illnesses. This was particularly true of bereaved people with heart disease, diabetes, and other major health problems. Chronic illnesses became worse during the first year of widowhood. In fact, the death rate of surviving spouses was ten times higher than among married people of comparable age and sex. Suicide rates were higher in the first year after the death of a spouse for both women and men. The study's findings point to the importance of support. It was discovered that those who received supportive psychotherapy for several months following bereavement to aid them in working through the grief process were less likely to need medical treatment or medication than those who did not get such care, and the study urges hospitals to establish "bereavement clinics."

Support Systems

One important aspect of grief is appealing to others for help. Adult children, particularly daughters, provide helpful emotional support. Women widowed in their middle years (earlier than most of their friends) often have parents to turn to as a resource. Siblings and relatives can be instrumental in helping a widow. For some fortunate widows, old friends, both married and single, deepen their relationships through the years:

> *I have been widowed for several years and most of my close married friends have continued to be a strong, enduring support network. There has been no diminution of their caring and reaching out to me. All through my husband's three-year illness, and in the years since then, the couple who live across the street from me have been superb friends—attentive to my moods, knowing how to bring a note of cheerfulness to each situation, including me in all appropriate social gatherings, and informally asking me to go for walks or to come over for a drink. I've been*

*very touched by their thoughtfulness and try to reciprocate when-
ever possible.*

*I have a sense that many widows sit back and wait to be
taken care of, expecting one-way friendships. It's really important for us to be interesting women, and interested in other people, to positively contribute to conversations and to give of ourselves to the same degree that others give to us.*

Cheryl, age 58

Other widows experience painful separations from former friends. Studies show that married friends often avoid the
recently bereaved woman. They restrict their visits or invitations
for fear that they might be confronted with painful emotional
outbursts, tears, constant talk of the deceased, and confessions of
loneliness, even when they are aware that this grieving process is
necessary. Lunch invitations around the kitchen table may replace
the "coupled" dinner party. Married friends may jealously guard
their own husbands, and few older women have the opportunity
to develop supportive male friendships that could help ease the
strangeness of the initial loneliness.

*You learn not to talk about your feelings—it only seems to em-
barrass your friends. I had to tell my friends I felt fine; otherwise
they stopped calling me.*

Susan, age 55

Helping the Older Widow

Friends who are eager to help might avoid well-meaning platitudes
and instead offer practical help, emotional support, and a ready
ear. A sympathetic person who has gone through similar experiences can be helpful. Often a visit or phone call from such a person
can act as proof that another woman has survived the devastation
the new widow is feeling.

Family and close friends can help with immediate decisions and funeral arrangements. They should not exclude the
widow, but instead support her in making the arrangements. Many
widows need immediate help with arranging their finances. This
help should come from a person outside of the family such as a
financial adviser or lawyer.

Each woman is a unique individual. Friends should allow
her to follow her own pace in grieving. Allow the widow to express

her grief, which peaks for many in the second week of bereavement. Give her the opportunity to talk openly about the death, if she chooses to. Don't be afraid of saying the "wrong" thing. To say nothing is worse.

Friends should encourage a widow not to make any major changes in her lifestyle for the first year.

Although relatives and some friends surrounding a widow will accept and even encourage her grief for a few months, a widow may also find it useful to turn to a counselor trained in bereavement. In recent years there has been an expanding national network of support groups initiated to help ease the impact of the loss of a loved one. Bereavement centers, which have been formed across the country, are places where small groups of widowed people can discuss problems, vent their feelings, and identify their strengths. Hope is enkindled that eventually things will change and each will soon be able to make it on their own. (See the Resources section at the end of the chapter for services for widowed persons.)

Some women are unwilling to or incapable of mustering the courage or energy to face widowhood and create a new lifestyle.

My husband of 42 years died quite unexpectedly last year. Since then I have been living the life of a lonely recluse. It's not that our friends don't invite me, but I feel awkward, and even more alone with them. My children continue to ask me to dinner or the movies, but I feel it's out of a sense of duty and I don't want to be a burden to them. Who wants an old person around all the time? It was different when J. was alive.

Nella, age 68

Most widows, however, after a period of normal grieving meet the challenge of widowhood. They readjust their lives in major ways, overcoming feelings of shyness, helplessness, and inferiority. They reschedule their daily routine and plan not to be alone on holidays, particularly birthdays and anniversaries. They strike out in new directions and find a job or do volunteer work or go to school. In the process they become more interesting to themselves and to others. As one woman stated, "A few minutes ago I was a widow, and suddenly I'm a whole woman again." Late-life widowhood can bring a woman, perhaps for the first time, to the full discovery of herself as an individual, as she succeeds in learning to live alone and to enjoy life.

> *Death is a great awakener. I have discovered another self, one that I remember dimly from half a lifetime ago. It is a leaner more alert warrior, but at the same time more grateful for friendship and more convinced of the necessity to embrace change. . . . I am alive, definitely alive.*
>
> Sarah, age 62

Resources: Lifelong Singlehood

Publications

Edwards, M., and E. Hoover. *The Challenge of Being Single*. Los Angeles: Tarcher, 1974.

Peterson, Nancy. *Lives for Ourselves: Women Who Have Never Married*. New York: Putnam, 1981.

Shahan, Lynn. *Living Alone and Liking It*. Los Angeles, Stratford Press, 1981.

Stein, P. *Single*. Englewood Cliffs, NJ: Prentice-Hall, 1976.

Washington, Mary Helen. "Working at Single Bliss," *Ms.*, October 1982.

Organizations

Holiday Dinner Club
P.O. Box 691
Wall Street Station
New York, NY 10005
Director: Sandra Fagen

Resources: Divorce and Separation

Publications

Baker, Nancy C. *New Lives for Former Wives*. Garden City, NY: Anchor/Doubleday, 1980.

Erickson, Nancy. *A Woman's Guide to Marriage and Divorce in New York State*. Woman's Law Center, 1414 Sixth Avenue, New York, NY 10019.

Frohlich, Newton. *Making the Best of It: A Common Sense Guide to Negotiating a Divorce*. New York: Harper & Row, 1971.

Gettleman, Susan, and Janet Markowitz. *The Courage to Divorce*. New York: Simon & Schuster, 1975.

Greene, Roberta. *Till Divorce Do You Part*. Know, Inc., P.O. Box 86031, Pittsburgh, PA 15221.

Hirsch, Barbara B. *Divorce: What a Woman Needs to Know*. Chicago: Regnery, 1973.

McConnell, Adeline, and Beverly Anderson. *Single after 50: How to Have the Time of Your Life*. New York: McGraw-Hill, 1979.

Mindley, Carol. *The Divorced Mother: A Guide to Readjustment*. New York: McGraw-Hill, 1969.

Ross, Susan D. *ACLU Handbook: The Rights of Women*. New York: Avon Books, 1973.

Van Buskirk, D. *Separation and Divorce Handbook*. 13 Huyler Road, Box 201, Setauket, NY 11733.

Women in Transition, Inc. *Women in Transition: A Feminist Handbook on Separation and Divorce*. New York: Scribner's, 1975.

Organizations

International Parents without Partners (PWP)
7910 Woodmont Ave.
Bethesda, MD 20014
301-654-8850

Local PWP groups are listed in the phone book.

*R*esources: Widowhood

Publications

Caine, Lynn. *Widow*. New York: Morrow, 1974.

Lindsey, Rae. *Alone and Surviving: A Guide for Today's Widow*. New York: Walker, 1977.

Lopata, Helena. *Women as Widows: Support Systems*. New York: Elsevier, 1979.

Mooney, Elizabeth. *Alone: Surviving as a Widow*. New York: Putnam, 1981.

Parkes, Colin. *Bereavement*. New York: Universities Press, 1972.

Petersen, James, and Michael Briley. *Widows and Widowhood*. New York: Association Press, 1977.

Porter, Sylvia. *Sylvia Porter's New Money Book for the 80's*. New York: Avon Books, 1980.

Shoemaker, Jane. *Widow's Walk*. Indianapolis: Newkirk, 1975.

Silverman, Phyllis. *Helping Each Other in Widowhood*. New York: Health Sciences, 1974.

Temes, Roberta. *Living with an Empty Chair: A Guide through Grief*. New York: Irvington, 1980.

Pamphlets and Other Material

"Commitment to a Better Life," by Federal Council on Aging, National Policy Concerns for Older Women, 1975
Superintendent of Documents
U.S. Government Printing Office
Washington, DC 20402

"Job Finding Techniques for Mature Women"
Superintendent of Documents
U.S. Government Printing Office
Washington, DC 20402

Lynn Caine's Lifelines
65 W. 90th St.
New York, NY 10024
Monthly newsletter to help widows

"Money in Your Life"
Women's Division, Institute of Life Insurance
277 Park Ave.
New York, NY 10017

"Retirement Widowhood Guide" and "On Being Alone"
American Association for Retired Persons
1909 K St., N.W.
Washington, DC 20006

Widow to Widow Program Kit
Laboratory of Community Psychiatry
Harvard Medical School
58 Fenwood Road
Boston, MA 02115

Organizations

Widowed Service Line
Boston, MA
617-371-0436
Telephone answering service by widows.

Widow to Widow Program
Department of Psychiatry
Harvard University Medical School
Cambridge, MA 02138
New widows are contacted about six weeks after bereavement. Person-to-person counseling, discussion groups, a 24 hour hot-line, and other services are available.

The Bereavement and Loss Center
170 E. 83rd St.
New York, NY 10028
Individual and group counseling for widowed, divorced, and separated persons.

NAIM Conference
109 N. Dearborn
Chicago, IL 60602
315-944-1286
Psychological, financial, legal, and spiritual help for Catholic widowed persons.

THEOS (They Help Each Other Spiritually)
11609 Frankstown Road
Pittsburgh, PA 15235
Nondenominational group for newly bereaved persons.

Widows Consultation Center
136 E. 57th St.
New York, NY 10022
212-688-8850
A nonprofit counseling service specifically for the widow. Some advice is given over the phone. Small fees are charged and arrangements made for those who can't afford them.

Bettye Lane

Chapter Three

New Beginnings

The resourcefulness of women seems to increase as they age. Although many choose the single state as their preferred lifestyle, others decide that remarriage and/or late-life children are their choice. Thousands of women are choosing a new partner in mid- or late life, and we are experiencing an almost epidemic number of women having first (or last) children in their fourth decade. Women over 40 represent the largest number of students returning to school and reentering the labor market. We are experimenting with new lifestyles and with innovative living arrangements. In the second half of our lives we are becoming more courageous and resourceful than ever before.

Remarriage after Forty

I've been remarried for nine years and have never been happier. My first marriage took place when I was 21 and lasted nine years. My former husband's increasing infidelities went against all my personal values, and I decided on divorce. I raised my son alone for the next fourteen rough years, during which I painfully reestablished my self-worth and self-esteem. This time around I

*was sure about what I needed . . . my basic needs were for a
mature man whom I could respect and trust without reserve. I'd
long since given up the idea of marrying again when I met a man
my age who'd been divorced ten years earlier. We were married
three months later. Although we enjoy each other's company, we
consciously work every day at improving our relationship. We've
learned how to honestly express our feelings and thoughts. We
are equal partners in this joint and loving venture—our marriage.*

Becky, age 52

Many happy second marriages have occurred in midlife
and late life. In fact, the number of marriages among older women
in the United States has more than doubled since 1960. An
estimated 16,000 women over the age of 65 will marry, most of
them for the second time, despite the fact that there are 150
women for every 100 men over the age of 65. Half to two-thirds
of second marriages last as long as their partners live. The people
most likely to remarry are:

- Divorced women (more often than widows)
- Four out of five divorced women in their twenties, within four years;
  two out of five divorced women over 40
- Women who are less educated
- Women over 45 (11 percent after five years)
- Five out of six divorced men of all ages
- Men over 45 (60 percent within five years)
- Men over 65 (seven times more likely than women over 65)

Sociologist Walter McKain studied one hundred couples
over age 60 who had been remarried for four to six years. He found
that seventy-four of these marriages were successful and only six
were hopeless. What makes for strong and happy remarriages in
the second half of life? Chances of success are maximized when
people have known each other for many years (often as the widowed spouse of a family friend); were in good health; were personally well adjusted; agree to set up a new home away from the home
occupied by a former mate; pool their financial resources and have
sufficient income to make the new relationship exciting; and have
children and friends who approve of the match. The resistance of
children and friends to a new mate can prove to be a major

Proportion of Men and Women by Age

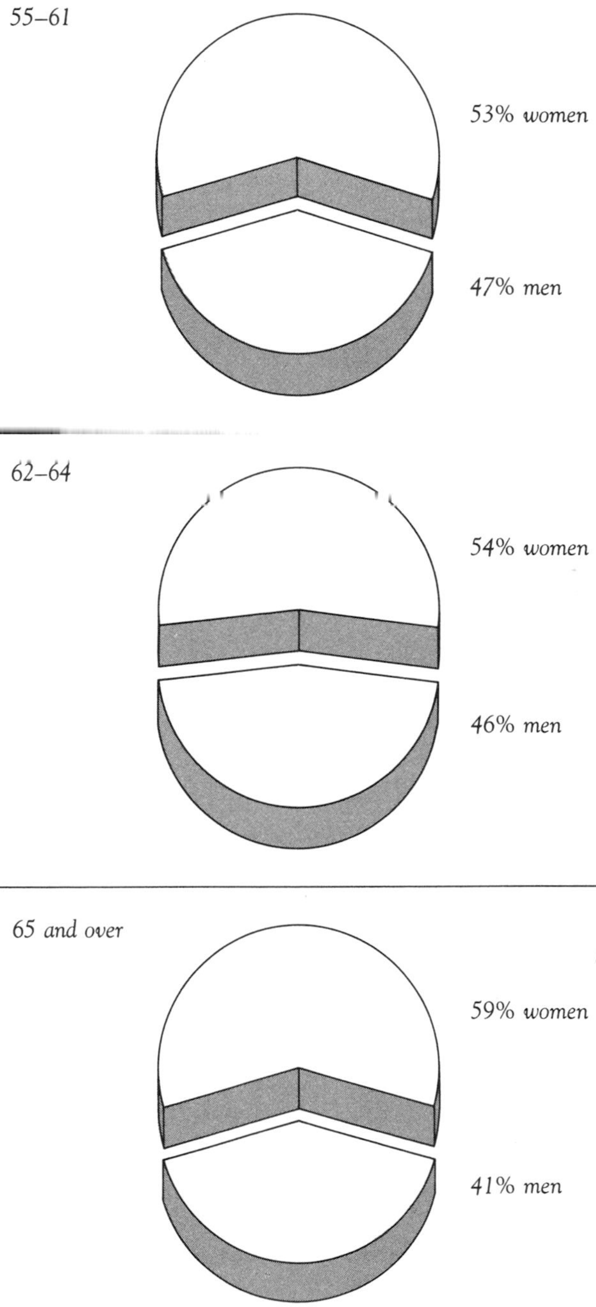

55–61

53% women

47% men

62–64

54% women

46% men

65 and over

59% women

41% men

stumbling block for many women. Some adult children actively encourage their widowed or divorced mothers to find new marriage partners. Others are very discouraging and assertively voice concerns over "loyalty" to their father. They may insist that their mother is acting "silly" or that she is being taken advantage of for her money. Many of these children find it painful to readjust their own lives to accommodate a new "father" or to relinquish dependency on their mother; some fear the loss of their inheritance.

For some older women the fear of going out to meet and date men is too overwhelming. Some may feel disloyal to a former mate or feel that no other man could live up to their former spouse. Other older women are obsessed with remarrying, spending most of their days trying to look younger to catch a man. Those women are often afraid to grow into self-confidence and independence. For some women remarrying is one way to continue the nurturing role that they lost when their husband and possibly their children left. They simply want someone to take care of, since their lives have always been lived for someone else. Many more formerly married women, however, are pleased to be single again and treasure their new found privacy and independence. Remarriage is not in their plans.

When women meet potential partners, they often find that remarriage is not as simple as marriage was, especially if each has grown children. Some of the questions they ask are the following:

- "Will my children be fully accepted by him?"
- "How will his children feel about me?"
- "Does this man simply want a caretaker?"
- "Will I be making a big mistake, at this late stage of my life?"
- "Will this new marriage improve the situation I'm living in?"
- "Do I really want to rearrange my life to fit in his time schedule?"

No one is predicting how long our marriage will last. This marriage business is give and take. And we don't have time to fight.

Louisa, age 78 (marrying an 89-year-old man)

Older women planning to remarry might consider: (1) seeking competent premarital counseling to allow them and their prospective spouses to explore their mixed feelings; (2) setting some long-range goals for the years ahead; and (3) discussing with a lawyer the possibility of drawing up a premarital contract or agreement. Most women wish to assure that part of their estate will revert to their children in case of death or divorce. A premarital agreement (which is different from a will) clearly defines how money and property assets are to be distributed. Such premarriage contracts are common in Europe.

Remarriage often means moving to another part of the country and making new friends. The Remarried Association, a Long Island, New York, group for couples embarked in second marriages, helps people face such changes. For more than ten years this group has successfully acted as a support group helping couples starting over again find new friends.

For some women, especially those who remarry quickly, the marriage proves to be a mistake. These women face the pain of a second divorce or the choice (which many make) to remain the rest of their lives in an unsatisfying relationship. But the majority of women who choose to marry in their later years report that their unions are satisfying and happy. Free of childrearing, in-law conflicts, and career ambitions, second marriages can be very rewarding, offering companionship and love that enhance the quality of life in later years. Each remarriage should be based on the hope that life will be enhanced with the new spouse.

I married at 18 and was divorced twenty-five years later, when my children were grown. I remarried in my fifties, returned to college for my first degree, and now, in my seventies, have acquired a doctoral degree and completed my second novel. My second marriage has lasted as long as my first, and within it I have undergone the long process of finally discovering what my own needs are. These later years within this good marriage have been the most challenging of all.

Sophie, age 78

Motherhood after Forty

After many years, and many doctors' examinations we were told we could not have our own child. We adopted two little ones and then—at age 41—I became pregnant for the first time. Sara was born beautiful and healthy. What surprises us most is the number of couples we discovered around us who are having their first children in their late thirties and early forties. Many of us are professional women. We felt safe, with amniocentesis, to postpone our family. Now many of our friends have little ones. We all feel "out of step" with other couples our age who have teenagers and college children, so we act as a support network for each other. We've no role models and are in a sense pioneers— but I must say it's been lots of fun to go to the zoo, the circus, and picnics in our middle years. My husband and I have never been closer.

Lynne, age 43

A new breed of women is emerging: those in their forties who are having children. A growing number of women feel they can best achieve their goals of both a career and a family by deferring marriage and/or postponing motherhood until their late thirties and early forties. Just a few years ago, women tended to be ashamed of a late-life pregnancy, but today it is often deliberately planned, with a clear knowledge of the increased risks involved. Sally Quinn, a well-known Washington journalist, wrote in the October 1982 issue of *Harper's Bazaar* that her marriage was good and her career secure. And yet she had an overwhelming feeling that she wanted more: "I needed to have a baby." She adds: "As I write this my baby is two months old, and I will be 41 tomorrow. I keep asking myself now, how could I possibly have ever contemplated *not* having this experience. . . . There is no way to describe the love that makes your chest ache when you hold your own child. . . . This child has simply added a marvelous new dimension to my life."

There are both positive and negative experiences confronting women who choose to become first-time mothers after age 40. These women have a mature appreciation of the problems and joys of motherhood. They've read and observed more, and as a result they know more about giving birth and rearing a child than many younger first-time mothers. They have had time to establish their independent identities, complete their education, establish careers, travel, and develop secure and open marriages. They are more likely to be financially secure and, therefore, able to afford help with housework and child care. Some leave their jobs for several years, finding that working interferes with the full-time joys and demands of motherhood. Others return to work after a maternity leave of two to twelve months. If they are established in their field, they may even be able to negotiate part-time hours while their baby is young.

Women who are well nourished and in good health and who obtain good prenatal care are often capable of delivering a normal baby throughout their middle years. The difficulties of achieving and maintaining a normal pregnancy should not be minimized however. Reproductive capacity begins to decline as early as the late twenties. There is some cause for women to worry that if they wait too long they may not be able to conceive. Infertility in older women is most often caused by infection, fibroid tumors, or endometriosis (cell growth that blocks and can damage the fallopian tubes). Late-life mothers are more likely to experience difficult labor, cesarean births, hypertension, and diabetes. Miscarriages in the first three months are almost four times more frequent for older women. They are at a higher risk of life-threatening toxemia (causing high blood pressure and excessive weight gain) and hemorrhaging before or during childbirth.

Women who have postponed childbearing are most often afraid of delivering a baby with Down's syndrome (mongoloidism) or other birth defects. Seven percent of all human fetuses are chromosomally abnormal. For older mothers this figure approaches 24 percent or more. Advances in modern technology, particularly the prenatal diagnostic technique of amniocentesis, make late pregnancy less risky than ever before. Amniocentesis, which was developed about fifteen years ago, is a simple procedure done, under local anesthesia, usually in a hospital during the fourteenth to seventeenth week of pregnancy by a qualified obstetrician. The fetus is located with ultrasound equipment. A small hollow needle is inserted through the abdomen and uterus of the pregnant woman and into the amniotic sac. A tablespoon or two of the amniotic fluid surrounding the fetus is withdrawn. The fetal cells from this fluid are then grown in a laboratory for two to three weeks. Physicians are able to identify more than eighty metabolic disorders and chromosome abnormalities with this test, including Down's syndrome, Tay-Sachs disease, and cystic fibrosis. They can also determine the sex of the unborn child and the presence of twins. If abnormalities are discovered, a woman has the choice of continuing the pregnancy or having a legal abortion (possible in many states up to the twenty-fourth week of pregnancy). Although amniocentesis is not without risks, such as fetal injury, infection, and spontaneous abortion, recent national studies found the risks extremely small and the diagnostic accuracy very high.

Another negative factor in late childbearing is that women may be out of sync with their peers, caring for new infants when their friends are sending children off to college. The difference in age between parent and child may pose problems later. Some women wonder what it will be like to raise an adolescent when they themselves are in their late fifties or early sixties, as well as whether the fathers will live to see their children through high school. Children born to older parents may never know the joy of having grandparents. Conversely, late-life mothers may miss becoming grandmothers.

Women who have their first children at an early age and then decide to have another child in later life may face similar problems as late-life mothers. Some become pregnant after many years to avoid the empty nest syndrome and to feel needed or to avoid the other challenges of later life, such as jobs or careers. Many have a sincere desire to have another child before it's too late.

I had my fourth child when I was 40 and my youngest daughter was 18. Despite the admonitions of most of our friends, this little one is the joy of all of our lives. There is simply no comparison between those hectic early days of childrearing in my twenties and the leisurely way Jennine is growing up now. She is three years old today, and I feel I've never been happier.

Meg, age 43

A practice of increasing popularity among women in their forties, single or married, is to adopt their first child.

Because of my age, I had a lot of difficulty adopting a baby. The agency finally agreed to give me a "handicapped infant," a ten-week-old girl who they thought was mentally deficient. Well, six months later, Suzanne is thriving. With the tender loving care I have been able to give her, all pediatricians agree that she is a particularly alert and bright child. I'm a college professor and have found a wonderful mature woman to care for my baby while I teach. I have never felt happier or more fulfilled.

Stephanie, age 41

Reentry to School

Being in your class on older women has rattled my thoughts and feelings—making me face issues head-on which I have been successfully circumventing for a long time. I am saying things out loud that I have never said before, like telling people my true age, that my oldest son is 32, and that I've been married for thirty-six years. I'm about to retire from one job but am back in school to consider my next career. I'm beginning to realize that age is good; the more the better.

Roberta, age 65

I remember the sinking feelings I had during my older son's last year of high school. He was making plans to go to college. My younger son was looking forward to his first year of high school come fall.

What was happening in my life? What plans did I have? What were my goals? What about my future? All of a sudden it hit me that I was almost out of a job, and now what?

This was the point in my life when I really took action. I said to myself, "Look, you have a great husband and two sons, ages 18 and 14. They don't need your full attention anymore. Now, get going and go back to school and get your own degree and a career before it's too late!"

There had been a long interruption between the time I had married, had my sons, and spent those 18 years involved with taking care of my family and meeting their needs.

"Now," I told myself, "if you're smart, you'll have the best of all possible worlds." I've had twenty years with my parents while growing up, twenty years with my own family raising them, now the next twenty years can be for me to go out in the world and see what I can do for myself!

Norine, age 45

Education is as important for older women as it is for younger women. It can be their connection to productive and personally satisfying lives as they advance in years. Most women over 40 who return to school are searching for self-expression, personal power, creativity, fellowship, the joy of learning, and, most important, an entrée to meaningful, well-paid jobs that will give them purpose and economic security during their later years.

Although equal numbers of women and men complete high school today, only 9 percent of women over 25, compared to 17 percent of men the same age, complete a bachelor's degree. Only 3 percent of women over 25 receive advanced degrees. This gap in education has resulted in low status and low-paid employment for women. As increasing numbers of women live to the eighth and ninth decade, the need to prepare women for economic independence is imperative.

While the proportion of older people returning to the campus is still relatively small (persons age 55 to 64 are only 6.6 percent of the total number of adult learners, and those over 65 represent only 3 percent), the actual numbers, some two million, are impressive. The largest numbers of women returning to school are those under 35 and over 55.

Today's over-65 population has completed an average of 9.5 years of schooling: 37 percent completed high school, while only 8 percent had four or more years of college. These figures will increase dramatically in the near future, as the more highly educated middle-aged and younger generations grow older.

Women over 40 constitute the largest group of students returning to school, for a variety of reasons: Some want to complete their high school education, some are attending specific trade schools, but most want to take up or complete academic programs at colleges and universities. Contrary to the myth that older people are less able to learn, older students have discovered they increase their learning capacity as they use their mental muscles. Women returning to school have generally been found to work harder, do more critical research, and perform as well as, if not better than, younger students.

I'll never forget my first day at school. As I was driving there, I realized I had the whole day to myself. I was alone! *I could make my own decisions: when to study, where, when to eat lunch, what to have and where. I was responsible to no one else's schedule but my own. I made new friends, thought about new ideas, became more enthusiastic about life than ever before. I was a little bit more me—and ecstatic.*

Peggy, age 42

This is a good time in history for women to return to school. Colleges are faced with an increasing loss of their student population and are turning to gray-haired women and men to fill up their empty seats. Older people are a brand-new constituency in postsecondary education.

I never had a chance to even start college until I became a widow at 63. I started by taking one course a semester. Now I'm taking four courses! I am always the oldest person in my class, but I don't mind at all. Instead of making fun of me because I'm old enough to be my classmates' grandmother, my classmates all treat me with respect and make me feel welcome. I am now starting my second year in college and hope to graduate when I reach 70.

Frances, age 67

Older women need a good deal of training to become advocates in their own behalf. This is a serious need. We must be able to speak out about the poverty and discrimination we face.

Judie, age 79

Obstacles in the Reentry Path

Poor self-image, lack of confidence in her ability to learn, a sense that she will feel out of place among young students, and "sabotage" by family and friends can be a woman's major obstacles.

My reentry process was very slow. I was so convinced that I couldn't learn, after thirty years away from school, that I decided to go forty-five miles away to the New School for Social Research in New York City, so that no one I knew would be aware of my "inevitable" failure. I can still taste the joy of those initial weeks—the recognition that I could still read with intelligence and participate hesitantly but as articulately as my younger colleagues. The return to self-confidence was a slow (but steady) process. Two years later, with the support of my consciousness-raising group and a women's career counseling course, I applied to the master's program of the School of Social Welfare. After some initial attempts by the school to ignore my application, be-

cause of my age (50), and some assertive steps by me to counteract this age discrimination, I was accepted. For the next two years, I was a full-time student, with a new kind of freedom, energy, and expectation of myself. Perhaps the biggest freedom was, for the first time in twenty-five years, to be just me. I didn't tell anyone for the first term that I was a wife and mother of seven. It was risky and scary to reclaim my individuality. Would people react positively to just me? (They did.) Another small but important freedom was to wear jeans and casual clothing every day. By my second year, my mind clicked back into gear. As a matter of fact, I have never had a more productive time in my life.

Anna, age 50

Family Sabotage

Some women report that their husbands and families are reluctant to accept their return to school and may even attempt to sabotage the process. They may say they are happy with the woman's decision, but in subtle ways they make it harder. Children continue the demands to take them shopping, to make their costumes for the play, or to bake for the school bake sale. Many men are threatened by their wife's schooling, feeling she's using it as an excuse to get out of the house and away from him. Others are afraid the "equilibrium" of their marriage will be shaken if their wives are successful. Husbands may promise to come home to care for the children and then don't, or they may choose the night before a final exam to provoke a quarrel or pout every night as their wives do their homework. Many others' husbands and children, however, totally support their wives' and mothers' return to school and are proud of the new exciting person "their" students become.

Pressure from Fellow Students

Most women reentering school are afraid of competing with bright young students. They feel self-conscious at age 40, 50, and 60 in a class full of 20-year-olds. They may initially feel paranoid that everyone is looking at them and wondering why they are there.

What a shock that first day was, in a classroom full of students my children's age. They all seemed so sure of themselves and initially very reserved with me. It took a few months for them to accept me as a fellow student—and for me to share with them my reasons for returning to school at age 50. Now I feel accepted by most; some of them even talk over their problems with me.

Margaret, age 50

When I returned to school after a thirty-five-year gap, I was strongly advised just to sit quietly and listen, not participate. I was told that my life experience would intimidate both young students and faculty. This lasted for about a week until I realized that I had a lot to learn from my colleagues and they from me. Another kind of pressure those first weeks came from friends and a few fellow students: "This is a hard school to get into, don't you feel guilty about taking the place of a younger student who could work for lots more years in the field of social work?" One thing we older students are succeeding in doing is shattering the myth that older people can't learn—and replacing it with role modeling of lifelong learning.

Kathy, age 57

Pressure from Friends and Relatives

The return to school is a lonely route for many older women. They may be the only one in their social set to chart this difficult path for themselves. Few people around them understand the total time commitment school involves. Friends can't understand why they aren't available for lunch or an afternoon in the city, anymore. Friends soon stop calling for weekend dinners since the older student has no more time to entertain. Aging parents and siblings are angry at feeling neglected.

Lack of Financial Resources

Reentry to college is financially difficult for most women. They are caught in the family budget squeeze, with their own children in, or about to enter, higher education. Married women are usually dependent on their husbands' salary for financial aid, and that is not always forthcoming. Many husbands refuse outright to finance their wives' education, but their salaries may make their wives ineligible for financial aid from the college. Many women feel that their needs are not important enough to justify taking a share of the family's money for their own education. Husbands', children's, and friends' attitudes may contribute to such feelings of guilt.

> *The only way I could deal with my own guilt in "taking" money from my husband and children for my own education was to sit down and monetarily add up the twenty-two years (8,030 days) I had put into our marriage. Eight thousand dollars would get me a four-year degree. That came out to one dollar a day for each of the days I was a full-time homemaker. That seemed reasonable. Only then could I justify returning to school.*
>
> Meredith, age 44

Sometimes women simply proceed, despite financial obstacles, to plan their return to school:

> *The worst year was when seven of us were in higher education at the same time (excluding only my husband and high school daughter). But with working summers and weekends, loans, and scholarship assistance, we made it through. It never even occurred to me to drop out. This was my turn and my need— equally as important as my children's. My husband supported me all the way.*
>
> Bobbie, age 56

Some midlife women recognize their need to become self-sufficient when they recognize that their marriages are beginning to flounder. Unfortunately in order to get the training necessary for an independent life, they often need to remain in unsatisfactory relationships. One woman reports: "I'm still living with my husband while I get my education. He's my only source of income, but I feel like a prostitute." Women over 40 and recently divorced or separated are particularly in need of financial assistance. Some divorce judges are awarding maintenance money instead of alimony for limited periods of time, and divorced women can use this money to finance their education. Child care often remains a problem for single women students over 40. Colleges could offer scholarships to help such women cover the expenses of child-sitters.

> *I didn't have enough money for college when I was young. But now, as a divorced single parent, I need that degree to be self-supportive. I was awarded a monthly maintenance check (in lieu of alimony) for a five-year period. By then, I have to be on my*

own or go on welfare. That's a lot of pressure, but I think I can do it. It feels good to be in control of my own life and time.

Sandra, age 45

Many women, however, cannot gain a skill and begin to earn a living wage in the few years alloted to them. Many are forced to compromise or abandon their hopes.

How to Finance Your College Education

Much of the available education funding is restricted to students working for credit on a full-time (or at least half-time) basis, despite the fact that two-thirds of all adult students are able to go to school only part-time. Many mature women students must remain involved with raising children or working while they pursue formal learning.

For information on relevant federal loans, scholarships, and work-study programs, older reentry women can do the following:

- See the financial aid officer of the school in which you wish to enroll.

- Write to The Division of Student Support, Bureau of Postsecondary Education, National Institute of Education, Department of Health and Human Services (HHS), 300 Independence Ave., S.W., Washington, DC 20202.

- Write to the Institute of Lifetime Learning, Department TS, 1909 K St., N.W., Washington, DC 20049, for a state-by-state listing of the 1,500 colleges and universities that offer free or reduced tuition to older people.

- If you are working, check with your employer to see if the company will provide financial aid to meet some of your college expenses or allow you to have time off to attend classes.

- Examine closely the following programs for potential financial aid ("hidden monies") for higher education:
  Adult Education Act
  Basic Educational Opportunity Grants (for low-income elderly)
  Economic Opportunity Act
  Fund for the Improvement of Postsecondary Education, HHS
  Title I of the Higher Education Act of 1965/76 (The Lifelong Learning Act)
  Library Services and Construction Act
  National Commission on Libraries and Information Science Act
  Older Americans Act

National Endowment for the Humanities
National Endowment for the Arts
National Institutes of Health and Mental Health
National Science Foundation
State agencies
Wonder Woman Foundation, 75 Rockefeller Plaza, New York, NY
    10020
The Business and Professional Women's Foundation, 2012 Massachu-
    setts Ave., N.W., Washington, DC 20003
Jeannette Rankin Foundation, P.O. Box 4045, Athens, GA 30602
    ($500)
Clairol Loving Care Scholarship Program, 345 Park Avenue, New
    York, NY 10022
Best Products Foundation, Box 112A, Londonderry Turnpike, R.F.D.
    7, Manchester, NH ($300–$1,000 for displaced homemakers)

Other programs that older reentry women should know about are
the following:

- Title IV of the Older Americans Act provides support for students who
  wish to make gerontology a career or to upgrade professional skills in
  the field. (It is estimated that some 30,000 gerontology specialists will
  be needed during the 1980s.)

- Under discussion are educational entitlement programs in which older
  people on social security would be entitled to a yearly amount of money
  for educational expenses. This would put the decision about how to use
  the money in the hands of the older person. The universities would
  have to provide what the older student wants.

- Scholarship Search, Student Assistance Council of America, 1775
  Broadway, New York, NY 10019, will electronically match sources of
  financial aid with eligible applicants.

New Legislation Is on Your Side

Two new federal laws can help you in your reentry process. The
Age Discrimination Act of 1975 (which became effective in January 1979) makes unlawful any unreasonable age discrimination in
programs or activities receiving federal funding. The Mondale Bill
on Lifelong Learning has now become Title I, Part B, of the
Educational Amendments of 1976. It recognizes for the first time
that older persons are a distinct group with a right to lifelong
education. Its proponents are assessing the educational needs of
older persons, identifying the barriers to reentry, and developing
appropriate curriculum and new funding sources.

Getting Credit for Life Experiences

Our life experience has taught us much that need not be learned all over again in a classroom. Women who have not completed high school may want to take a high school equivalency test to earn their high school diploma. Returning women can take the College-Level Examination Program (CLEP) exams to gain advanced college credit for knowledge they have acquired on their own. More than 1,800 colleges and universities now award credit or placement through CLEP. Other colleges have a challenge program of credits that allows mature students to challenge almost any course in the university by taking the final course examination. A group called the Council for Advancement of Experimental Learning (CAEL) has developed ways to help colleges evaluate what people have learned from different kinds of life experience. For further information, contact CAEL, American City Building, Columbia, MD 21044.

Women need to be able to translate their years of experience as homemakers and volunteers into the language of skills and competencies required by college admissions boards. The book *How to Get College Credit for What You Have Learned as a Homemaker and Volunteer* (see Resources: Reentry at the end of this chapter) is an invaluable guide for women who are reentering school or the job market. The authors developed competency lists "to help women review their experiences and take credit for their years of work in the home or as volunteers in the community." They list typical jobs performed by homemakers in professional terms such as home nutritionist, financial manager, child caretaker, designer, clothing and textile specialist, and horticulturist. Volunteer competencies may include the skills of administrator, financial and personnnel manager, trainer, public relations/communicator, problem surveyor, researcher, fundraiser, tutor, group leader, and counselor. These words have a special meaning to employers, unlike "homemaker" or "volunteer." The specific skills and knowledge acquired through each of these jobs are described in detail. This information is useful to a woman assessing her skills and then filling out a college admission form or writing a résumé.

Making It Work

Some of us need a mentor or an advocate to assist our return to school. One woman single-handedly helped more than one hundred low-income minority women over the age of 40 reenter the school system. Some women needed guidance in preparing for and taking the high school equivalency tests, others needed help looking for financial support. She discovered that guidelines for economic help on most college campuses specify "for the economically and educationally disadvantaged person," and realized that many returning women meet both of these criteria. Another model for helping women who want to return to both education and the job market is the displaced homemaking program described on page 122.

The Goddard-Cambridge Graduate Program in Social Change in Cambridge, Mass., has developed a program called Breaking the Silence for adult and adolescent women whose access to education and employment has been limited because of race, sex, and class discrimination. It is offered in communities, in prisons, and in high schools. Seven separate courses (each consisting of six one-hour sessions) use consciousness raising, skill building, and resource sharing to support women's efforts to create change in their lives.

Sometimes a teacher or professor can become a mentor:

Thank God for one of my first professors who kept assuring me that I could do the work. She pushed me to share some of my life experiences in her classes and was always there for me when the going got rough.

Maureen, age 51

Professional counseling is essential for midlife and older women returning to school. They need help with setting realistic goals; deciding what to study and how to study (after being away from the classroom for thirty to fifty years); searching out the resources of the campus; and how to best use these resources. Career guidance throughout the college experience will help older women consider appropriate options and will direct them to paid or unpaid work consistent with their abilities.

Many reentry women need the support of other older women returning to campus. Groups like consciousness-raising groups, workshops on assertiveness training, and small groups of reentry women, such as the Women in Transition (WIT) program at State University of New York at Stony Brook which meets once a week for lunch and mutual encouragement, are good models. Support groups deal with such topics as the following:

- What is it like adding the role of student to the many roles you already occupy?
- What are the skills needed to navigate a large university?
- How can you become a visible and effective student?
- How do you get help, such as career counseling, with long-range planning?

If older women are not to be second-class citizens in the school of their choice, they should receive the full range of special services provided for younger students—personal, educational, and career counseling, health services specifically designed for women over 40, and recreational programs. The staff providing these services should be knowledgeable and sensitive to the special concerns of the mature woman. Simplified registration procedures, by mail or phone, would be helpful. Support in coping with the role conflicts and role overload most reentry women experience is also helpful. Each campus should provide a full range of services designed for reentry students.

Older women are a varied mix, needing a wide diversity of programs. Often the routine of lecture, test, grades, long-term commitment made in today's college classrooms is inappropriate for mature adults. Faculty are often ignorant of the unique concerns and life experiences of older people, and orientation or in-service training could be provided to increase their sensitivity to the aging experience.

Educational Programs for Returning Women

Specific Reentry Programs

- Project Reentry, Boston, Mass., offers workshops to assess skills and counseling to build self-esteem; half-time internships in a variety of businesses.
- Mundelein College, Chicago, Ill., offers career-oriented programs for older women in a schedule especially designed to meet their needs.
- Goucher College, Baltimore, Md., has a six-month management course followed by a three-month internship. (Job offers often follow the internship.)

◆ A community college in New Jersey offers a three-credit course for reentering students called "The College Experience," which discusses use of the library and other campus resources, how to organize and write a term paper, and other essential bits of knowledge. This same college also has graduate students who act as mentors one-to-one with older reentry students.

Intergenerational Schools

◆ The Bridge Project, Fairhaven College, Bellingham, Wash., has forty retirees (aged 55 to 82) who live in resident halls on campus and attend classes with younger undergraduate students. Most get degrees but some audit classes for personal enrichment.

◆ Pioneer Program, New England College, Henniker, NH, gives students over age 55 the chance to audit or take courses for credit with undergraduates. Students are housed in dorms or local homes and a few commute daily.

Age-Segregated Education

◆ The New School for Social Research, New York, NY, has a special program for 650 persons aged 56 to 88 who pay a modest annual tuition to attend two classes a week.

◆ University Seniors, New York University School of Continuing Education, New York, offers a meeting place for members to socialize, take classes, and participate in informal discussions. Membership is $90 per semester.

◆ Hofstra University, Hempstead, NY offers retired professors and executives the opportunity to manage their own educational program using their own expertise as well as the college faculty.

◆ LaGuardia Community College, Brooklyn, NY sends its faculty into local communities to offer college courses to women who can't get to the campus.

◆ The State University of New York at Stony Brook (and a consortium of four other colleges) offers college-level courses to older people in local libraries.

◆ Long Island University C. W. Post Center, Brookville, NY offers a weekend college for 3,000 mature students. Its Life Plus Program gives life-experience credit.

◆ Elderhostel, a nationwide network of 500 educational institutions in the United States and abroad, offers week-long summer programs for persons over age 60. Tuition ($140) covers room, board, and a choice of three courses taught by college professors. Canada, Great Britain, and Scandinavia also offer courses in their colleges through the Elderhostel program at minimal costs. Elderhostel, Suite 200, 100 Boylston St., Boston, MA 02116.

My husband was 60 this year and we were finally eligible for an elderhostel. We'd always wanted to see the Rocky Mountains and so chose a small community college in Leadville, Colorado, which offered a course that interested both of us. It was a fantastic week—living at 10,000-feet elevation with fifty diverse people from all over the country (from a nuclear physicist to the owner of a flower shop). We had fun and learned a lot about the mountains and the old mining town we lived in and had an excellent course on Biofeedback. Can't wait for next summer!!

Ginna, age 59

Returning to school may open a new world—new interests, opportunities, people, and skills. The costs, in terms of courage, time, and money, will be balanced against the many advantages for better living in the second half of your life. Anyone who keeps learning stays young, whether at age 20 or age 90.

I have one thought about aging that has stayed with me for a good many years. The later years of life are the ideal years for new learning. Keeping the mind alive and growing is the best insurance against deterioration. I think many psychosomatic complaints arise out of boredom, out of a sense that the best things in life are over. But a sense of one's own growing capacity to learn creates a sense of fullness—as though, well, I can't afford to be sick now, there is too much to do and see and learn about. So cultivation of mental muscles is my personal recipe for my old age, and so far it has been successful.

May, age 73

Resources: Remarriage

Publications

Butler, Robert, and Myrna Lewis. *Sex after 60: A Guide for Men and Women in Their Later Years.* New York: Harper & Row, 1976.

LeShan, Eda. *The Wonderful Crisis of Middle Age.* New York: McKay, 1973.

Peterson, James and Barbara Payne. *Love in the Later Years.* New York: Association Press, 1975.

Jacobs, Ruth, and Barbara Vinick. *Reengagement in Later Life.* Stamford, Conn.: Greylock Press, 1979.

Resources: Motherhood after Forty

Publications

Daniels, Pamela, and Kathy Weingarten. *Sooner or Later: The Timing of Parenthood in Adult Lives.* New York: Norton, 1981.

Price, Jane. *You're Not Too Old to Have a Baby.* New York: Farrar, Straus, Giroux, 1977.

Wikler, Norma. *Up Against the Clock.* New York: Random House, 1979.

Resources: Reentry

Publications

Ekstrom, Ruth, Abigail Harris, and Marlane Lockhead. *How to Get College Credit for What You Have Learned as a Homemaker and Volunteer.* Educational Testing Service, Princeton, NJ 08541, rev. ed., 1979.

National Advisory Council on Women's Educational Programs. *Neglected Women: The Educational Needs of the Displaced Homemakers, Single Mothers and Older Women.* National Advisory Council, 1832 M St., N.W. #821, Washington, DC 20036.

Weinstock, Ruth. *The Graying of the Campus.* Educational Facilities Laboratory, 850 3rd Ave., New York, NY 10022. Paperbound $8.00.

"The Age Discrimination Act of 1975 and Women on Campus." The Project on the Status and Education of Women, 1818 R St., N.W., Washington, DC 20009.

Services

Nexus
800-424-9775
Free telephone service with information about educational opportunities for older persons with a high school diploma (weekend colleges, free education for older persons, women in higher education).

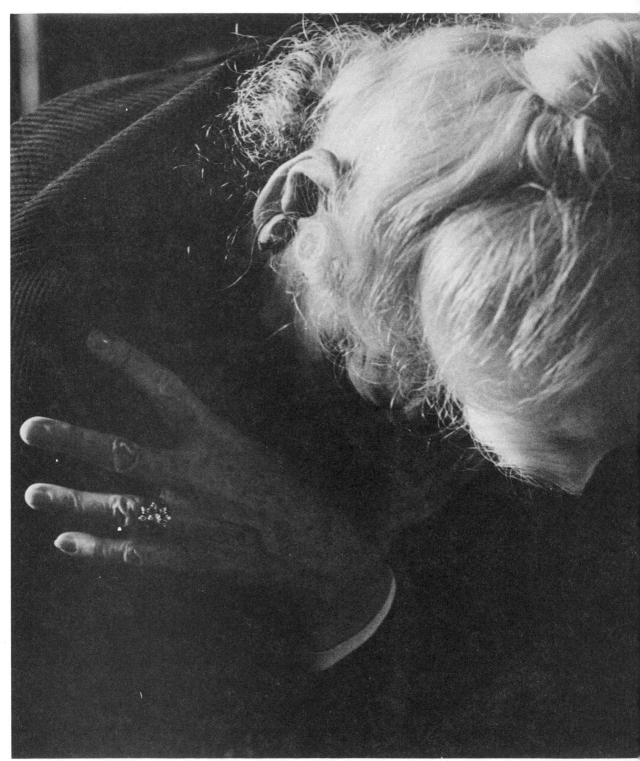

Chapter Four

Women in Crisis

Despite the transitions many of us have achieved, all too many women remain survivors of abusive husbands, or we are caught in the "sandwich generation," needing to continue nurturing our adult children, a disabled spouse, and/or our aging parents. We are entangled in the complexities of a world we didn't design, and it is difficult to find leftover energy to devote to our own personal growth and development. As the following chapters divulge, there is a new recognition of the need for supports for these women in crisis—and new resources offering this support.

Aging Parents

We recognize that the support system for older persons remains anchored in the family and extended family and therefore national policy should be redirected to provide greater resources, particularly home health care, in-home supportive services and a variety of reimbursement systems, such as family allowance, tax credits, etc., to families who are caring for older members.

Recommendation, 1981 White House Conference on Aging

Immediate family (spouse, children, and siblings) are usually our major supports during times of illness and need. We tend to turn for help first to family, then to friends and neighbors, and last to the formal, governmental network. Contrary to the popular stereotype, families do not abandon their older members; the vast majority of care (an estimated 80 percent) is offered by immediate and extended family and friends. Most older people live within an hour's drive of at least one adult child. Money cannot buy the caring, individual services and commitment most families offer.

All of us, as we age, fiercely guard our self-reliance and independence. We often choose to live in our own homes (usually near one of our adult children) with our own activities and circle of friends. Most older people prefer intimacy with distance in their relationships with their children. For as long as possible we should receive the supports necessary to retain control over our lives.

A number of alternatives exist to make this possible. Younger people (or other physically able older people) can be recruited for heavy yard work and housework (putting up screens, shoveling snow, and so on), for transportation services (when we can no longer drive or find public transportation too difficult), to provide meals (either at congregate nutrition sites in the community or through Meals on Wheels, which brings meals into the homes of housebound elderly), to serve as home health aides (taking care of minor health needs and perhaps helping with daily household chores), and as friendly visitors (who come for a couple of hours each day to keep us company). Many of these programs are funded by aging programs in the community, which keep costs generally low.

Multipurpose senior community centers exist in most towns and cities of the United States, providing places for older people to congregate and benefit from recreational, educational, health, and legal services. In some areas day-care services are available to provide a social and therapeutic environment during the day, enabling us to return to our own homes (or to the home of an adult child) each night. Transportation to these programs is often available. Shared housing with other people our own age or with an intergenerational group (hiring a live-in homemaker if necessary) is a rapidly growing alternative that helps us maintain independence throughout our lives. Our children can usually be counted on to help out financially and to offer emotional support and help in locating services.

Until recently, society assumed that a woman (usually the nearest of kin) would care for her aged relatives and handicapped family members, even if that meant quitting a job or abandoning educational plans. Usually a woman would give this home care without pay or support services. Eleanor Polansky, Ph.D., in the book *Women's Issues and Social Work Practice*, says:

Millions of caring and concerned wives, daughters and mothers are, in effect, forced to devote up to 24 hours a day, sometimes for years on end, to the care of relatives. This role and function is often taken on by women who are themselves aging and ill, who know little about nursing tasks, and who are confused about their right to their ambivalent feelings and their need to ask for assistance in performance of this hard work. Many women are assigned this role without adequate inquiry into their ability to do the work, their other needs and responsibilities, or their own health care.

How do we handle the time when supplemental care is no longer enough—when the parent who has cared for us all our lives becomes dependent on us? This may occur when one parent dies, leaving the other alone, or when an elderly parent has an accident resulting in a serious injury or disability or exhibits the first signs of senility. Adult children are faced with questioning how much responsibility they can, and want to, accept for an ill, dependent parent.

I really don't want to give up my job and my freedom to stay home now. But if I don't care for my parents, how will my kids treat me when I'm old?

Dottie, age 50

For many women, this new caretaking role arrives just at the time she is beginning to feel free from full-time childrearing. She may be thrust into the triple role of caring for her spouse, her children, and her parents. The following quote from Silverstone and Hyman's *You and Your Aging Parents* typifies the emotions aroused in this situation:

"What's happened to me? I'm like the rope in a tug of war between my parents and my children. I always seem to be needed in two places at the same time and I'm never in the right one. When I'm with my parents I'm always asking myself, what am I doing here? I ought to be with my children. And when I'm with my children, I'm always asking myself, what am I doing here? It's awful to feel so guilty all the time. But do you know there's something even worse? It's that little voice inside my head that's always crying out—What about me? When is there going to be time for me? Doesn't anybody care?"

Most of us are unprepared for the changes in the well-being of our parents, partly because we lack sufficient knowledge of the physical and emotional aging process. Usually we are unaware of available community resources or how to obtain access to them. We see few options other than moving our parents into our own home or moving them to a nursing home. In a few cases, unmarried adult children move in with their elderly parents to care for them.

Sometimes, innovative solutions can be found. One woman, with eight sisters and brothers reported:

As my father became increasingly feeble, and my mother increasingly worn down by his care, we held a family confab. We each decided to help out one three-day weekend a month (which meant only once in a two-month period). We would drive to my parents' home alone, leaving our active children with our spouse. This has worked out wonderfully for almost a year now. I don't ever remember feeling closer to either of my parents and I've come to look forward with pleasure to "my turn."

Mila, age 42

The decision to take an aging parent into your home is a difficult one. Your concern and sense of responsibility for your parents may conflict with your own needs for independence. All family members can benefit from this intergenerational living arrangement, however. As one woman writes:

When my father died, my mother came to live with us. She was healthy and anxious to help with my three children and the housework. Her presence enabled me to take a job, and we all were quite happy. The kids adored her; one even came home for lunch each day to "keep Gram company." There were of course hard moments, but mostly we feel we're very lucky.

Bev, age 47

When either physical or mental disabilities overtake an aging parent, the constant caretaking responsibilities that are required may become overwhelming for all generations involved. Restrictions of freedom and privacy coupled with interpersonal conflicts can become overwhelming.

I can't stand it another day. My children are finding excuses for staying overnight with friends. My husband is threatening to leave me. My mother sleeps all day and wanders around the house all night. None of us can sleep, worrying about her falling or absentmindedly starting a fire as she fixes her tenth cup of tea. I worry about her all day at work. This just can't go on. This family is falling apart.

Megan, age 51

Many older people themselves find that living in an adult child's home is not always the most stimulating environment for them.

I get so bored all day living with my son's family. If no one is home to take me out, I go crazy. Some days when all the family is busy I just feel I'm no good anymore—useless!

Catherine, age 72

Under such conditions the caretaker and aging parent may feel in need of supportive help and respite care (overnight or week-long care that gives the caretaker time for needed relaxation). Without such intervention, problems can increase and communications decrease.

A Disabled Spouse

Mutual support groups have been formed in California for older women coping with disabled husbands. Women Who Care is a model program formed by Clemmi Barry and sponsored by a community senior day-care service. Wives who are caretakers come together weekly for mutual support and to advocate home care and other programs that will give them some needed respite from their full-time burden. The handicapped husbands (mostly stroke victims) are transported to the center several days a week.

> *My husband had a stroke after twenty-three years of a wonderful marriage. For the next seventeen years I was his twenty-four-hour-a-day caretaker. A totally different man shared my life than the man I had experienced such joy with before. His stroke was a little like a death. There was a loss of closeness, because he was no longer able to respond in any way to my love. Gradually friends and relatives dropped away, unable to bear the anguish of seeing this once strong, handsome, vital man so diminished. I was alone—his only life support system. There was no one to help with his care. He recently died. Today I am working hard to make sure that other women will not have to be caretakers, abandoned by the world, but that they will receive the respite help and support they so desperately need.*
>
> Clemmi Barry, age 78

The labor involved in the caretaking role is usually exhausting. Often the patient cannot be left alone, forcing the caretaker to be homebound, and to feel angry and guilty. Consequently, her physical health often declines. Caretakers lack the technical skills they need to care for their aged spouse or parent. They also lack adequate community services that could help reduce their stress, guilt, and frustration.

A major issue discussed by the 1981 White House Conference on Aging was financial incentives for families who are willing to care for their aged relatives. This, plus respite and day-care services, would give caretakers a temporary escape from the daily caretaking role.

Nursing Homes

Deciding that some type of nursing home is necessary may be one of the most painful experiences for an adult child and his or her parents. Less than 5 percent of this country's elderly live in any type of an institution; 75 percent of nursing home residents are women, most of whom have no living family. The average age of admission to a nursing home is 80.

There are two categories of nursing homes: health-related facilities (HRF) and skilled nursing facilities (SNF). In an HRF the resident must be able to care for all of her personal needs and to get to the dining room for meals. An SNF provides round-the-clock nursing services. For some women a good health-related facility or a skilled nursing home is the most appropriate living choice.

> *My mother's doctor called to say she could no longer safely live alone in her apartment, after two minor heart attacks. We discussed with her the possibility of living with one of her five children, but she decided that the daily strain of living with little children and teenagers would be too much. And so I began the search for a health-related facility near enough to us for back-and-forth visiting. Two months later we found a home she liked and she moved in, walking with a cane and looking ten years older than her 78 years. Within a few weeks, the cane disappeared, along with many of her symptoms. The relief of being taken care of day and night was just what she needed. For the next six years she lived happily there, acting as an informal "social director" and visiting one of us on all family occasions. She was beloved by all the staff, and chose not to go to the hospital during her last illness, but to be cared for "in her own home."*
>
> Jody, age 59

For those older women who have no alternative to living in a nursing home (because of failing health and/or no living relatives who can become caretakers) and for those adult children with no alternative for aging parents but a nursing home, the Illinois Council for Long Term Care has issued some guidelines to help in evaluating nursing homes:

1. Is the home licensed? Ask. If the answer is yes, ask to see the license.
2. Does the administrator have a current state license? If the answer is yes, ask to see it.
3. Is the nursing home approved by Medicare and Medicaid?
4. What other insurance plans are accepted?
5. Are there additional charges for personal laundry? Does therapy cost extra? If so, how much?

6. Are residents allowed to furnish their rooms with their own furniture? Can residents have their own radio or television?

7. Can a husband and wife share the same room?

8. Can residents have alcohol? Can they smoke in their rooms if they are able to do so unsupervised? Are there other convenient places where smoking is permitted?

9. Are there restrictions on making or receiving phone calls? Is a phone readily available?

10. What are the visiting hours? Is the resident allowed to visit friends and relatives outside the nursing home?

11. Where is the resident's money kept? Are there provisions for personal banking services? Are accurate records kept of residents' financial transactions?

12. Does each resident have his or her own closet and chest of drawers?

13. What is the capacity of the home? How many residents are presently there?

14. Are the residents encouraged to leave their rooms when able?

15. When was the last state or local inspection? You may want to see the most recent inspection report.

16. How often are fire drills held for staff and residents?

17. What types of activities are available to residents? Don't hesitate to ask to see the schedule of activities.

18. How are residents' medical needs met? Does the nursing home have an arrangement with a nearby hospital to handle emergencies?

19. Is there a dining hall, or do residents eat in their rooms? Are special diets available for those who need them? If they are not, is there a professional dietitian on the staff available as a consultant?

These are all valid questions. Don't hesitate to ask them.

The decision that a nursing home is the best choice brings about a period of crisis for everyone involved. Women report feeling guilty that they're abandoning their parent, anxious about how she or he will adapt to a routinized living situation, and concerned that they will be able to visit frequently enough to satisfy their parent's needs.

These anxieties may be relieved by professional intervention. A social worker on Long Island, for example, has established a counseling/resource service for adult children and their aging parents to alleviate family stress. Support groups have been organized all over the country for children of aging parents. (Children of Aging Parents—CAPS—in Levittown, Pa., for example, provides training, education, counseling, rap sessions, information, and referral services related to caring for older people. See Resources section at the end of this chapter.)

Legal Intervention

When older people can no longer care for their own affairs, the legal intervention of a middle-aged daughter or son may be necessary. Monies may be put in a joint bank account (to be drawn on by both adult child and parent) or into a trust account to be drawn on only by the older person during her life time but automatically inherited by adult children at the parent's death. When mental incompetency is not being questioned, an older person may legally give another person the power to act on her or his behalf in financial matters. This is called the power of attorney and can be revoked at any time. A living trust (*inter vivos*) gives an adult child even more control over the properties in the trust they legally manage. The terms of the trust determine the inheritance.

When mental competency is in question, the older person may be legally declared incompetent and made the ward of a guardian in arrangements called guardianships and conservatorships. The individual then loses for the rest of his or her life the right to engage in business or professional activities, to draw up a contract, to decide where to live, or even to vote. Too often guardianships are decided without due protection to the aged person. It might be wise for a guardian *ad litem* to be appointed for protection of the rights of the older person in court. The court-appointed guardian/conservator may be a relative, friend, or even a corporate entity such as a bank. The guardian has complete authority over not only property but also the older person (even to the extent of being able to place the ward in an institution). It would be wise for all of us to determine beforehand whom we would want to act as our guardian/conservator in case of mental or physical incompetence.

As life expectancy increases, we are witnessing four- and five-generation families. The younger-old family members become caretakers of the older-old. Since families are, and probably will remain, the primary nurturants, most of us will face the issues of aging parents for ourselves, our parents, or our relatives. If we are prepared with practical information, the process will be smoother.

Domestic Violence

The President and Congress should declare the elimination of violence in the home to be a national goal. Local and State governments, law enforcement agencies and social welfare agencies should provide training programs on the problem of wife battering, crisis intervention techniques, and the need for prompt and effective enforcement of laws that protect the rights of battered women. Programs for battered women should be sensitive to the bilingual and multicultural needs of ethnic and minority women.

National Women's Conference, 1979, Houston, Texas

> *Mrs. J. (89) was admitted to the hospital in a state of fear of her son, with whom she had been living. She said she did not have enough to eat and her body showed evidence of physical abuse. It was discovered that her son was an alcoholic, living on his mother's social security income. He did not work outside the home or help with household chores; he slept all day and went out each night. He physically and verbally abused his mother, who was too ashamed to tell anyone about this problem.*

Wife Abuse

The needs of battered women have emerged recently as an issue of major national concern. Wife beating cuts across all ages, classes, races, and economic levels. More and more women married fifteen to thirty years are reporting abuse. The Women's Bureau of the Department of Labor suggests that approximately 40 percent of all American marriages will experience at least one incident of violence, 15 to 20 percent will experience violence periodically, and at least 5 percent will be plagued by chronic wife beating. Occasional, periodic, or chronic beating is abnormal and unhealthy behavior, probably the result of pathological conditions. Women experiencing more than one violent episode are in serious difficulty and should seek immediate help. Alcoholism plays a major role in wife abuse. Long-term illnesses and financial difficulties are also significant sources of stress that can lead to brutality.

The House of Ruth, the first shelter in the country to meet the needs of homeless, destitute women, reports that 12 percent of the women who sought assistance in their first two years were over 40. "Many, many of the women we serve are older women. Some of the abused have suffered with abusive marriages for thirty years," the shelter's spokesperson reported.

Most wife abuse goes unreported, primarily out of fear of retaliation and further violence. Abused women are usually psychologically intimidated and almost always financially dependent on their husbands. This seems to be especially true of older women, who often have no skills of value in the job market, no support system, and no economic independence. After her children are raised, a woman might dare to leave, but the psychological damage caused by years of abuse makes this difficult. Older abused women are afraid and ashamed to tell anyone that their husbands beat them. It seems true that large numbers of people consider domestic violence an acceptable form of marital behavior. A woman who believes that living with a violent man is preferable to living alone or to getting help for herself and her husband is in need of help, and she needs information about where she can find that help.

Women who are physically abused by their husbands need refuge, medical attention, counseling, legal advice, and referral to community services. Fortunately, the number of family shelters throughout the country is growing rapidly. Women can call their local women's center or community mental health center to find out where such a service exists near them. Many of the women directing such programs are particularly sensitive to the issues since they themselves have been battered wives. Most programs provide the woman who has just been beaten with temporary emergency shelter for herself and her children. In such a safe, supportive environment a woman can take time to think of the decisions she must make, with the support of professionals and other women in the same situation. Most programs for battered women have twenty-four-hour hotlines that provide telephone counseling and referral services. Many groups have a volunteer transportation service to help women get away from their attackers or to get essential medical care.

Counselors help women consider their alternatives, which usually include the following: to do nothing, to seek professional counseling for herself and her spouse, to leave her attacker, to enlist the deterrent powers of the district attorney, or to press criminal charges. In many shelters the abused woman's children are encouraged to express their feelings about their parents and themselves by means of art and drama therapy and noncompetitive games. Without such help, officials estimate that 60 percent of the children will become either abusers or victims themselves as adults.

Assistance is given in long-range planning, for getting a divorce (including a "do-your-own-divorce" if finances are a problem), for finding a job, or for locating permanent housing.

A major problem with wife abuse is the reluctance of the police to intervene in what they consider family squabbles. Many police have been taught to avoid arrests, restore the peace, and leave. This undermines the battered woman's attempts to get protection and help at a time when she may be in mortal danger. Most women are not aware of their right to tell the police that they wish to make a citizen's arrest, although in twenty-three states a spouse may not bring civil suit against the other spouse, even in the case of physical violence.

If you are one of the thousands of older women who has suffered silently in a marriage that has been abusive to you, either physically or emotionally, it is imperative that you reach out for help. The Resources section at the end of this chapter contains essential information about how to find such help.

Elder Abuse

The home can be a dangerous place for some older women, but only recently has the nationwide problem of elder abuse received attention. Abuse of the elderly may be defined as physical or psychological mistreatment, including neglect (failure of the care-taker to provide for the basic human needs of food, warmth, shelter, or health care), physical or sexual assault, or financial exploitation. An increasing number of older women living with their families, in foster homes, and in institutions are victims of abuse. Nationwide the estimated numbers range from 500,000 to one million cases each year. There is a natural reluctance to admit publicly that your adult child is abusing you. Some women would rather face daily abuse than the shame they might face in reporting it.

The typical abused person has been described as a woman over age 75, middle class, in poor health, and socially isolated. She is usually dependent on her abusive caretaker for survival. The average abuser is also described as a woman aged 45 to 65, white, middle class, and under heavy work-related or economic-related stress. Many abusers are alcoholics, are addicted to drugs, or are psychologically unstable.

The most common cause of elder abuse is stress—internal stress experienced by a family that cares for an elderly relative without any community supports. Inadequate housing, economic problems, alcoholism, and medical problems suffered by the caretaker are potential causes. Violence breeds violence. Many children who are now the abusers were themselves abused as children.

Few services are available to families in which elder abuse exists. Short TV and radio public-service announcements urge abused persons to call their community Protective Services for Adults (PSA). Community emergency shelters for victims and respite care and day-care services, when available, seem to successfully relieve the daily family stress. Many states have passed mandatory reporting laws requiring professionals to report suspected cases of abuse. It is estimated that 70 percent of those reports come from third parties such as social workers, psychologists, and counselors.

When counseling and support services are available to abusers, the success rate of prevention has been high; stress is lessened and the quality of care at home improves.

Resources: Aging Parents and Disabled Spouses

Publications

Circirelli, Victor. *Helping Elderly Parents.* Boston: Auburn House, 1981.

Galton, Lawrence. *Don't Give Up on Your Aging Parents.* New York: Crown, 1977.

Norman, Elaine, and Arlene Mancuso, eds. *Women's Issues and Social Work Practice: Women and the Health Care System.* New York: Peacock, 1980.

Otten, Jane, and Florence Shelley. *When Your Parents Grow Old.* New York: Funk & Wagnalls, 1976.

Percy, Charles H. *Growing Old in the Country of the Young: A Practical Resource Guide for the Aged and Their Families.* New York: McGraw-Hill, 1974.

Polansky, Eleanor. *Women's Issues and Social Work Practice.* New York: Peacock, 1980.

Ragan, Pauline, ed. *Aging Parents.* Los Angeles: Andrus Gerontology Center, 1979.

Schwartz, Arthur. *Survival Handbook for Children of Aging Parents.* Chicago: Follett, 1977.

Silverman, Alida, Carl Brahce, and Carol Zielinski. *As Parents Grow Older: A Manual for Developing Community Based Support Groups for Families of Aged Persons.* Ann Arbor, MI: Institute of Gerontology, University of Michigan, 1981.

Silverstone, Barbara, and Helen Hyman. *You and Your Aging Parents.* New York: Pantheon, 1976.

Organizations

Children of Aging Parents (CAPS)
2761 Trenton Rd.
Levittown, PA 19056
215-547-1070 (hotline)
Director: Mirca Liberti

Caregivers Assistance and Resources
for the Elderly Relatives Series
Center for the Study of Aging
State University of New York
Buffalo, NY 14214
716-831-3834
Director: Gary Brice
Training program for family members who have primary
care responsibilities for an aged relative.

Women Who Care
Marin Senior Day Services
Box 692
Mill Valley, CA 94941

Resources: Wife Abuse

Publications

A Comprehensive Bibliography: Domestic Violence Crisis Intervention and Programs Providing Services to Battered Women. Center for Women Policy Studies, 2000 P St., N.W., Suite 508, Washington, DC 20036.

Fields, Marjory, and Elyse Lehman. *Handbook for Beaten Women: How to Get Help if Your Husband or Boyfriend Beats You.* Brooklyn Legal Services Corporation, Brooklyn, NY 11201.

Warrier, Betsy. *Working on Wife Abuse.* 46 Pleasant Street, Cambridge, MA 02139.

Nationwide Networks

Assisi Family Shelter
P.O. Box 203
Upper Marlboro, MD 20870
Executive Director:
Elizabeth Fischer

The House of Ruth
459 Massachusetts Ave., N.W.
Washington, DC 20001

Resources: Elder Abuse

Publications

Block, Marilyn, and Jan Sinnott. *The Battered Elder Syndrome: An Exploratory Study.* College Park, MD: University of Maryland.

Massachusetts Legal Research and Services for the Elderly Demonstration Project. *Elder Abuse in Massachusetts: A Survey of Professionals and Paraprofessionals.*

Lau, Elizabeth, and Jordon Kosberg. "Abuse of the Elderly by Informal Care Providers." in *Aging* (September–October 1979).

Chapter Five

Lifestyles in Transition

Housing is a major variable physically, socially, and psychologically, in the lives of older people. It is an integral part of the trinity that perks up one's quality of living, the other two being sufficient income and good health.

Forum III Conference, Housing for the Retired, January 1979

There are thousands of wonderful old people, living alone in thousands of houses all over America. More often than not, they are lonely, isolated and frightened. There are also thousands of younger people who would like to live with them, not as boarders, but as friends. I emphasize the word "friends," because that is what multigenerational living is, at its best.

Maggie Kuhn

Current Census Bureau reports reveal that six out of ten American women live by themselves. In the 1970s there was a 40 percent increase in the number of women over 65 who lived alone;

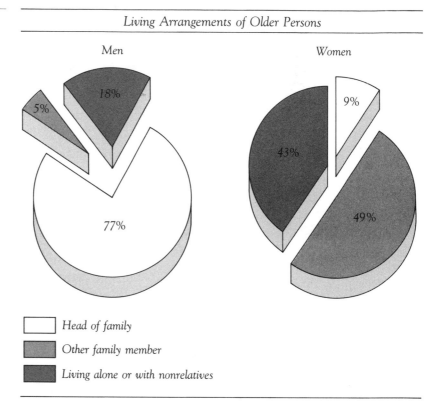

Living Arrangements of Older Persons

Men

Women

18%

5%

77%

9%

43%

49%

☐ Head of family

▨ Other family member

▩ Living alone or with nonrelatives

millions of women between the ages of 40 and 64 also lived alone. Almost four times as many older women as older men live alone. Many of these women—single, widowed, divorced, or separated—prefer to live alone, but most of them live by themselves because they don't know any other alternative.

Remaining in Your Own Home

Most older women own their own homes and choose to remain in them, even if that means living alone. This is often possible when an adult child lives nearby and can offer a strong, supportive relationship.

Let me pass along one idea we worked out for my mother-in-law, a widow of three decades (she is now 88). She still lives in an apartment by herself on street level—an apartment house on the same street where we live. We rent the apartment across the hall from her and then, with her permission, sublet it free to a young couple, usually graduate students, who provide company, interest in a new field (be it archeology, psychology, or religious studies) and who increasingly do the marketing, cooking, and so on. It has worked well for six years now.

Betty, age 58

It was once common for a widow to sell her family home and move in with one of her adult children, especially a daughter. This could mean sharing a room, having a separate apartment in the family's house, or living in "mother-daughter" houses. In such houses, built for two separate families, older people can be close to their grown children yet maintain their independence. Some families build an addition to their home for their aging parents. The parents' apartment is separate from the younger family's quarters and has its own entrance. They can share meals but maintain their own private lives. Often this arrangement makes everyone involved feel more secure.

Distribution of Population Age 65 and Over

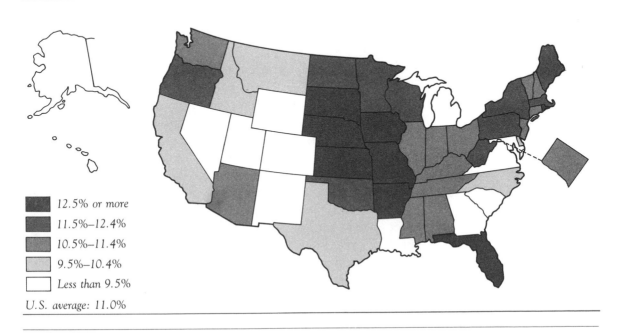

12.5% or more
11.5%–12.4%
10.5%–11.4%
9.5%–10.4%
Less than 9.5%

U.S. average: 11.0%

Australia's "granny flats" are also capturing the interest of Americans as a way for older parents to maintain their independence while living near their families. Granny flats are small, detached, portable homes designed for easy installation and removal on the property of adult children. In Australia they are subsidized by the government and cost $14 a week for an individual and $21 a week for a couple to rent. California has enacted legislation for granny flats and two private developers in Pennsylvania and California are working on prototypes, one called the Elder Cottage. As with several other housing options for older women, zoning laws are a major obstacle.

Most older women who choose to live alone need some outside help with maintenance—seasonal chores, home repair, energy costs, and property taxes. Additional services such as home health services, home-delivered meals, and transportation to church, stores, and health and recreational centers make their decision to live alone possible. The cost of such support services is minimal compared to the $2,000 to $3,000 per month charged by many nursing homes.

> *My $60,000 home is paid for but I can't eat it or make it supplement my income. Still, I'd much rather live here than elsewhere.*
>
> Nancy, age 74

Several programs are currently available to help older women remain in their homes even though they feel the effects of increased costs of living and no longer have borrowing power. The *Home Equity Living Plan (HELP)* in Buffalo, N.Y., aids house-rich, cash-poor elderly homeowners. HELP assumes all tax and insurance obligations and performs repairs and maintenance. The owner receives a monthly check as long as she or he lives. When the homeowner dies, the home reverts to HELP. A *Lifetime Income Plan*, from American Homestead, Inc., Morristown, N.J., guarantees a lifetime flow of income to homeowners over age 65. A single, 70-year-old woman who owns a house valued at $100,000, for example, would receive $286 monthly for life. *Reverse annuity mortgages* in many states allow elderly homeowners to borrow up to 70 percent of the value of their house for a period of five to ten years. The house is sold if the owner dies, or the loan must be paid back at the end of the five to ten years.

Sharing a Home: A Nontraditional Lifestyle

The latest census figures indicate that more than 25 percent of American households are made up of people living together. With increasing taxes and fuel costs, and with almost half of all older women living alone, housesharing has become an economically and socially viable living alternative for older women.

The major impetus is financial. Housing is our single largest budget item. For years college students have shared apartments and houses to save money, and this practice is spreading nationwide among older women, who are finding that housesharing suits their needs, too. The housing may be city apartments, suburban split-levels, small-town colonials, restored convents, or empty schools. It is estimated that sharing housing helps women cut their housing costs by one-third to one-half.

Another major reason women over 40 are seeking roommates is companionship. Loneliness is a way of life for too many older women.

> *Living alone is not a human way to live. You come home to a dark house, cook your own dinner, eat by yourself. You go to bed by yourself, and you get up by yourself. It's just too lonely.*
>
> Kitty, age 90

Disability is another reason for a woman's decision to share a home. A woman with a minor disability may feel secure knowing someone else can take care of the heavier tasks and is available if any emergency arises. Safety is also often a key factor.

One type of shared housing is communal living, with people of the same age and sex or with a more diverse "intentional" family. Communal living requires dedication to share not only a home but also a lifestyle. Not unlike the families most of us have lived in, communal living requires a daily effort to work out the frictions that are generated when any group of people live together. But the rewards can be great: affordable, comfortable, and secure housing and an increased quality of life with supportive people who share one's interests.

> *I've been living in a twelve-member intentional family for the last two and a half years. We live in an old twenty-five-room house in the city. Each of us is single, aged 18 to 53. Four of us are middle-aged women. We cooperate in buying food, preparing meals, housekeeping chores, and maintenance. It's ecologically (as well as economically) sound to have two refrigerators, stoves, and washing machines rather than twelve. We even share our cars. I feel respected and valued by my housemates, nurtured in our sharing, caring family.*
>
> Joanne, age 45

The following are some organized intergenerational communities in which members share their lifestyle:

* Gray Panther Intergenerational Housing, Philadelphia, Pa. Maggie Kuhn, founder of the Gray Panthers, shares her home and an adjoining brownstone with seven people of varied ages. Each has a separate room and all share common space, rent, and housekeeping chores.

* Syracuse University Intergenerational Living Project, Syracuse, N.Y. Connecting high-rise buildings house 400 elderly and 750 undergraduate students on the university campus. Dining hall, library, and activity areas are shared.

* The Movement for a New Society, Philadelphia, Pa. A collective of twenty-two homes in a ten-block radius where 150 people of all ages (many of whom are older women) live communally. Each person works part time in the community and participates in training others in nonviolent social actions the remainder of the time. A collective called WOW (Wonderful Older Women) meets weekly as a support group.

* Findhorn, Northern Scotland, and Sirius Community, Amherst, Mass. A spiritual community whose members are of all ages from many countries. They live together in bungalows and trailers. Daily work tasks include gardening, carpentry, teaching, weaving.

* Lavender Hill, Elk, Calif. A small community of older and younger women living on 160 acres of woodlands and meadows. The grounds are also used as a woman's retreat.

The simplest and most common form of housesharing is house or apartment sharing. Housesharing agencies in various parts of the country are successfully matching older people who need housing, most of whom are widowed females. People who are willing to share a home register with an agency, and prospective renter and tenant meet several times to decide compatibility. Expenses and household tasks are shared. Preplacement and postplacement counseling is available, ensuring a smooth adjustment in the housesharing experience. Project Share, Hempstead, N.Y.; Project Match, San Jose, Calif.; Housing Alternative for Seniors and Share Program, both in Los Angeles; and the Senior Housing Assistance Program in Venice, Calif. prefer to match senior homeowners with seniors. Homesharing for Seniors, Seattle, Wash., is open to intergenerational matching.

The following programs provide safe family-type living arrangements for small groups of older people. They bridge the gap between independent living and institutional care for ambulatory older people who are able to maintain a semi-independent lifestyle.

- Share-A-Home, Winter Park, Fla. Nineteen homes throughout the country with semicommunal living. Older people live together as a family, paying a monthly rent that includes mortgage costs and all expenses. Most homes hire live-in managers.

- The Weinfield Group Living Residence, Chicago. Sponsored by the Council for Jewish Elderly. Twelve residents live in a renovated townhouse with a staff that includes housekeeper, cook, nurse, nutritionist, and therapist.

- A shared living project in Boston, cosponsored by the Back Bay Aging Concerns Committee and the Boston Gray Panthers, has purchased and renovated a building that opened in 1979. This is a cooperative, self-sufficient household shared by a group of people over age 50 and a few younger people. Rents are very low and residents are carefully screened and matched.

- Small Group Homes, Honolulu. Six small-group homes in a residential neighborhood each housing three to five compatible older people aged 51 to 85. Each resident has a private room, and all residents organize cooking, shopping, and housework. Each house has its own rules and holds regular house meetings.

- Apartment Sharing, Washington, D.C. The Jewish Council for the Aging operates a program of shared apartments for older people. Eight three-bedroom apartments and four two-bedroom units are located in age-integrated high-rise rental buildings. Each group has a homemaker who shops, cooks, and cleans five days a week and a social work supervisor.

Each form of shared living has its own advantages and disadvantages for individual women. Most people who try alternative living arrangements report a high level of satisfaction. A growing number of real estate brokers specializes in group housing, including interviewing prospective clients and negotiating agreements.

Group living is not the appropriate choice for every woman, but it does widen our housing options and has the potential to become a personally enriching experience.

Traditional Housing Options

There are many ways that women can have the advantages of living in their own homes within a supportive community.

Adult Retirement/Leisure Communities

Many older Americans with middle or high incomes are moving to the leisure communities that are springing up throughout the country. Leisure communities are concentrated in the south and the west, in warmer climates. Homes cost between $50,000 and $150,000, with a monthly maintenance fee. After years of work, many older women and men want to enjoy the recreation and leisure opportunities this type of housing provides, often in a country club atmosphere. Many married couples move to these villages shortly after they retire. Often older women choose to remain there after they are widowed; in fact, women outnumber men in most of these communities, by as large a ratio as six to one. The median age of residents in leisure communities is between 70 and 80, with most villages requiring that one member of each couple be 50 or older. Children under 18 are not allowed.

Rossmore Leisure World is a typical retirement/leisure community, with established communities in New Jersey, Florida, Maryland, and California. The California Leisure World is set on 600 acres and has a capacity of 26,000 people. Residents never have to leave the community unless they choose to. Rossmore has private homes, apartments, a full-scale hospital for sick care, and a nursing home providing extended care. Residents may take part in a wide variety of daily activities, such as the daily cocktail hour, dance classes, golf, tennis, swimming, and the communal clubhouse. Most are happy to be free of the responsibilities of snow removal, grass cutting, painting, and seasonal maintenance. A twenty-four-hour security guard alleviates many fears of crime and victimization.

Disadvantages to such leisure villages are that they are too expensive for many retirees and that many people do not want to live their lives only among older people. As one woman wrote, "Retirement villages take you out of the mainstream of society."

Friends Village in Newtown, Pa., is a moderate-cost, Quaker-sponsored community for seventy people. Four housing clusters provide eight one- or two-bedroom apartments each. A larger building houses twelve single rooms and dining and recreational facilities. The noon meal is provided and apartments are furnished by their occupants. Residents find that they are able to enjoy their later years in an atmosphere of comfort and companionship. In fact, the turnover rate in this and other communities has been estimated to be as low as ten percent.

> *As for myself, it is perfect. So much is offered to us, from protection to good food and service to stimulating events, right here, as well as cultural happenings in nearby communities. You'll have to come and experience for yourself the warm spirit that dwells among us.*
>
> Laura, age 84

Retirement communities for people who shared similar careers before retirement are also successful. York States, a New York state teachers' retirement center in Syracuse, N.Y., is a two-story housing development run by the New York State Retired Teachers' Association. The Film Industry Retirement Community in Woodland Hills, Calif., is a large residential community with fifty-four cottages on forty-one acres. It has 275 residents whose average age is 82 and who have retired from different aspects of the movie industry. A hospital and health-care facilities are on the premises.

> *It means a lot when you get old to be with people who understand the magic of the stage. We don't have to search for topics of conversation, because we all love show business.*
>
> Carolyn, age 82

Mobile Homes

Mobile homes are becoming increasingly popular among older people. They offer a reasonably low-cost housing alternative for older women, selling for $13,000 to $40,000. There are about 12,000 mobile-home parks in this country, with 11 million residents. Over half the residents of many trailer courts are retired, strongly represented by the white working-class community. Most mobile-home parks are found in states with mild climates, such as Arizona, California, and Florida, and usually in suburban areas. Mobile homes can be large and quite luxurious. Many include appliances and wall-to-wall carpeting. "Closed" mobile-home parks require that new homes be purchased from the developer, usually at higher prices than at independent dealers. "Open" parks allow residents to move in with their own mobile homes (although some parks will not allow homes that are older than five years). Mobile homes depreciate in value, unlike permanent homes whose value increases.

Women wishing to experience this kind of lifestyle are advised to rent a mobile home and to use it for several weeks' vacation first. For many people, the space is too limited and a trailer park lacks privacy. Most trailer parks are in isolated areas, away from shopping, police and fire protection, and medical care. A car is a virtual necessity. Some parks are very restrictive, prohibiting pets, children, and visitors who stay more than a week.

Movable trailers satisfy many older women's desire to travel. One 83-year-old single woman has traveled in her large self-contained Winnebago to every state in the union, to Canada and the Maritime provinces, and to most of Europe since her retirement twenty years ago. It has become an enjoyable way of life for her.

Federally Subsidized Low-Rent Apartments

More and more cities are building and renovating apartment complexes for people over 60 or designating one or two buildings and/or floors for older people. In most of these complexes the rent is subsidized, and people pay about 20 percent of their income for rent. They have provided much-needed housing for lower-income older women who cannot afford private housing, but the number of available apartments is far lower than the number needed.

I'm living, for the first time in many years, in a lovely, spacious apartment (after forty-seven years in my gradually deteriorating *one in the city). It's a public housing project for senior citizens and I was one of the first chosen in a lottery (with 800 others still on a waiting list). I have three and one-half bright, sunny rooms and even an outside porch. My total rental costs are $72 a month (the apartments are subsidized). We have a van which takes us to the nearby village to shop once a week and a central building for our many recreational programs. A neighbor drives me to the Retired Senior Volunteer Program twice a week, where I type and regularly call on other homebound seniors. I feel secure. There are buzzers in every room, in case I need help, and a round-the-clock manager. I've never been happier.*

Amy, age 80

My mother is living in a state-subsidized public housing project in Brooklyn. There are three buildings set aside for seniors among twenty buildings. These three contain 200 apartments. Each apartment is individual and lovely. She is able to maintain her independence, and yet she's not alone. She always knows someone will be there when she needs help.

Meredith, age 47

In Cambridge, Mass., a local housing authority purchased a former convent and converted it to three-bedroom apartments for older people, with a central dining room, lounge, laundry room, porch, and gardens. Merril Court, an apartment community in San Francisco, has forty-three residents (thirty-seven of whom are women) aged 69 to 89. Each resident lives independently, but supportive services are available and residents have developed supportive, sharing relationships. The town of Gloucester, Mass., converted an unused grammar school in the central business district into apartments for older people.

Other Options

Groups of middle-aged and older individuals can join together to buy or build small apartment complexes. Four semi-retired in South Bend, Ind., sold their own homes and built an apartment complex near Indiana University. The couples own their own two-bedroom apartments and share communal areas (laundry and recreational rooms, porch, and yard).

Midlife and older women are experimenting with a wide variety of lifestyles. One innovative woman spends ten months a year on freighters, sailing around the world and returning to visit relatives and friends during the summer. She uses her federal pension and a small social security check to finance her ocean-going adventures. It costs her about $6,000 for ten months at sea, compared to $2,000 for her two-month home stays. At age 70 she boarded a Polish Ocean Line freighter for a cruise to the Far East, saying:

> *For me, there is no better way to find absolute freedom from responsibility or worry than getting on a freighter and sailing wherever the ship will take you. And you make new friends on every trip, meeting people you ordinarily would never have a chance to meet.*
>
> Dora, age 70

Some women join the Peace Corps and head for foreign countries to offer volunteer services. Others stay in this country with VISTA.

In New Jersey, the Unitarian Universalist Fellowship actively recruited people of all ages, both men and women, who were looking for a family. Though each person lives in his or her own home, the members of the group agree to be "related" to each other in many important ways. They are in touch at least once a week and always on holidays. They exchange both emotional and physical support and are there for each other in moments of need. A 70-year-old couple that has belonged to such a family for three years feels it takes away their loneliness for their children, who live far away. They often act as counselors and confidants for younger group members, both married and single. Occasionally they baby-sit for younger families. Often the whole group goes into New York City for a day's adventure, sometimes leaving the children behind and sometimes including them in trips to the zoo and museums. When they are ill, they are helped by other members of this "family." One 75-year-old woman was supported by the group in continuing her creative art and opening a small crafts shop. It is an arrangement that makes life richer for all involved and that offers many options for older women, especially those who are alone.

Tish Sommers, director of the Older Women's League (OWL), and other women are planning their own alternative to nursing homes so they can control their own lives to the end. It will be called "Last Perch," a live-in community of compatible people, some ambulatory and others living their last days in a joyous and beautiful setting.

There are obviously many more ways that women can and do live out their later years. Older women need a wide variety of choices to suit the wonderful diversity we represent. It's never too early to begin planning a lifestyle suited to the unique needs of the second half of your life.

Resources: *Lifestyles in Transition*

Publications

Call for Decent Housing. Gray Panthers National Task Force on Housing, Quarterly Newsmagazine, 4534 47th St. NW, Washington, DC 20016.

Center News. National Policy Center on Housing and Living Arrangements for Older Americans, The University of Michigan, 200 Bonisteel Blvd., Ann Arbor, MI 48109.

Intergenerational House Sharing. The Andrus Gerontology Center, University of Southern California, Los Angeles, CA 90007.

Mobile Homes: The Low Cost Housing Hoax. The Center for Auto Safety, 1223 DuPont Circle Bldg., Washington, DC 20036.

Planning and Developing a Shared Living Project. Action for Boston Community Development, Inc., 178 Tremont St., Boston, MA 02111.

Raimy, Eric. *Shared Houses, Shared Lives.* Los Angeles: J. P. Tarcher, 1979.

Organizations

Apartment Sharing
The Jewish Council for the Aging
Washington, DC

Elder Cottage
Coastal Colony Corporation
44 North Cupe Hill Dr.
Lititz, PA 17543

Findhorn, Findhorn Bay, Northern Scotland
c/o Shared Living Project
67 Newbury Street
Boston, MA 02116

Friends Village
Newtown, PA 18940

Granny Flats, Flair House
P.O. Box H
Santa Maria, CA 93456

HELP, Home Equity Living Plan
Buffalo, NY
Donna Guillaume, Project Director
716-892-2141

Homesharing for Seniors
522 19th Ave. E
Seattle, WA 98112

Housing Alternative for Seniors
351 N. Fairfax
Los Angeles, CA 90036

Lavender Hill
1085 Greenwood Rd.
Elks, CA 95432

Movement for a New Society
4722 Baltimore Ave.
Philadelphia, PA 19143

Project Match
277 W. Hedding St.
San Jose, CA 95110

Project Share
129 Jackson St.
Hempstead, NY 11550

Small Group Homes
Catholic Social Services
Honolulu, HI

Share-A-Home, Inc.
1950 Lee Rd.
Winter Park, FL 32789

Share Program
1450 Venice Blvd.
Los Angeles, CA 90006

Sirius Community
P.O. Box 388
Amherst, MA 01002

The Senior Housing Assistance Program
635 Venice Blvd.
Venice, CA 90291

Weinfield Group Living Residence
1 S. Franklin St.
Chicago, IL 60606

Bettye Lane

Chapter Six

Financial Independence

Ageism and sexism combine forces to create a set of issues that critically affect our mothers, our sisters, and ourselves. Without question, the number-one priority for midlife and older women right now is economic security. The poverty rate for women is about 65 percent higher for older women than for older men . . . 25 percent of all women working now can expect to be poor in their old age. . . . I am amazed at how little we, as women, know about our economic status and destiny. In order to make intelligent and informed choices we must be aware of our rights as they exist and of our options for change.

Mary Rose Oakar, Congresswoman

Women in the Work Force

Today, for the first time in history, more adult women are paid workers outside the home than are homemakers—and many of us are both. One-third of all working women—more than three million—between the ages of 35 and 54 returned to the labor market in the 1970s. Women over 50 have also entered the job market at a rapid pace. If current trends continue, two out of every ten women over 55 will remain in the labor force.

We are reentry women who have changed jobs in midlife or are in our first paid employment after ten to twenty years of homemaking. Many of us returned to a job or career because of a pressing need for money. We are women who married in the 1950s and 1960s. We were raised with the expectation we would stay married forever, raise a family, keep a clean and beautiful house, help build our husband's career, and therefore be supported for life. We weren't aware of the possibilities of widowhood, divorce, a floundering economy, or the personal desire to find lucrative work after raising children. Unfortunately, the majority of us have been forced by circumstances to be "survivors" in our later years as we struggle merely to cope with the financial difficulties of old age.

There are 25 million Americans over age 65. Of these, older women are the largest proportion: There are 14.6 million older women and 10 million older men. With an increased life expectancy, women will live eight years longer than men; it is projected that in the year 2035 there will be nearly 10 million more older women than older men.

Older women have the lowest median income of any age or sex group and are the fastest-growing segment of the nation's poor. Women over 65 make up 70 percent of all poor people. The average single woman retires with less than $1,000 in personal savings. Social security payments average $233 a month per person. For the majority of older women, this is 85 percent of their total income. For those women lucky enough to receive them, pension benefits average only $157 a month; 90 percent of women workers in private industry never receive any pension benefits.

Older black women are three times as likely to be poor as elderly white women. Almost two out of three aged black women live in poverty, compared to about one out of seven older white women. Black women 65 or older who live alone or with relatives are especially disadvantaged. In 1978, elderly, unrelated, black women had a median yearly income of $2,828, well below the poverty line of $3,116. Older black women also experience a higher unemployment rate than older white women.

Almost half of all older women who work are widowed, divorced, or single. This means that many older women are the sole support of themselves and their dependents, despite the fact that it is becoming necessary to have two incomes in order to raise a family above poverty level. Older women play an increasingly important role in the economy: The number of older women in the work force has risen dramatically in the past two decades. One out of every three women (about 12 million) in the work force is 45 or older.

Women who work outside the home often find themselves segregated into jobs that offer low pay and little chance for advancement. Older women are frequently denied access to training programs or promotions despite years of experience. The earning gap between men and women also increases with age. Older women earn only 55 percent of what older men earn. In many cases, new employees earn just pennies less than women who have worked ten to twenty years.

Because many women drop out of the labor force after a prolonged and unsuccessful job search or believe they cannot obtain employment because of their age, a substantial amount of hidden unemployment exists among older women. After age 40, unemployment rates are one-third higher for women than for men. Half a million women work part-time involuntarily, because they cannot find full-time work.

Women are the victims of discrimination on the basis of both age and sex, and then encounter serious barriers when looking for a job as well as discrimination on the job. Older minority women face triple jeopardy.

Since my husband of thirty-five years took off I have walked the streets looking for a job. I have been to agency after agency. No luck. My worst moment came when a young employer, who had interviewed me for an hour, said, "I thought the job would be too much for you." Well, I got so angry, I said, "I've been to Switzerland twice, raised three daughters as old as you, owned an antique shop, been across the United States six times, took care of a 90-year-old stroke victim. . . . I hardly think anything in your office would be too much for me!"

Fay, age 58

Only when we have full employment will the old attain dignity. After a year of continuous rejection, after loss of esteem, I no longer want to return to work. I am becoming one of those women who spends her time in unrewarding busywork.

Emmy, age 67

> *I am finding it nearly impossible to find a job in the small com-*
> *munity I live in. I've only a high school education, but I do have*
> *office skills. It's so degrading to be offered $2.65 an hour. . . .*
> *It's very depressing but I'll keep trying because I need a job. I'm*
> *scared about my old age without any retirement fund.*
>
> Bernice, age 47

Because so many of us have postponed employment while bearing and caring for children, entering the job market presents overwhelming obstacles. It is hard to find even low-level jobs. We face greater barriers in applying for nontraditional or high-paying jobs. Many of us take part-time work or jobs that do not utilize our skills and experience. Others cannot find work at all.

Most employers label our earlier education "outdated" and will not consider any of the skills we have acquired as unpaid homemakers. Those of us lucky enough to have acquired an education and/or salable skills are often rejected as being "overquali-fied," which is merely an excuse for discrimination.

The well-known poster of Golda Meir with the caption "But can she type?" expresses older women's frustrations and the typical lack of regard of employers.

> *The ironic thing about [the poster] is if she could have typed one*
> *hundred words per minute, she'd still have had a hard time get-*
> *ting a job. She was too old. Employment counselors would have*
> *told her kindly, "Don't you think you should go home and enjoy*
> *your grandchildren?" Or a personnel manager would have said,*
> *"You appear to be somewhat overqualified for this typing job,*
> *Ms. Meir. I don't think you'd be satisfied here."*
>
> Muriel, age 60

Women experience discrimination on the job when they are passed over for advancement or training programs that could increase their earning power. Nearly 80 percent of all working women are employed in low-paying, low-status, and low-benefit jobs. The so-called women's professions—nursing, teaching, and social work—are service professions, which have a low rating as professions and are low in pay.

I have a good friend who is 48, and a more qualified administrator you will never find. Last year she found one door after another closed to her on the job because of her age, although that was never given as the reason. I have worked side by side with her; she is attractive, articulate, gracious, warm, sophisticated—a competent and mature individual. On one hand, I could cry for her hurt feelings and wounded pride. On the other hand, I am so angry . . . she simply is not wanted.

Cynthia, age 40

Fighting Job Discrimination

The two basic laws that help women fight sex discrimination in employment are Title VII of the Civil Rights Act and the Equal Pay Act.

Title VII prohibits discrimination on the basis of race, color, religion, national origin, or sex. It is enforced by the Equal Employment Opportunity Commission (EEOC), which unfortunately has not actively helped enforce this law for older women.

The Equal Pay Act requires that equal wages be paid for equal work. Older women who feel they have a legitimate claim against an employer can bring their case to the Department of Labor (Wage and Hour Division) or hire a private attorney and sue for their back wages.

Up until 1974 the Age Discrimination in Employment Act (ADEA) protected only people aged 40 to 65. It was then amended to extend coverage up to age 70. This law prohibits age discrimination in employment agency referrals, hiring, promotion, training, layoffs, pay, firing, and labor union membership. There is no upper age limit for federal employees under ADEA. However, state and local elected officials, tenured college and university employees, apprentices, and those in jobs for which age is a "bona fide occupational qualification" are excluded from ADEA.

How to Spot Age Discrimination

Applying for a Job

- Were the job qualifications made clear by the employment agency or employer? If you feel you are qualified, ask for a list of minimal qualifications or a job description.

- Did the job advertisement mention age or recent graduation?

- Did the application ask your age? (Although this is not illegal, there must be a clear indication that this will not be used against you.)

- If your rejection was based on an interview, ask what the employer was looking for and what you were lacking. Ask to speak to a superior if you're not satisfied.
- Did a younger person get the job? Was he or she less qualified?
- Were you told you were overqualified?
- Were you told the job might be too strenuous for you, without an accompanying physical checkup?
- Were you asked whether you would mind working under a younger person?
- Were you tested only on skills needed for the job?
- Did you notice only younger people working there?
- Did the personnel office prominently display the Age Discrimination in Employment Act notice, required by law?

On the Job

- Were you passed over for a promotion or training program that you were eligible for?
- Were you involuntarily "promoted" into a new job you didn't want or weren't qualified for? Were you put on a faster schedule or a more physically demanding job?
- Did you suddenly begin to get bad job performance evaluations after several years of satisfactory evaluations?
- Were you asked to take an early retirement?
- Were you fired before your pension rights vested? Were you replaced by a younger, less qualified person?

Adapted from National Association of Office Workers

The National Association of Office Workers has begun to wage war against age discrimination in a nationwide campaign. Their goal is to impress upon public and agency officials the need for stronger enforcement of age discrimination laws as well as increased protection for older working women during their work life and retirement.

If you feel you have been discriminated against under the provisions of ADEA, file a charge within 180 days with the EEOC, which administers ADEA. If you live in a state that has laws against age discrimination, you must first file with your state employment discrimination agency. It is wise to file immediately with both the state and federal government. If you then receive notice of your state's termination or dismissal of the case you have only 30 days (not the usual 180) to file with the EEOC.

How to File a Charge of Discrimination

1. File your charge with the intake officer at the EEOC.
2. He or she will interview you and do a minimal investigation but will not make a determination of probable cause.
3. He or she will attempt a reconciliation with the employer.
4. If a reconciliation is not reached, the EEOC officer will advise you to retain a lawyer and file a private suit in court.

Women who are victims of age and sex discrimination are often frustrated by the expense and length of time involved in seeking remedies through EEOC and the federal courts. Despite the high incidence of discrimination, few older women have actually filed charges. Many of those who have fought back, however, have won employment, reinstatement, promotion, and even back pay and damages.

The American Civil Liberties Union has a Women's Rights Project that publishes a quarterly report of interest to women over 40 who are facing age and sex discrimination in the work force. A recent report noted a relatively new and untried provision that is an inexpensive, speedy, and effective means for challenging discrimination practices:

The Revenue Sharing Act prohibits any state or local government receiving Revenue Sharing funds from discriminating in employment or services on the basis of race, national origin, religion, sex, handicapped status, or age. . . . In most cases state and local governments will enter into corrective agreements containing specific and long-term relief to avoid loss of these funds. Any citizen may file a complaint . . . not necessarily the individual who has been discriminated against. . . . The complaint can be broad and include patterns and practices of discrimination in hiring and promotion . . . discriminatory appointments to city, county and state boards. . . . There is no time period, no forms. The complaint must be in writing.

Those who are frustrated or discouraged in seeking aid against discrimination may be interested in writing for a manual for filing such complaints prepared by the ACLU of Georgia (88 Walton St., N.W., Atlanta, GA 30303, $7.50 prepaid).

Displaced Homemakers

A displaced homemaker is a middle-aged women under 62 who has not worked in the labor force for the many years she has provided unpaid services to her family. She has been displaced from the role of wife (through death, disability, divorce, or separation) and the role of mother (because her children are grown). She is too young for social security and often considered too old and inexperienced for employment. Many widowed and divorced women become suddenly poor, forced to enter the workplace with little or no paid work experience and are ill-prepared to compete in a highly competitive job market. There are about 4.1 million displaced homemakers in this country, and the number is growing.

The Displaced Homemakers Program, conceived and activated by Tish Sommers and Laurie Shields (themselves displaced homemakers), has been set up in all fifty states and is an excellent model for the retraining of all mature women. Their first step in helping the displaced homemaker is helping her solve her immediate life crises. If a woman needs legal help, she is referred to a sympathetic lawyer. If she is left destitute, as many are, she is helped to find short-term public assistance.

In helping the displaced homemaker reenter the job market, counselors assist women in defining their goals and setting up personalized plans of action. Decisions are made about what education and training each woman needs to build on her existing skills, to explore her occupational alternatives, and to develop new job skills. Practical workshops are held in résumé writing, interviewing skills, and job-hunting techniques, as well as self-assessment, decision making, assertiveness training, and skills in handling finances.

An ingenious new tool in displaced homemaker programs is the "transferable skills" concept. Most homemakers have already developed numerous skills—such as organizing, mediating, budgeting, counseling, delegating responsibilities—both in the home and in community volunteer work. In reassessing her qualifications a woman might discover that she is a logical candidate for a management or other professional position despite her limited experience in the world of paid work.

By fostering employment, these programs are an investment in the economic future of the country. Working in the later years promotes better productivity and health for older women and improves society's regard and respect for us. None of us wants to be dependent on the government and family in our old age. It's our worst fear. But as the number of women over 65 doubles in the next three decades, government intervention—preferably in the middle years—will be essential in helping us attain the financial independence we desire. The training of women in midlife is cost-effective, because we have many productive years of work ahead of us.

Eleanor Smeal, president of the National Organization for Women, proposed a Homemakers Bill of Rights to the U.S. House of Representatives:

Mid-life women discover the actual value society places on homemaking and motherhood when employers refuse to consider their years in the home as work experience, and when social security records show "zero" for each year they've invested in nurturing and serving the family. The mid-life homemaker discovers the false security of marriage. She can be "fired" from her job at a moment's notice, with no unemployment compensation, no retirement benefits, no profit sharing. . . . Women have been, in essence, society's built-in, unpaid, houseworkers, caring for the very young, the sick, the elderly, the disabled—those for whom society is unwilling to provide. But these services are not being rendered for free. Women are paying for them with their lives.

The Homemakers Bill of Rights, for women who want or need to return to the labor market after age 40, would offer low-interest educational loans, tax deductions for educational expenses, more available child care, increased benefits in part-time employment, and incentives to business to employ these newly trained women.

The legislation N.O.W. is proposing is similar to the G.I. Bill of Rights, which was offered to World War II veterans who served America for at least 180 days. Women have served their country for years as mothers and homemakers and should be recognized, valued, and aided in return.

My husband recently divorced me and I am in a desperate situation. I am over the hill agewise, my skills are rusty, and to be thrown out into an accelerated "young bunny" world is devastating. . . . All I want is a job, even an insignificant one . . . a job of any kind would do wonders for me.

Nan, age 57

Reentering the Work Force

A first step for many women who want or need to reenter the work force is to attend a career counseling workshop. This is a time to evaluate both priorities and skills. Workshop leaders will suggest that you write a personal profile, including the tasks you most enjoy, earlier work experience, hobbies, and recreational activities. This is for your own morale, not for a prospective employer. You may be asked to fantasize what kind of job you'd like to have in five years. The counseling programs offer both group and individual counseling. Women are helped to analyze their achievements as homemakers and volunteers, to define realistic career goals, to write intelligent résumés, to learn job interview skills, and to work out a job search plan.

Some programs offer intensive help in writing "functional" résumés, which focus on your job objectives and skills and are designed to best illustrate your value to a potential employer. Your résumé must prove to the employer that you are worth talking to, and you should tailor your résumé to a particular position. Counselors advise using action words in your résumé such as *manage, negotiate,* or *authorize.*

With the help of counselors and friends, you can identify fields that would make best use of your skills and interest. Speak to people employed in these fields. Learn more about them at the public library. *Occupational Outlook Handbook* and the *Dictionary of Occupational Titles* are two reference books you may find particularly helpful, and career literature and trade association magazines are also good sources. After you've identified employers in your field, send your résumé with a brief cover letter that describes the job you want. Do this whether or not an announced vacancy exists.

Before you go for an interview, learn as much as you can about the prospective company, including the names of company officers. In the interview, be self-confident and assertive. Stress the links between your skills and the job being offered. Ask some questions of your own. Follow up the interview with a letter thanking the employer for the opportunity to speak with him or her. Remember that even a lower-level, entry job is often a step to a better position.

While you are job hunting, set daily goals: phone calls to make, résumés to send out, follow-up letters to write. When you're looking for a job, it's important to use all your contacts: your spouse and his associates, children, friends, relatives, and so on. Talk to people and let them know you're available. Have lunch or a drink with people who might be able to help you or who might suggest someone else who can. When you are in a position to return the favor, you'll be able to lend this kind of support to others.

As women, we have used networking informally all our lives. If we want a good tailor or efficient plumber we call a friend who can recommend someone or who will call someone else on our behalf for a recommendation. The same method works when job hunting. There are women's networks in most American cities that can be valuable as job contacts, support groups, lecture groups, and lobbying organizations. These can include groups with common professional or political concerns, such as the Congressional Women's Caucus, the National Alliance of Homebased Working Women, or the Boston Secretarial Network.

Such all-female groups are often started by women who are already successful in their careers and who want to help other women meet each other for support in their respective careers. Networks usually meet monthly at a lunch or dinner where informal contacts are developed. Members exchange resources, provide moral support, and bring women into contact with other women in similar situations.

The woman over 40 is a rich and often unused talent. She is mature, with half a lifetime of experience behind her, and she has half a lifetime ahead of her. Employers need to be educated about the vitality, experience, and motivation older women bring to the job:

♦ Older women workers are less likely to leave the labor force or change jobs than are young workers. The turnover rate for women in their fifties is one-sixth that of women in their twenties.

♦ An employer who trains a 40-year-old woman has the possibility of *twenty-five* more years of service.

- Older women are highly motivated, as evidenced by their job stability and sense of responsibility and commitment to their work.

- Women over 45 register fewer disability days than men over 45.

- Women are particularly adept at jobs that require juggling several tasks at once; we've learned the art of compromise on the job raising our families.

Women over 40 need to explore job possibilities within traditional, nontraditional, and entrepreneur fields. Learn your own market value and ask for the money you deserve. Among the top fields of the 1980s are those in which we've had good volunteer experience: accounting, personnel, marketing, promotion, and public relations. We should think about training for sophisticated fields such as computer technology and word processing, instead of automatically accepting low-paying clerical jobs. Instead of heading for the local department store, look for jobs selling equipment and other high-priced items in industrial sales. If you want to enter retail sales, your experience as an Avon or Tupperware saleswoman may be translated to a higher-paying job. The rapidly expanding hotel industry has in recent years successfully employed women of all ages. You might get the credentials you need for such a career in a hotel/restaurant educational institution. Mature women can also become skilled in seeking funding on a large scale, learning to write proposals to foundations and companies, skills that are very much needed by public and private agencies.

Many women over 40 will create their own jobs rather than passively accepting the concept of a shrinking work force. Tish Sommers believes that "we should all be in the business of creating new jobs, second and third careers, and part-time options." The following are a few examples of women who creatively solved their own employment problems:

- An older woman in Manhattan who started a service called "Let Millie Do It." She charges $20 an hour and will do anything, from taking people or pets to the doctor, taking documents across the country to be signed and returned, to feeding plants while owners are away on vacation.

- A grandmother who offers lunchtime exercise classes for the employees of a company in her town.

- A mother-and-daughter construction company that renovates, paints, and decorates homes with their own skilled electricians, cabinetmakers, and plumbers.

- A retired Vermont physician who started a new career at age 78. She is a mender of everything from clothes to dolls. She's even written a book about the art of mending.

- One woman who learned all about weatherizing houses to make them warmer. She organized a crew of women who teach individual home-makers how to insulate, and a few women are hired to actually install insulation.

- A middle-aged woman in Massachusetts who designs beautiful hand-made quilts and pillows, which are in high demand by exclusive shops in Boston.

Paralegal training is being offered to retired people in major cities. This training would enable a woman to work as a lawyer's assistant in a law firm, corporation, or government agency after three or four months of study.

Many women have found working for a temporary agency helpful because it gives them the opportunity to observe different kinds of businesses. You might want to try this before or during your own job search, to get some experience in the business world. It also would give you a chance to see what professional women wear and how they act on the job.

You might try starting your own small cleaning business—not just private homes, but hospitals or businesses. Or, if you are handy, you might try selling your crafts at markets, fairs, and flea markets.

Mature women have also been successful at selling homes. Some people feel that women, who usually make the final decision about home buying, are more comfortable with a woman realtor. One real estate agent added another service: She finds her clients reliable service people after they've moved in, from plumbers to baby-sitters. Women who love to cook have translated their ability into catering businesses. Try working for an established caterer for a while to learn the business.

Home care for the elderly and child care for the young are two traditionally female fields of work that offer opportunities for older women. You might begin a business in your home (perhaps in partnership with another woman), or offer your services in someone else's home. Two other service careers that offer exciting opportunities are the Peace Corps (several hundred Americans over 50 serve in thirty-nine countries around the globe) and VISTA, which seeks women, particularly those who speak a second language, to work with ethnic groups.

> *After my husband died, I was bored . . . unfulfilled. One night I was looking at television, and I saw, "Join the Peace Corps— Age No Barrier." I wrote that night for an application. I knew my children were not going to let me go. But Jimmy said, "Mother, I think that is fine." Billy said, "Mother, what in the hell are you going to do?" Gloria said, "Mother, who will go fishing with me?" Ruth said, "Please go because I have never been to Bombay, and I'm dying to go." So I had to go to the Peace Corps to keep from losing face with my children.*
>
> Lillian Carter, age 85

Alternative Work Plans

A 1981 Harris Poll pointed out that most older Americans would like the option of working part-time, and many would like the opportunity to do so in their present job. Some flexible work arrangements now being considered by various businesses and institutions include the following:

- Greater availability of part-time work. Individuals work a reduced number of hours on a permanent or temporary basis. This might mean part of a day, week, or year.
- Work sharing ("piggy-backing"), which allows more than one employee to work part-time to fill one full-time position.
- Flex-time, which allows employees to set their own starting and quitting time, provided they work during certain periods. Women could take a two-hour lunch break, for instance, or they could come in early and leave before rush hour, or arrive after their children go to school.
- A compressed work week, which involves a four-day work week of ten hours daily.
- A seventy-hour work schedule arranged over a two-week period.
- Leisure sharing, which is reduced salary or no pay raise in exchange for additional time off.
- A job allowing a day or two of work at home.
- Sabbatical leaves, paid blocks of time away from work for leisure or second-career pursuits.

♦ Phased retirement, blocks of time off for older employers before full retirement.

Only seven percent of American workers are now on alternative work plans. That small number, however, has proven to management that such programs not only humanize the work week but result in improved productivity, reduced absenteeism and lateness, and less employee turnover, as well as greater job satisfaction and morale. Such alternative work patterns make employment more available to the woman over 40.

Retirement: His and Hers

The 1981 Harris Poll found that most adults across the nation agree that no one should be forced to retire because of age, if they want to and are able to continue working. Yet retirement at 65 is still the rule, rather than the exception, and older people must face this dilemma at some point. Older women have differing reactions to retirement. Some look forward to large blocks of time for relaxation and pleasure; others change one job for another, perhaps a less demanding and more satisfying one; but still others enter this stage of life feeling useless and lost.

The successful woman retiree has usually planned for her postretirement years. She becomes involved in new activities and friendships. Women who have a good, strong self-image during their lifetime usually carry it into their retirement years.

When I retired this December, my colleagues feted me at a dinner in which I was deeply touched by the warmth, fellowship, friendship, and love publicly expressed. When my husband and I stopped for a nightcap the waitress, seeing we were dressed up, noting my lovely white orchid and the happiness that engulfed us both, said in a conspiratorial whisper, "Did you two just get married?" For us, who will soon celebrate our thirty-eighth wedding anniversary—and now a new beginning—life felt especially great at that moment.

Jennifer, age 68

I have no intention of retiring to nothing. Next year I can retire from my time-consuming job as head librarian. I'm in college now, preparing myself for part-time work with the elderly after retirement. I am looking forward to some days when I don't have to jump up when the alarm clock rings and when I can plan social events during the day and even read some nonprofessional books.

Millie, age 59

Nevertheless, retirement is often a hollow dream for many older women many of whom have an overall lack of preparedness. This is often true among older women, who may be the least able to cope financially with retirement. Many who have looked forward to retirement are disillusioned by the inadequacy of their retirement income. Retirement may be even more difficult for reentry women. Because they have had a late career start, their retirement is likely to come before they have achieved all their job goals. Many women are pressured to retire long before they are ready or legally need to (although the nation's mandatory retirement laws now allow most people to work until they are 70).

Studies indicate that more retired women than men miss their friends at work. They also miss the structure of the workday, the feelings of productiveness and the status that accompanies working. Retirement often triggers fears of inadequacy and death. Some women, like many men, have made their career the source of their identity. For them, retirement may cause dissatisfaction and depression.

In spite of good health, devotion, and years of experience, I was forced to retire. I feel like I've been relegated to the trash heap, like an old shoe, just because of my age. To be considered unfit for a job I do well is the cruelest injustice.

Tish, age 66

For some couples, a husband's retirement is a time for deepening their relationship. They embark on trips they planned years earlier and on mutual projects. For others, a lifetime of daily patterns is suddenly disrupted. The change may be so traumatic that the wife will choose to go back to school or work for the first time. Many women feel that retirement is a time of reckoning, similar to the time when their children left home.

My biggest problem now is not my retirement, but my husband's. He is 65 and plans to leave work next year. I'm a reentry woman and I've worked only twelve years. I love my job and want to continue for at least ten more years. My husband is quite insistent that we retire together and go live in one of those condominiums in Florida. After thirty-six years of marriage we have come to a frightening impasse.

Eleanor, age 58

Many crises of retirement are caused by women's sudden inability to live adequately on their incomes. Most retire without pensions, and social security income is woefully inadequate. The average payment to retired women workers in 1980 was below $4,000 a year. Most of the oldest women have effectively outlived their retirement resources.

Social Security

Today women are caught between yesterday's pedestal and to-morrow's self-sufficiency.

Pat Schroeder, Congresswoman

There is a built-in sex bias in our existing social security system, which is the major source of retirement income for the vast majority of Americans.

Social security was designed in the 1930s, when men were the primary wage earners and women were economically dependent. It does not successfully provide for today's changing aging population when almost half of all married women of necessity work outside their homes. The average number of years of widowhood is eighteen, and close to one in two marriages ends in divorce. Sixty-three percent of the beneficiaries of social security are women. Our benefits are much lower than men's because most of us were absent from the labor force for fifteen to twenty years while we raised children. These years of homemaking are not recognized as work when social security credits are computed. Moreover, women tend to be more dependent on social security payments because they have few other sources of income in their old age.

Many of the inequities of the social security system can be traced to inequities in employment. Women employed outside the home earn, on the average, fifty-nine cents for each dollar paid to male workers. At the same time as wages for women begin to

131

decline after age 34, they begin to increase for men after age 34. Women college graduates are paid $400 *a year less* than men who have finished only elementary school. Despite being systematically excluded from high-paying jobs all our lives, the amount of our social security benefits are based on these low earnings. Many working women who are married receive no more social security benefits on retirement than if they had never worked at all. Two-earner families often receive lower benefits than families in which only the husbands worked.

If a woman has not worked outside the home she must contend with the fact that she will not have social security protection if her marriage lasted less than ten years even if, during this period, she left the labor force to care for their children. Even if the marriage has lasted more than ten years (ending either through widowhood or divorce), the most she can expect to receive is half of her husband's social security benefits, while he receives 100 percent benefits. A widowed homemaker is not entitled to any social security benefits until she reaches age 60, unless she is still caring for minor children. If she is disabled, her benefits can start at age 50. Even then, the average benefit received by disabled homemakers in 1978 was only $1,992 a year.

Changes must be made not only to remedy the inequitable treatment of women under social security but also to provide adequate retirement income for all older women. This can be accomplished by the following programs.

Homemaker credits: Homemakers would be given credit for the years they worked within the home. In some European countries, women are given "dropout" social security credit for the years they left the labor force to bear and raise children.

Mandatory earnings sharing: This plan would combine the earnings of both husband and wife during their marriage and divide the total into equal social security eligibility.

Voluntary earnings splitting: Either spouse could elect to split earnings that occurred during their marriage upon the retirement of either—or both—or within two years of their divorce. This would result in equal social security benefits much as under mandatory shared earnings.

Inheritance of earnings credits by the surviving spouse or surviving divorced spouse: When a spouse dies, or leaves through divorce, the surviving spouse would inherit all earnings credits gained during their marriage. The couple must have been married for five years before the spouse's death or before the date when divorce became final.

Transition benefits: Benefits would be paid to a surviving spouse who is at least fifty years old, for the month in which the wage earner's death occurs and for the next three months.

Disabled widows/widowers: Under age 60, the disabled spouse would be entitled to no less than 71½ percent of the social security benefits he or she would be entitled to at age 60.

Divorced spouse: when the marriage lasts for at least five years, the late-life divorced spouse would qualify for benefits.

Approximately 70 percent of older women elect to take their social security benefits at 62, the earliest possible age. Many don't realize that the amount of social security they receive will be reduced throughout their lifetime if they don't wait until age 65. By claiming their benefits early, they will receive only 75 percent of the maximum for an average of twenty-one years, rather than 100 percent for eighteen years.

It is crucial that as women we actively resist any cuts in social security benefits and constantly reaffirm to ourselves and our legislators that homemaking is unpaid labor that must be recognized in the social security system of the future.

Supplemental Security Income (SSI) Program

The Supplemental Security Income Program (SSI) was established in 1974 to provide a guaranteed minimum income to needy aged, blind, and disabled Americans nationwide. SSI is administered by the Social Security Administration and is a very important source of income for women over 65 who live on low social security benefits. Ninety-four percent of SSI recipients are women living alone. Without this program, many older women would not have enough income to survive, and even with it their total income may be below the established poverty line. Twenty-two percent of elderly blacks and 25 percent of elderly Hispanics receive SSI, compared to 5 percent of elderly whites. The current monthly grant to a couple is $357 and to an individual, $238; this amount is pitifully inadequate in today's economy. Some states supplement this amount. Even this small sum, however, is reduced by one-third when other family members live in the same household. This is a disincentive for families who wish to care for the elderly relatives instead of sending them to an institution.

Pensions

Lack of pensions is a serious problem for older women. Women who worked in temporary or part-time jobs are not covered by any pension plan, and 80 percent of all retirement-age women have no access to private pensions. Only 21 percent of women have private pension coverage on their longest-held job, contrasted with 49 percent of men. The reality, however, is that only 13 percent of these women actually receive their pension benefits.

Most married women fully expect that their husband's pension coverage will include them if he dies. This is a dangerous assumption and often not true. The survivor's option is *not* mandatory. Your spouse has the right to sign a form (without notifying you) before his retirement that waives your survivor's benefits. Many men choose this single annuity option rather than the joint survivor option because it provides more money for their retirement days. However, this choice leaves many unsuspecting women penniless upon their husband's death. Only nine percent of all widows receive survivor's pension benefits. Most women will receive only half the benefits their husbands receive during their husbands' lifetime and no benefits at all if their husbands die before retirement. Although some states have liberalized their laws so that divorced women can claim a share of their husbands' pension benefits at the time of a divorce, the laws are still variable. Unjustly, many divorced women receive no share of their spouses' pension rights, even after twenty years of marriage.

The Employment Retirement Income Security Act (ERISA), enacted in 1974, is expected to improve the likelihood of women workers' receiving pension benefits. Workers with over one thousand hours of work a year are to be included in all pension plans.

As women we should be knowledgeable about pension plans, for ourselves and our spouses. Careful planning can make a significant difference in the financial comfort of our later years.

Resources: Financial Independence

Publications

Marketing Yourself: The Catalyst's Women's Guide to Successful Resumes and Interviews. New York: Putnam, 1980.

"Older Women and Pensions: A Gray Paper." The Older Women's League, 3800 Harrison St., Oakland, CA 94611.

Women and Private Pension Plans, U.S. Department of Labor, Government Printing Office, 1980.

Women's Networks: The Complete Guide to Finding a Better Job, Advancing Your Career and Feeling Great as a Woman through Networking. New York: Lippincott, 1980.
A state-by-state guide to networking groups.

Organizations

ACLU Women's Rights Project
1001 E. Main St., Suite 710
Richmond, VA 23219
Publishes quarterly report on women's rights

The Business and Professional Women's Foundation
2012 Massachusetts Ave., N.W.
Washington, DC 20036
Provides information on educational scholarships for mature women interested in broadening their job prospects.

Displaced Homemakers Network
755 8th St., N.W.
Washington, DC 20001
202-347-0522

National Commission on Working Women:
Center for Women and Work
1211 Connecticut Ave., N.W.
Washington, DC 20036
202-887-6820
Focus is on the 80 percent of women in low-paying, low-status jobs in service industries, clerical occupations, retail stores, factories, and plants. Publishes a new report, *Women, Work and Age Discrimination: Challenging the Workplace Myths*, a compendium of survey research data and case studies, a series of recommendations for employees, and information about discrimination against women.

Senior Women's Group, Polaroid Corporation
750 Main St., 2A
Cambridge, MA 02139
617-864-6000, ext. 3654, Joline Godrey
Women employees, over 45 meet to discuss their common issues; support groups have formed; a dialogue with management has been initiated; and specific proposals are being formulated.

Women's Equity Action League (WEAL)
805 15th St., N.W., Suite 822
Washington, DC 20005
202-638-1961
Publishes a series of fact sheets on age discrimination for women.

Women's Bureau
Office of the Secretary
U. S. Department of Labor
Regional Offices
Washington, DC 20210

Women Organized for Labor
127 Montgomery St.
San Francisco, CA 94104
Publishes free newsletter "Downtown Women's News."

Working Women: National Association of Office
    Workers
Program for Older Women
1224 Huran Road
Cleveland, OH 44115
Offers age workshops for local groups. Publishes "Vanished Dreams: Age Discrimination and Older Women."

Women's Work Force:
A Project of Wider Opportunities for Women (WOW)
1511 K St., N.W., Suite 345
Washington, DC 20005
202-638-3143

Career Planning

Contact your local NOW chapter about career counseling and assertiveness training workshops.

Catalyst
14 E. 60th St.
New York, NY 10036
212-759-9700
Makes referrals to career counseling and continuing education programs across the country. Provides résumé preparation manual written especially for women.

Womanspace
211 Lewisohn Hall
Columbia University
School of General Studies
New York, NY 10027
212-280-2820
Director: Dr. Lorna Edmundson
Conducts nine-week career exploration workshops in winter and spring with an eight-month career internship project possible.

Alternative Work Schedules

Women's Research and Education Institute of the
    Congresswomen's Caucus
204 Fourth St., S.E.
Washington, DC 20003

National Council for Alternative Work Patterns
1925 K St., N.W., Suite 308
Washington, DC 20006

Association of Part-Time Professionals
P.O. Box 3419
Alexandria, VA 22302
703-370-6206

Pensions

The Citizens Commission on Pension Policy
P.O. Box 40123
Washington, DC 20016
Ralph Nader's committee to protect individuals' pension interests.

Pension Rights Center
1346 Connecticut Ave., N.W.
Washington, DC 20036
Speakers and publications available.

The President's Commission on Pension Policy
736 Jackson Pl., N.W.
Washington, DC 20006
Compiles case histories of complaints and pension policy gripes.

Ellen

Chapter Seven

Thriving

Maintaining Mental Health

The second half of life can be a time of new growth, a time to try new activities and new ways of life, and a challenge to do more than just survive. It can be a time to *thrive*, to participate fully in life, to share our love, and to grow in our ability to be creative and open to new ideas.

Although women over 40, with the help of the women's movement, have come a long way in the last fifteen years, these transitional years are difficult. Because of wider choices, the lines separating traditional roles are now blurred. We are confused by conflicting commitments to job, home, husband, and children. There are few role models or road maps to show us how to deal with our new longevity; many of us will live for more than forty years after our children leave home.

I've reached the age when my grown children no longer demand daily care and attention, but my older parents are increasingly needing my help. I feel an enormous resentment (accompanied by no small amount of guilt) as I strive for a measure of what I think is a well-deserved time for personal freedom and moments of solitude.

Britt, age 52

In the 1970s the number of females over age 65 rose by 31 percent, while the male population of the same age increased by 23 percent. At ages 65 and over there are three women for every two men, and at age 85 there are more than two women to one man.

A 1980 Metropolitan Life Insurance Company survey on older white women showed that the most favorable longevity was enjoyed in Florida, where expectation of life at birth was highest, 79.2 years. Seven other states reported a life expectancy for women of at least 78 years: North Dakota, Arizona, Minnesota, Nebraska, South Dakota, Utah, and Colorado. At the other extreme, the expectation of life among women in West Virginia was only 75.4. In every state there was a greater probability of survival among women than among men.

Loneliness

In a survey conducted by the State University of New York at Stony Brook, loneliness was one of the major mental health problems mentioned for women over 40. Loneliness and isolation should not be confused with the choice to live alone that some women make, retaining their rights of decision making and mastery over their environment. We all need the attention, support, and companionship of another person, however. Maintaining at least one stable, intimate relationship in our lives can protect us from the depressive effects that accompany the losses of old age.

Women are usually better able than men to receive and offer friendship. Because of our socialization as nurturing, caring people, we tend to be more sensitive to others, more responsive to emotional cues, and better able to talk over personal problems with children or close friends. This ability to hold many reciprocal friendships may account in part for our greater life expectancy. Older men rely primarily on their spouse as a confidante and are often devastated when they are widowed.

Stress

Stress is something each of us experiences in our lives, and yet few of us really know what it is. Stress is the chemical reaction of the body to tension-producing circumstances. Our muscles tense, our heart beats faster, our blood pressure goes up, and our nervous and digestive systems are negatively affected. A certain amount of positive stress is beneficial because it adds zest and excitement to our lives; without some stress life would be boring. Many of us thrive on stress; we're at our best when we're completing a job within a given deadline or juggling several important roles at once. Negative stresses, however, have been demonstrated to be a major predisposing factor in all diseases. For older women stress is frequently caused by societal factors such as inadequate income, unsafe environments, and a socially imposed sense of powerlessness and uselessness. Other stresses arise from relocation, a serious or prolonged illness, death of a loved one, and social isolation. Our goal should be not to eliminate stress but to be aware of times when we're overwhelmed. It is how we react to the stresses in our lives that is important.

The Holmes Stress Scale, developed by Dr. Thomas H. Holmes of the University of Washington's School of Medicine, assigns a numerical number to each stress-producing situation. The death of a spouse or family member is more stressful, for example, than a change in sleep or eating habits. One's score from answering forty-odd questions gives an indication of how stressed you are—and how susceptible to illness you are as a result of your stress overload. The "average" score is 150 points. Much above that level one enters stress overload. Many of us are on stress overload. It would be helpful and healthful to try to think of ways we can alleviate some of the most stressful situations in our lives.

> *I recently did the Holmes Stress Scale and find my score is well over 300—really an overload. I can't say I'm depressed all the time or at an emotional or physical standstill, but I am bewildered, at times overwhelmed, and feeling very much alone. I am fairly young for a widow (54), in good health, I have a profession (nursing), and my children are grown and fairly independent, and yet I often feel simply overwhelmed.*
>
> Della, age 54

We can be taught to identify the stressors in our lives and to learn better communication, decision-making, and assertiveness skills. We should not be afraid to express our anger, but we should also learn when it's appropriate to do so. There are times when it may be wiser to disengage ourselves from the situation. Relaxation techniques such as the following can be very helpful.

Short relaxation exercises can take place in a quiet environment. You can break the stress cycle, help your muscles to relax, and relieve some of the strain by doing the following:

1. *Stretch up to the ceiling, then slowly collapse.*
   Like a balloon letting out the air, let your body hang loose.

2. *Shrug your shoulders up as high as you can, then release.*
   Do a few head rolls.

3. *During a stressful period, try to break away.*
   Take a few deep breaths.
   Tell yourself you are calm.
   Close your eyes and relax for a moment.
   Starting at your head, produce a wave of calm throughout your body, feeling it all the way down to your feet.

4. *Sit back in your chair and take a deep breath.*
   Let your whole body go limp and become a rag doll.
   Breathe in and out, relaxing completely.

The relaxation response is a method that was developed by Dr. Herbert Benson, a Harvard cardiologist at Beth Israel Hospital in Boston, and has been used successfully to lower blood pressure. It involves the following steps:

1. Sit quietly in a comfortable position.

2. Close your eyes.

3. Deeply relax all your muscles, beginning at your feet and progressing up to your face. Keep them relaxed.

4. Breathe through your nose. Become aware of your breathing. As you breathe out, say the word *one*, silently to yourself. Breathe easily and naturally.

5. Continue for ten to twenty minutes. You may open your eyes to check the time, but don't use an alarm. When you finish, sit quietly for several minutes before you stand up, with your eyes opened.

6. Maintain a passive attitude and permit relaxation to occur at its own pace. When distracting throughts occur, try to ignore them.

7. Practice the technique once or twice daily, but not within two hours after any meal, since the digestive processes interfere.

Women can also work off stress by engaging in vigorous activities such as walking briskly, jogging, or swimming. It helps to get enough sleep and to eat regular, nutritious meals. Be sure you schedule time for relaxation. Do what gives you pleasure: gardening, reading, dancing, or playing a musical instrument. This reenergizes you. When you are distressed, get your mind off yourself by helping someone else. Talk out your stress with a friend, relative, or professional counselor.

Depression

> *In my consciousness-raising group for women in the middle years, almost every one of us was concerned about depression. For me, it's not just the neurosis I've always had off and on throughout my life, but feelings of depression that extend for long periods of time, which I feel I can't handle. I feel like I simply can't cope with some of the harder problems of my life.*
>
> Tracy, age 48

Depression is the most common mental disorder among women in the second half of life. It is estimated that it affects twice as many women as men. Depression describes a broad range of moods and behaviors that produce mild to severely impaired functioning. It is a physical sign, like a headache, that tells us that something is not quite right in our lives, that we need to move in new directions. Its causes can be biological, psychological, and social.

Certain drugs can cause depression in vulnerable women. Antihypertensives, antiparkinsonian agents, corticosteroids, hormones, and anticancer drugs are some common ones. A number of diseases, including brain tumors, Parkinson's disease, thyroid disease, pernicious anemia, and even flu, can cause depressive symptoms. Changes in our hormone and enzyme systems can also make us susceptible.

We can recognize depression in ourselves when we exhibit several of the following symptoms:

- Loss of interest and pleasure in most activities
- Inability to carry out routine functions
- Feelings of worthlessness or guilt

- Change (increase or decrease) in appetite, weight, or sleep patterns
- Fatigue, especially in the morning
- Abject and painful sadness
- A pervasive pessimism
- Diminished ability to think or concentrate
- Decrease in sexual interest and activity
- Frequent thoughts of death or suicide

More severe depressions occur in women between 30 to 49 years of age. Major depression episodes can last from eight months to two years. There is a natural tendency for depressive illness to improve on its own after several months, but depression is frequently responsive to therapy. To shorten the course of the illness, treatment in the form of therapy and/or drugs (when necessary) will lead to speedier recovery and will lengthen the time between relapses.

Treatment
More and more women over 40 are acknowledging their need for professional help in trying not only to solve transitional emotional problems but also to improve their potential for happiness in their later years. An estimated 6.7 million Americans received some form of professional help for mental and emotional problems in the year 1981.

All of our lives are filled with a series of emotional ups and downs. It's normal occasionally to feel low, guilty, depressed, fearful, or inadequate. But if you can answer yes to some of the following questions, those feelings may be extreme enough for you to seek some professional help.

- Do feelings of guilt, depression, fear, or inadequacy dominate your home, work, and social life?
- Are you overwhelmed by feelings of hopelessness and helplessness about your life? Do you feel demoralized?
- Are you unable to bounce back from real crisis events?
- Do you have unexplained and erratic shifts in mood?

- Are you less able than usual to think clearly about everyday events or to make decisions?
- Is your life feeling out of control?
- Do you have thoughts of suicide?
- Are you aware of long-lasting physical problems such as headaches, intestinal disorders, or asthma?

It is important to have a thorough medical examination to rule out symptoms of distress that have physical causes. Then you can begin to plan a course of treatment that will help relieve your emotional stress.

How to Select a Therapist

There are many types of professional therapists. The differences have to do with training, philosophy of treatment, insurance coverage, and ability to prescribe medication.

Psychiatrists are medical doctors who have completed a three-year residency in psychiatry. Among therapists, only psychiatrists are permitted to prescribe drugs. They are certified by the American Board of Psychiatry and Neurology.

Psychologists have a Ph.D. and a year of supervised practice.

Psychoanalysts for the most part are psychiatrists or psychologists with extra years of training in an accredited psychoanalytic institute.

Psychiatric social workers have a master's or doctoral degree with special training in therapeutic work. They provide most of the psychotherapy offered today and are accredited by the Academy of Certified Social Workers.

Psychiatric nurses have a master's degree with a specialty in mental health.

Pastoral counselors include clergy with special training in psychology or psychiatric social work.

There are also many different types of therapy to consider. The major traditional schools of therapy are psychoanalysis and analytical therapy, both based on Freud's theory of uncovering unconscious conflicts. Psychoanalysis allows the patient to talk about early memories and dreams while relaxing. Analytical therapy provides a more direct therapist-patient dialogue. These therapies usually continue for several years. The newer human potential therapies began with Carl Rogers's client-centered technique in which the therapist builds up the client's self-image. The therapies have expanded to include Gestalt therapy (which deals with the current needs of the person) and bioenergetics (which uses exercise and physical manipulations). Group therapies are available for individuals, couples, and families. Some specific group forms are transactional analysis, which interprets behavior according to three states—parent, child, and adult—and psychodrama, in which group members take turns acting out their personal conflicts. In the last few years biofeedback therapy has helped people become more aware of their bodily stresses through electronic equipment. They are then able to use deep muscle relaxation during stressful moments as a self-treatment.

Many women find that the choice of an individual therapist is more important than the specific method of therapy. It is important to choose a therapist who has had reputable training and experience. Since therapy is a mixture of art and science, the personality of the therapist is very important. A therapist should be nonjudgmental, easy to talk to, and respectful. She or he should be skilled enough to identify some life options you might not have been aware of.

Ask a friend or relative to recommend a therapist who has been helpful. Your family doctor, clergy, women's center, and local mental health association may be good reference sources. Women often, but not always, find women therapists more understanding and more able to inspire trust. Since 90 percent of practicing psychiatrists and 67 percent of clinical psychologists are white males, it may be difficult to find a woman therapist. Many therapists do not understand or acknowledge fully the role society plays in women's problems. They frequently see our problems as *personal* failures and use therapy to help us "adjust" to our environment. For many women, an alternative approach is essential.

Some women search for a feminist therapist, one who can help them discover personal strengths, respect for other women, as well as an ability to view themselves as independent and equal in their primary relationships. Such a professional will be more inclined to help a woman develop an identity that is not predetermined by children or the men in her life.

Throughout our lifetime we may need different therapists at different times and for different reasons. Remember that psychotherapy is only part science. It is also part art, and no one can guarantee you success.

In finding a therapist it is advisable to consider your first appointment a consultation, to see if you and the therapist are compatible. (Ask in advance about the fees and check to see if your medical insurance will cover this type of care.) It is wise to ask how often the therapist will want to see you and the approximate length of therapy. After two or three vists ask yourself several questions: Do I trust my therapist? Is this therapist alert and attentive when I'm talking? Does she or he understand me? Do the therapist's suggestions make good sense to me? Don't hesitate to leave a therapeutic environment that is cold and distant. If you do not like your therapist, or if after several months you feel no improvement, seek another therapist.

Private psychotherapy is expensive, from $40 to $100 for a "fifty-minute hour." Some insurance policies have limited mental health coverage (typically up to $250 a year) and others cover 50 percent of all costs for an unlimited period of time. Medicare will pay 50 percent of outpatient mental health expenses or $250, whichever is less, per year. Women in a psychiatric hospital are covered by Medicare only up to 190 days in a lifetime. Medicaid (determined in each state) has low reimbursement rates (about 25 percent of the costs, or under $10 per visit). This makes the availability of mental health care very limited for many women.

Community mental health centers offer therapy with sliding-scale fees. Many communities maintain telephone hotlines for people in an immediate crisis situation (rape, suicidal feelings, and so on).

Alternative Programs

One program that holds a lot of hope for older people is Senior Actualization and Growth Exploration (SAGE). In 1974, twelve adventuresome people (aged 63 to 77) led by Dr. Gay Luce, met to explore ways to develop a positive image of aging. Their philosophy is that we can, as we age, tap into all of our potential; we can be healthy, vital, and alive, we can learn new things, make new friends, and fall in love. Small groups (ten to twenty persons) meet in weekly sessions for about one year. They use a wide variety of techniques—indeed, anything that works—exercise, relaxation techniques, meditation, biofeedback, group interaction, massage, art, music, and dance. As the weeks progress, participants get more in touch with their bodies and with each other. Many radically change their situation: Those who were sick get well, others emerge from their loneliness and depression, people's minds and memories become refreshed and alert, and even those diagnosed as senile show a marked improvement. SAGE is a holistic mental health approach to life, encompassing the idea of personal responsibility. Astounding results and impressive transformations make this program worth investigating.

An international co-counseling community that can be very helpful is reevaluation counseling, or R.C., founded thirty years ago by Harvey Jackins. The premise of R.C. is that we all are very intelligent and able to create new and unique responses to each new experience; yet we use only about ten percent of our vast potential. R.C. is a process whereby people of all ages and backgrounds can learn how to exchange effective help with each other to free themselves from the effects of past distress. We should be able to go through life feeling zestful, enjoying living, and relating to other human beings with enjoyment and affection. However, we each have been so hurt as we've grown up that we've lost some of that innate ability. This can be changed if someone listens attentively to us, allowing us to discharge some of those previous hurts by crying, trembling, laughing, and so on. Weekly group classes are held to train people to be active listeners, and two-hour co-counseling sessions follow in which partners take turns listening to each other with full interest. The counselor is a helper (not an authority) who believes that the client knows best what she or he needs. Questions are asked only to steer and guide the client, and discharge is encouraged. The counselor never judges, interprets, advises, or tells of a similar problem she or he has had. With experience and increased confidence and trust in each other, co-counselors work better and better together. Individuals can become part of an existing local community of co-counselors that has close ties with other such communities in many parts of the world.

Senility/Dementia

Many of us, as we age, are concerned about senility or intellectual impairment. About 20 percent of what is *mis*diagnosed as dementia is caused by depression, drugs, alcohol, malnutrition, infection, tumors, and endocrine disorders. Cases of confused behavior with such causes are potentially treatable. A thorough medical, neurological, and psychiatric evaluation is essential to distinguish treatable "dementias" from the progressive dementias of the Alzheimer's type.

Alzheimer's Disease/Senile Dementia

Alzheimer's disease and senile dementia are very similar in characteristics and are usually considered a single disease. They are *not* a part of the normal aging process. Alzheimer's disease afflicts more than two million people over age 65 in this country, from a moderate to a severe degree (five to six percent of the older population). It is more common in women than in men (three to one), and half of all nursing home residents suffer from some form of dementia.

Alzheimer's is an incurable disease in which abnormal changes in the tissue of the brain result in a slow and gradual deterioration. It is, however, similar in its early stages to other conditions, so a thorough examination is required for diagnosis. In the first stage of the disease, which may last from two to four years, memory loss, particularly recent or short-term memory, is noticeable. Mild personality changes are observed (less spontaneity, increased apathy, or a tendency to withdraw from social situations). As the disease progresses in the next two to twelve years, problems increase in intellectual functioning and abstract thinking (inability to figure out bills, not understanding what one has read, not being able to organize the day's work). Behavior changes appear, with the victim becoming agitated, irritable, quarrelsome, and less neat in appearance; inappropriate eating and toilet habits are often observed.

In the third or terminal stage, which lasts about a year, the victim becomes mute and unresponsive and is unable to perform any purposeful movement; a rapid weight loss is noticed. Alzheimer's victims rarely die directly from the disease, but from a secondary condition such as heart failure or pneumonia.

Researchers do not know what causes Alzheimer's, although it is theorized that a slow-acting virus, changes in the brain chemistry, or excessive amounts of aluminum in the brain may be involved. Alzheimer's is a progressive disease, with no known treatment. We can help the afflicted individual maintain as much comfort and dignity as possible through understanding, support, therapy, and the judicious use of drugs when severe symptoms are present. Not to be overlooked is the need for assistance to the family members, who experience tremendous pain and stress at seeing a loved one deteriorate.

> *My husband was a handsome vital, athletic man, a civic leader and a highly respected businessman. . . . He is now permanently hospitalized . . . not knowing his family or speaking a word in the past 4 years. He requires total care as the physical deterioration takes its toll. . . . We have lost a loved one in this slow devastating process that diminishes one to a shell that simply breathes.*
>
> Journal of Gerontological Nursing, February 1982

Alzheimer's disease family support groups have been so needed and so successful that they have spread rapidly throughout the country (see Resources section at the end of this chapter).

Our pursuit in life is, of course, for happiness. Recent studies show that a large number of older women today are optimistic about their future. Maintaining good mental health depends on planning what we're going to do in the second half of our lives. Whether it's in a job or as a professional volunteer, our search should be to find stimulating and interesting activities to which we can commit ourselves.

Some beneficial changes seem to occur with women and men as they age. Men become more openly dependent, emotional, and nurturing; women become less dependent and more assertive in their relationships. As we strive for equality, control over our own lives, and some measure of independence and freedom, we forge new ground. Those who live long and well seem to have a common attribute: a tremendous eagerness and drive to face the future as a challenge.

> *At 67 I'm continuing to explore, reach out, and try different things in order to become what I want to be, to find out who the real me is. I've managed to do most of the things I've wanted to and I've got a lot to look forward to—like learning Spanish well, playing the guitar better, and keeping my body really fit. I feel like I've got it together and am finally able to make my life go the way I want it to.*
>
> Nora, age 67

*B*eing Our Age and Learning to Like It

> *Consciousness raising has been the single most helpful process in helping me transform my life. Through it I've been helped so much to know that other women felt the same way I do. I no longer felt alone. I discovered new truths about myself—and new possibilities for my life. The group helped me explore new choices and supported me in my first tentative steps to return to school after a thirty-year absence. CR has moved me into action.*
>
> Sylvia, age 50

For many of us, joining groups with other women our own age can be a first step toward awareness and action. Increasingly, women over 40 are turning to each other, without experts, to articulate our own issues and problems. In doing this, we begin to overcome the isolation many of us feel as we grow older. As we find the support we need to move forward in our lives, we increase our self-confidence and can take pride in ourselves.

These groups fall into three categories—consciousness raising (CR), mutual self-help, and action groups. Each helps us achieve new perspectives of ourselves and the world.

Consciousness Raising

Consciousness-raising groups have been successful in helping women to get to know themselves and to value themselves as women. They are small, informal groups of women who meet weekly, in each other's homes, to identify and act on the problems of their lives. Through sharing insights and feelings we learn to recognize those experiences that are not unique to us but that are common problems in a sexist, ageist society. The anger women feel at the oppression they have suffered often galvanizes them into action. Consciousness raising seems to work best, as a first step, when women around the same age work out their common potentials and problems. They share similar life experiences and the same historical perspectives. A second step may be to join consciousness-raising groups that include women of all ages.

> *My late forties were rough years for me. I was feeling roleless, useless, hopeless, and depressed about the years ahead. By*

chance, I met another woman my age who was also worrying about the first signs of change in her appearance and in her physical abilities. She had tried a consciousness-raising group in which she was the only older member. She felt she could share her own life experiences, but could not receive information pertinent to her present stage in life.

We decided to start our own consciousness-raising group, each seeking out women to join us who were over age 40. Within a few weeks we were ready to begin, with ten women who agreed to meet weekly and to give it at least a three-week trial run. The local NOW chapter sent a trained organizer to help us get started.

At our first meeting, we were all a bit nervous and not at all sure that this was for us. We began by sharing anything about our lives we wanted to and by telling why we thought such a group might be helpful to us. The organizer came only for the first three meetings, sharing guidelines and possible topics for future meetings. Eight of us continued to meet weekly for nine months. It was indeed a turning point in my life.

Marian, age 55

Guidelines for Successful CR Groups

- Confidentiality. What is shared in the group is never repeated outside.

- Take turns talking. Each woman tells her own story within an agreed-upon time (five to ten minutes). She may pass, if she doesn't wish to talk, but she is not interrupted when it's her turn. This allows shy women, as well as more dominant, articulate ones, to get their fair share of the group's time. One exception to this rule occurs when one member is in a crisis situation and has an immediate need to talk out her problem and receive group support. No one is argued with or put down for what they say.

- Avoid generalizations. Women are asked to speak from their own experiences. Each of our lives is unique. Although we developed different insights as we grew up, it is amazing how many similar feelings we've kept hidden.

- Feelings can be openly and honestly expressed. Anger, hostility, fear, sadness, and joy are often ventilated as women drop their usual defenses and find a safe place to discharge their feelings. Both defeats and successes are shared.

- Close the group to new members after the second or third meeting. This is essential for women to get to know and trust each other as they discuss sensitive subjects. It is wise to start with ten to twelve women, since it is not unusual for women to drop out in the early stages.

♦ Always choose the topic for discussion at the end of the previous week's meeting. This allows members to clarify their thoughts before the next meeting. Some subjects may require a second session. Suggested topics include

Our mothers as role models
The influence of our fathers
Important people in our childhood—siblings, friends, teachers, etc.
The impact of paid work in our lives
Marriage and how it affects us
The role of children in our lives
How we feel about menopause, aging, sex, our bodies, retirement, religion, death
Women and economics
Committed relationships
Experiences of violence and rape

♦ Choose a different moderator for each meeting. The moderator will be responsible for the meeting's beginning and ending on time, for making sure each member has time to speak, and for interrupting women who talk too long. This gives each woman an opportunity to practice leadership.

A group of us who are single women in our middle years have begun meeting every three weeks at dinner and afterward, we discuss our lives and feel supported by this new network. Most of us are at a point where our previous lifestyle has ended and we are forced to find new directions and new goals. We are women in transition. We don't know if some of the answers lie in shared housing, a small business to supplement incomes, or other practical measures. What we do know is we're sharing friendship, dealing with issues before they become problems, and challenging each other. It's exciting.

Ginger, age 51

Self-Help Groups

Self-help groups are clusters of women who share a common condition and who join together to offer one another the benefit of mutual experiences, support, and counsel. Such groups have sprung up to answer the needs of widows, diabetics, women who act as caretakers, alcoholics, postmastectomy women, and many others.

The National Self-Help Clearinghouse at New York University and the Self-Help Institute at Northwestern University have compiled files on where such self-help groups exist (see Resources section at the end of the chapter). They also aid individuals in joining the group that meets their needs. Self-help groups may or may not have an expert leader. Many use guidelines similar to those of consciousness raising.

Action Groups

Women over 40 are coming together all over the country in action groups to help champion the cause of older women and to fight for legislation to improve the quality of their lives. The National Action Forum for Midlife and Older Women (NAFOW) helps women over 40 by increasing public awareness to their problems and potential through a quarterly newsletter, *Hot Flash,* national lectures, and conferences. The group's goal is to establish a national resource center and hotline for midlife and older women. The Older Women's League (OWL) is a national advocacy organization for middle-aged and older women. It is a grass-roots movement, with local chapters in all fifty states.

The National Coalition of Older Women's Issues is a network of Washington-based national groups concerned about the status of women in midlife and late life. It encourages, through education and advocacy, the development of public policy responsive to the needs of older women. The Older Women's Caucus of the National Women's Political Caucus works to correct the social and economic injustices faced by midlife and older women, specifically in the areas of access to medical care, pensions, social security, and employment. This group offers training in model political action techniques and supports both issues and candidates appropriate to its goals. Women's Equity Action League (WEAL) lobbies for legislation to reform social security and improve retirement income of older women. The Women's Division of the American Association of Retired People (AARP) is a clearinghouse for all established national women's organizations concerned with older women's policy, issues, and programs.

We could have real voting clout! But will we use it? Will enough people realize their potential power and capitalize on it? Imagine laws that protected everyone—imagine a dignified old age for all people. What a good feeling. How many of us could spend some time enriching our lives if we didn't have to worry about losing our medical insurance, getting social security, and being able to live out our lives with an adequate income? I've read articles about senior citizens foraging for food in the trash bins of super-

markets, eating cat food because it was less expensive. I'm glad the power is switching to older people. I have to smile at the picture of older women forming a voting bloc with so much power that all politicians would have to listen to them if they wanted to be elected or reelected. That would be real woman power!

Chris, age 50

Resources: Maintaining Mental Health

Publications

Benson, Herbert. *The Relaxation Response*. New York: Morrow, 1975.

Butler, Robert, and Nyrna Lewis. *Aging and Mental Health* (Third Edition). St. Louis, MO: Mosby, 1982.

Collett, Betts, ed. *Women and Therapy* (a quarterly journal). 435 Split Rock Road, Syosset, NY 11791.

Friedman, Susan. *A Women's Guide to Psychotherapy*. Englewoood Cliff, NJ: Prentice-Hall, 1979.

Luce, Gay Gaer. *Your Second Life: Vitality and Growth in Middle and Later Years*. New York: Delacorte, 1979.

Miller, Jean Baker. *Toward a New Psychology of Women*. Boston: Beacon Press, 1976.

Ogg, Elizabeth. *The Psychotherapies Today*. Public Affairs Committee, 381 Park Ave. South, New York, NY 10016.

Porcino, Jane, Elaine Friedman, and Peggy Brahn, eds. *Health Issues of Older Women: A Projection to the Year 2000*. The State University of New York at Stony Brook, 1981.

Powell, Lenore, and Katie Courtice. *Alzheimer's: A Guide For Families*. Reading, MA: Addison-Wesley, 1983.

Selye, Hans. *Stress without Distress*. New York: Lippincott, 1974.

Woolfold, Robert, and Frank Richardson. *Stress, Sanity and Survival*, New York: New American Library, 1979.

Organizations

Alzheimer's Disease and Related Disorders Association, Inc.
360 North Michigan Ave.
Chicago, IL 60601
312-853-3060

Center for Studies of Mental Health of the Aging,
National Institute of Mental Health
5600 Fishers Lane, Room 11A-16
Rockville, MD 20857
301-443-1185

Reevaluation Counseling
719 Second Ave., North
Seattle, WA 98109
206-284-0311

Resources: Being Our Age

Organizations

National Action Forum for Midlife and Older Women
(NAFOW)
The School of Allied Health Professions
State University of New York
Stony Brook, NY 11794
Director: Jane Porcino
Publication: *Hot Flash* (quarterly); annual subscription
$10, overseas $15

National Coalition of Older Women's Issues
Suite 822
805 15th St., N.W.
Washington, DC 20005
Membership: $35 (organization), $15 (individual)

The National Self-Help Clearinghouse
Graduate School and University Center
City University of New York
33 W. 42nd St., Room 1227
New York, NY 10036

Older Women's Caucus:
National Women's Political Caucus
63 Monte Vista
Novato, CA 94947
Director: Annette Klang Smail

Older Women's League (OWL)
3800 Harrison St.
Oakland, CA 94611
Directors: Tish Sommers and Laurie Shields
Publication: *OWL Observer* (monthly)
Membership: $5 per year

Harriet M. Perl
1121 H. Point St.
Los Angeles, CA 90035
Publishes "Guidelines to Feminist Consciousness Raising" (3rd ed.), $6.00

The Self-Help Institute
Center for Urban Affairs
Northwestern University
2040 Sheridan Road
Evanston, IL 60201

Women's Division: American Society of
Retired People (AARP)
1909 K St., N.W.
Washington, DC 20049
Director: Margaret Arnold

Women's Equity Action League (WEAL)
805 15th St., N.W.
Washington, DC 20005
Director: Maxine Forman

Hilda Biju

Part II

Our Changing Bodies

Introduction

All of us want good health, but many of us don't know how to achieve lifelong wellness; in fact, we often believe the myths that tell us old age is a time of disease and illness.

Our health depends on a combination of things: knowing everything we can about our body and the preventable nature of most diseases; the personal traits we've inherited; the environment in which we live and work; the attitudes and care of the health professionals to whom we turn for help; the exorbitant costs of health care today; and our daily personal behaviors that influence our health. Good health is not a matter of luck. We have to work at it.

It has been estimated that as many as seven of the ten leading causes of death in the United States could be reduced through common sense changes in health style. This section will assist you in knowing the facts and some of the preventive alternatives that can actually help you add years to your life and promote good health in those years.

This portion of the book focuses on the physical and mental health issues of women in the second half of life, beginning with menopause. Neither traditional medicine nor the thirty or so existing feminist health clinics in the country have given women over 40 sufficient information about our health needs. Researchers have neglected the health problems important to us. Breast cancer, for example, which affects one in eleven women, receives only 4 percent of all cancer research monies. We don't yet know how to prevent or diagnose early osteoporosis, which affects one out of four postmenopausal white women. There are few health professionals who are knowledgeable about our problems and who offer us any alternatives other than drugs and surgery. Although women use health-care services 25 percent more often than men, practitioners seem disinterested in older women. Although women constitute 80 percent of the health work force (86 percent of health aides, 97 percent of nurses, and 71 percent of health practitioners), 93 percent of all American physicians are male. This imbalance will be changed in the near future, as 25 to 30 percent of all medical students are now female.

> Older women cannot count on the medical profession. Few doctors are interested in them. Their physical and emotional discomforts are often characterized as "postmenopausal syndromes" until they have lived too long for this to be an even faintly reasonable diagnosis. After that they are assigned the category of "senility."
>
> Robert Butler, M.D., and Myrna Lewis, M.S.W., *Aging and Mental Health*

Many changes are needed in the traditional relationship between doctors and women in midlife and late-life. Sexism and ageism are the twin prejudices of most health-care professionals, who treat the problems of women over 40 as if they were either purely physical (curable by drugs) or completely psychological ("It's all in your head"). Women have long suspected the bias of their physicians, but the May 1979 *Journal of the American Medical Association* reported on a scientific study that supports our assumptions. The study analyzed the responses of nine male family physicians to fifty-two middle-aged married couples who came to them with five common medical complaints (back pain, headache, dizziness, chest pain, and fatigue). The study found that the men received more extensive workups than the women for *all* five complaints, particularly low back pain and headaches. Since lower back pain is an early symptom of osteoporosis, this bias has a serious implication for women. The data bear out the fact that physicians tend to take illness more seriously in men than in women, perhaps responding to the current stereotype of all women over 40 as hypochondriacs.

If a man is suffering from stress on the job, his doctor will diagnose the symptoms and attempt to treat his specific complaint. A woman worker in a similar situation is much more likely to be dismissed with a tranquilizer, a pat on the head, and the rest of the day off.

Matilda White Riley, D.Sc. "Implications for Middle and Later Years," Department of Health and Human Services, 1982

Part of the responsibility is ours. We tend to view all doctors as God and passively relinquish to them complete responsibility for the well-being of our bodies.

> *What stupefies me is how many women will simply go to a doctor and do whatever it is he tells her to do even though she may have just heard about him from a friend or even walked in from the street knowing nothing whatever about him. The next thing you know the person's in surgery. . . . She's putting her life on the line.*
>
> Burton B. Caldwell, M.D., Yale University

We have for too long allowed ourselves to be treated as dependent, inferior human beings by physicians who are often condescending, judgmental, and paternalistic. We have given docile consent to such medical abuses as hormonal manipulation and unnecessary surgery. Maggie Kuhn has called for a new "atheism" in our relationships with our physicians. American physicians hold the same stereotypes about older women as does the rest of society. Their medical training gives them little information about the aging process and almost none about the unique health problems of women over 40, their largest constituency. They are also influenced by advertisements in medical journals that depict postmenopausal women as drab, unattractive, and a nuisance to their husbands and children.

A recent Harris poll indicates that 72 percent of those surveyed think doctors charge too much, over half feel doctors aren't interested in them as people, 53 percent said their physicians weren't willing to take time to explain things to them, and 35 percent said their doctors were too quick to prescribe medicines. This report is disconcerting to us as patients and it should be disconcerting to the nation's physicians as well.

How can we older women who are the major consumers of health care in this country change the way our physicians treat us? First, we can search for a knowledgeable, empathetic doctor while we are still well; we can ask questions, take the time to tell our doctor when we don't understand, and expect that she or he will explain the diagnosis and treatment in language we can understand. Don't continue going to a doctor who resents your questions or is too hurried to answer them. We should expect to be equal partners in determining a satisfactory treatment plan, and we should be able to discuss honestly our financial situation, expecting that the doctor's fees will be adjusted if necessary. As we become better informed about our bodies and the normal processes of aging, we will be better able to articulate our problems and accurately describe our symptoms. Then, *together* with our physicians, we will be able to accept or refuse any medications or procedures and make informed decisions about our own health care.

The patient and physician must understand and trust one another so that painful questions may be asked and frankly answered, with real knowledge of the medical, emotional, and socioeconomic consequences.

Robert Butler, M.D., *Health Issues of Older Women: A Projection to the Year 2000*, The State University of New York at Stony Brook, 1981.

Resources

Publications

Huttman, Barbara, R.N. *The Patient's Advocate: The Complete Handbook of Patient Rights*. New York: Penguin Books, 1982.

Porcino, Jane, Elaine Friedman, and Peggy Brahn, eds. *Health Issues of Older Women: A Projection to the Year 2000*. The State University of New York at Stony Brook, 1981.

Vickery, Donald, and James Fries. *Take Care of Yourself: A Consumer's Guide to Medical Care* (rev. ed.). Reading, MA: Addison-Wesley, 1981.

Ellen Shub

Chapter Eight

Menopause: A Turning Point

There are encouraging signs that women are beginning to get more information about menopause, and to share it with each other. . . . Menopause often causes a woman to focus on herself for the first time after many years of concern for her family. It may be a catalyst for her to take time out, to think and talk about her feelings and doubts. It can be a time of reevaluation, and of setting new goals—the beginning of a new phase of life.

Joan Cohen, Karen Coburn, Joan Perlman, *Hitting Our Stride*, New York: Delacorte Press, 1980.

Menopause happens to all women who live long enough. The word is from the Greek, meaning "month" and "cessation"— the monthly flow ceases. Thirty-one million women in this country are undergoing or are past menopause. Many incorrectly associate it with disease, believing menopause to be a pathological condition requiring treatment by hormones, tranquilizers, or surgery. Menopause is not an illness or a deficiency disease, though it may be a major transition, signifying a turning point in your life. It brings with it the experiences of finiteness, an awareness of the life left to live and how you want to live it. At the beginning of this century, few women lived long enough to go through menopause. Today women can expect to experience more than twenty-five postmenopausal years.

The climacteric—that twenty-year period of change between reproduction and nonreproduction—takes place in three phases: premenopause, menopause, and postmenopause. The whole period can begin as early as age 40 and end as late as the early sixties. Heavier women often seem to have later menopause. Premenopause is marked by a decline in ovarian function in which a woman's ovaries stop producing eggs and significantly decrease their monthly production of estrogen. The monthly menstrual flow becomes less frequent until finally it stops altogether. Menopause is complete when twelve consecutive months have passed without a menstrual period. This usually takes about two years from its onset. At this point, a woman can feel safe from the concern of future pregnancies. The average age of menopause is 50, although it can begin as early as age 40 and as late as age 58.

I know that at this point of my life, even though I'm just 42, I'm starting to go through menopause. When I consulted a physician with heart palpitations and hot flashes, I was told, "Come back and talk to me when you're 48." That makes me furious. I'm the one who knows my own body.

Brenda, age 42

It is estimated that 20 percent of women experience no menopausal symptoms, 60 percent report minor discomforts, and less than 20 percent suffer symptoms severe enough to seek medical help. Women who have "surgical" menopause (removal of the ovaries) or "artificial" menopause (caused by radiation or chemotherapy) experience even more severe symptoms than those women who go through "natural" menopause.

Signals of Menopause

Women may experience one or more of the following signs that menopause is occurring:

Irregular monthly flow: The menstrual flow may become lighter or more profuse; it may occur more frequently or at intervals of several months; spotting may occur. Some women's periods are regular until they come to an abrupt end. For other women, symptoms and irregularity continue for several years. Note, however, that a woman with profuse bleeding should consult her doctor, as this may be a sign of a benign or malignant tumor.

Hot flashes: In medical terms hot flashes are caused by "vasomotor instability," when the nerves overrespond to decreases in hormone levels. This affects the hypothalamus (the part of the brain that regulates body temperature), causing the blood vessels to dilate or constrict. When the blood vessels dilate, blood rushes to the skin surface, causing perspiration, flushing, increased pulse rate and temperature. When the blood vessels constrict, chills are experienced. Hormonal imbalances due to menopause can cause a "shut-off" of the pituitary hormones (LH or FSH). When LH levels are high, the heat control vasodilating mechanisms are affected. Hot flashes occur in 75 to 85 percent of all postmenopausal women. They may occur as frequently as every hour and last for as long as three to four minutes and are characterized by a sudden sensation of heat in the upper body. A hot flash usually starts in the chest and spreads up to the neck, face, and arms. It can also be felt elsewhere. Frequently, the sensation will be accompanied by reddening of the skin and profuse sweating, sometimes followed by chills. It can occur during the day or at night. Hot flashes are not as noticeable as some women think. However, many women are embarrassed by the sweating caused by hot flashes. No common symptoms seem to precede hot flashes, but many women report a rapid heartbeat marking their onset. A few women experience feelings of suffocation. In most instances, however, the disturbances are mild and can be controlled by removing a layer of clothes. They occasionally interfere with a woman's sleep or normal routine, and a few women with severe hot flashes must cease all activity and consequently suffer feelings of inadequacy and distress. Some women report only an occasional hot flash; most hot flashes cease within one to two years, although a few women experience episodes for five years or more after the cessation of the monthly flow.

Vaginal changes: The lining of the vagina becomes thinner as you age; the length and width is somewhat reduced and the color changes to a lighter pink. A gradual loss of elasticity of the vaginal walls also occurs. This is sometimes called "the mature vagina" or "vaginal atrophy." Many women experience a lack of lubrication during sexual intercourse, causing pain and sometimes infection. An itching or burning sensation sometimes results from the dryness of the vagina. Masters and Johnson report that older women who maintain a regular pattern of sexual activity (through intercourse or masturbation) continue to lubricate well with little vaginal constriction. Use of natural nonoily, water-soluble oils (sesame or coconut oil, for example) helps provide lubrication during intercourse. These are readily available in drug and health food stores.

Other physical symptoms: Women may also experience weight gain, swelling of breasts, heart palpitations, water retention, and frequent urination.

Complications

Along with the physical stresses brought about by hormonal imbalances during menopause, many women experience psychological and emotional complications. It is thought that those women who experience a rapid drop in estrogen are more likely to experience distressing symptoms such as nervousness, lethargy, insomnia, irritability, unexplained mood swings, or depression.

> *I have had some difficult problems with menopause during the last several months. I have always had excellent health and high energy and I had expected to breeze through this period of my life with no difficulties at all. However, there have been days and weeks when total panic has gripped me, when the simplest decision is almost impossible, and when everything seems totally hopeless. It is as if someone who looks like me is walking around in my shoes, because this frightened and indecisive person, with no energy, is not me at all.*
>
> Rosa, age 50

At the time of menopause other family changes may also occur that affect a woman's role and relationships. Often elderly parents need more help and attention; husbands may experience their own midlife crisis; children may be struggling with adolescence and young adulthood, beginning their process of separation. All of these factors may provide stress during a woman's menopausal years.

Any combination of these stresses can contribute to the depression that is frequently associated with menopause. Because symptoms vary so dramatically from one woman to another, and because there is so little accurate scientific data, we believe that it is important for women to share with each other their personal experiences of menopause.

> *Somewhere in my middle years, I began to feel unexpectedly different—volatile moods, feeling up one minute and down to the depths the next. I felt irritable, had trouble sleeping, and seemed to be losing my ability to think (one day I could not remember how to measure my windows for new curtains). This deepening depression was a new experience for me and for almost a year I kept pushing it away, feeling I could handle it, as I had all other crisis periods of my life. My gynecologist patted me on the head like a little girl and said, "This too will pass. It's just menopause." He prescribed 1.25 milligrams of estrogen daily. One morning I just didn't want to get out of bed. I could see no reason for my being alive. I felt that there was no meaning in my life and was sure that the world and my family had no further use for me. There were a number of social reasons for this depression. I had seven children (three of whom had already left home) and it was apparent that in a few short years they would all be gone, leaving me with no clear role. My husband and I had just left the church which had been the foundation of our lives for some forty-five years. But more than all of these life events, I believe that I was among the approximately 20 percent of all women who suffer a sharp and abrupt drop in estrogen. At that time, it was difficult for me to understand why this was happening to me. I was a modern, liberated, active woman, with never a thought about menopause being a difficult time. All of the scant literature on the subject, and my doctor, suggested that menopausal problems only occurred to neurotic, unfulfilled women and that my symptoms were purely psychosomatic. Now I know that most of the stress of that period, which was the worst time in my life, could have been avoided if I had been more knowledgeable about menopause and had received some support from other women. I thought I was alone in experiencing these traumatic symptoms.*
>
> Claudia, age 56

The Estrogen Therapy Controversy

Estrogen therapy is one of the most controversial issues in medicine today. Estrogen is one of the female hormones responsible for the changes that occur in our breasts, uterus, cervix, and vagina. It acts with the natural progesterone of our body in a system of checks and balances. During the climacteric that system of checks and balances is thrown temporarily out of kilter. There are three types of estrogen: estrone, estradiol, and estriol. Estrogen levels (mostly estradiol) remain relatively constant in women (except during pregnancy) until age 40. At menopause the type of estrogen in our bodies becomes mainly estrone, and our ovaries secrete it at reduced rates. We are never totally estrogen-depleted, however, for the adrenal glands and fatty (adipose) tissues continue to produce small amounts of both estrogen and progesterone. About 40 percent of postmenopausal women retain their premenopause levels of estrogen throughout old age. Heavier women have higher levels of estrogen in their bodies, and research indicates they may be at higher risk for uterine tumors. It is believed that women need higher levels of estrogen during their reproductive years and much lower levels after menopause.

In 1966 Dr. Robert Wilson in his book *Feminine Forever* urged that estrogen be artificially replaced in all women at the first sign of menopause and that replacement continue throughout life. He falsely reasoned that menopause was a hormone deficiency disease and that estrogen replacement therapy would therefore keep women young forever. His method was called the "youth pill." Wilson's work received wide publicity, and millions of women began taking estrogen for a variety of symptoms. This widespread use of estrogen, usually in the form of premarin, continued for more than a decade. Though in 1965 some 8.5 million American women were taking estrogen (unaware of its serious risks), the number jumped to 26.7 million women in 1975, the peak period of estrogen use.

Epidemiologists noticed a corresponding increase in the rise of endometrial (uterine) cancer after the use of estrogen therapy became widespread. More than 15,000 cases of endometrial cancer were reported from 1971 to 1975. Studies about the potential links between estrogen and endometrial cancer were cautiously published in the *New England Journal of Medicine* in 1975. The following year, new studies provided clear evidence that estrogen was causing breast cancer in animals. Four years later a study reported in the *Journal of the American Medical Association* found an association between long-term use of 1.25-mg estrogen doses by postmenopausal women and a doubled risk of breast cancer. The researchers found that a woman who starts at age 50 taking estrogen daily for three years increases her risk of getting breast cancer by age 75, from 6 percent to 12 percent. Although these few studies are not conclusive (much more research is needed), when this information was published women began questioning their physicians about estrogen replacement therapy, and estrogen use began to decline.

One of the difficulties in our lack of knowledge of estrogen-caused health problems is the long latency period of cancer. It takes anywhere from three and a half to fifteen years after a woman starts taking estrogen for a cancer to become apparent in her body. Since estrogen use more than tripled between 1965 and 1975, we may have to wait several more years before researchers can prove all of the adverse effects of estrogen replacement therapy. The picture is even more complicated because estrogen is the major ingredient in birth control pills.

The National Institute on Aging sponsored a conference in September 1979 on estrogen use and postmenopausal women. Two questions that were asked at the conference were: Why are we tinkering with hormonal medications when we know so little about them? and How much risk is a woman willing to take to be free of menopausal discomfort? Although estrogen is used less today than it once was, it is estimated that 50 percent of all American menopausal women are still taking it! Many physicians reported at the conference that their patients were no longer asking for estrogen; instead they were saying, "Do anything to relieve my symptoms, but don't give me estrogen." Other specialists at the conference urged that women be told all that is presently known about estrogen—both its benefits and its risks—and be kept informed of all new developments. We each must insist on getting this information from our physician.

Estrogen therapy alleviates: the severe vasomotor symptoms called hot flashes; vaginal changes that occur in menopause including atrophy, dryness, itching, pain during intercourse, frequent urination, and urethral irritation; bone loss in osteoporosis, which seems to be retarded as long as estrogen use is continued. As soon as the estrogen is stopped, however, dramatic bone loss begins again. Relief from these symptoms is temporary. They return when estrogen use is discontinued. When estrogen is stopped, even twenty years later, symptoms will reoccur, and at an age when we may be less able to cope. Other therapies to alleviate these symptoms involve less risk.

Estrogen therapy does not help: the aging progress; depression so often associated with the menopause; insomnia; the risk of heart attack or stroke. (High doses of estrogen may even increase this risk.)

The Risks of Estrogen

Cancer of the endometrium (the lining of the uterus) occurs four to thirteen times more often after two to four years of estrogen use than without estrogen replacement. The rate of occurrence declines after estrogen is stopped. Gallbladder disease increases 2.5-fold with estrogen use. There is some evidence that both cardiovascular disease and hypertension may be increased with estrogen use. Some women who use estrogen replacement therapy report breakthrough bleeding, sore breasts, bloating, and headaches.

Estrogen should never be taken by women with untreated vaginal bleeding, liver disease, thrombophlebitis, endometriosis, gallbladder disease, seizure disorders, or migraine headaches.

With new information available each year about the risks of estrogen, it is frightening to find a recent Ann Landers column recommending menopausal medication as a "godsend" and to find Dr. Robert Taylor's 1976 book *A Doctors Guide: Welcome to the Middle Years* advising women to

take estrogenic hormones after menopause . . . indefinitely . . . merely to replace a deficiency . . . in a sense to correct one of nature's mistakes . . . to help preserve youthful feminine tissues.

Other Forms of Estrogen

Most replacement estrogen is taken orally in the form of a pill, and for years it was felt that estrogen cream was safe for vaginal use. The cream is quickly absorbed into the bloodstream, however, and entails many of the same risks as oral estrogen. Another form of estrogen of which many are unaware is the estrogen sometimes ingested when one eats beef. Many cattle in this country are fed DES (di-ethyl stilbestrol—artificial estrogen) to fatten them up. If you eat beef, you add the artificial hormone to your own natural supply. DES has also been implicated in the last several years as a cancer-causing agent in the daughters of women who were given the drug in the 1950s as a preventive against miscarriage. Estrogen has indeed become the "wonder drug we should wonder about."

Progesterone

Many doctors prescribe estrogen in combination with progesterone, another female sex hormone. Its effects are not known, and the panel of experts at the National Institute on Aging conference in September 1979 felt it was not safe to prescribe progesterone. At least one study shows an increased risk of heart attack for premenopausal women who have used the estrogen-progesterone combination.

The decision to use estrogen is a personal one although it seems obvious that its use should be restricted to more severe menopausal problems. It remains a very attractive and alluring drug therapy, however. Knowing the facts, women need to make their own choice.

> *I can understand why five million women are currently taking estrogen. The fear of aging in some of us is almost as powerful as the fear of cancer and death.*
>
> Donna, age 52

Women who choose to use estrogen, despite the known risks, should use the lowest possible dose (.3 mg estrogen or .01 mg estradol) for the shortest possible time. It should be taken in a cyclical pattern, from days 21 to 25 each month, with progesterone added the last seven to ten days. Estrogen should not be used for more than one to two years. An endometrial biopsy should be performed if any unexplained bleeding occurs or after a one- or two-year period of estrogen use. Remember, estrogen merely postpones menopausal symptoms.

Alternative Treatment for Menopausal Symptoms

Many women and physicians are experimenting with alternative ways to relieve menopausal symptoms. Vitamin E is thought to bring relief to about half of the women using it. A *Prevention Magazine* questionnaire on vitamin E brought responses from 2,000 menopausal women who found that vitamin E largely or totally relieved the problems associated with menopause. They reported more energy, an increased sense of well-being, and relief from leg cramps and hot flashes. Vitamin E is most often recommended in dosages of 200 or 400 IUs. Some therapists advise using both vitamin E and B-complex supplements to alleviate hot flashes. The B-complex vitamins are commonly available in 50-mg tablets. Eliminating coffee, alcohol, and sugar from the diet may be helpful.

Sexual activity stimulates lubrication of the vagina, which relieves dryness. K-Y jelly, cocoa butter, or vegetable oils (such as coconut oil) can be used during intercourse to prevent dryness.

Barbara and Gideon Seaman, in their book *Women and the Crisis in Sex Hormones,* suggest some natural remedies to achieve optimal health at menopause. They recommend nutritional therapies and the use of minerals and vitamins, and discuss women who found relief from hot flashes by using ginseng, an ancient Chinese herb. Some of the latest studies, however, say that ginseng acts like estrogen in the body, with the same side effects. For hot flashes, herbalists recommend black cohash (which contains natural estrogen) licorice root, red raspberry leaves and sarsaparilla. These should only be used under the guidance of an experienced herbalist. Biofeedback has also been a useful technique for hot flashes. A promising method of stopping hot flashes by using acupressure has been used successfully by a physician in New York City with a small group of women having severe hot flashes.

One doctor on Long Island holds rap groups to educate and support women in menopause. She advises women to lose weight and cut down on their salt intake for relief of menopausal symptoms. If problems remain three months later, she puts the women on low doses of phenobarbital for a short period of time. She warns, however, that long-term use of phenobarbital may be habit forming. As a last resort, and informing the woman of the known risks, she prescribes low doses of estrogen for no longer than six months.

Commonly known natural diuretics like cranberry juice, watermelon, and asparagus may reduce the unpleasant bloating many women experience. Warm milk is a natural sedative. Camomile tea and wine help some women alleviate the discomfort of sleeplessness that is occasionally found during menopause. Regular exercise during and after menopause contributes to relaxation and an overall sense of health and well-being.

In a highly recommended book, *Menopause: A Positive Approach,* Rosetta Reitz lists several practical solutions:

- For irritability, insomnia, or depression, pamper yourself.
- Try an herb or milk-and-honey bath. Instead of estrogen for dry skin, try lubricating jelly for your delicate vaginal tissue and natural oil treatments for your face.
- If you're down, instead of bottling your blues up, call a close friend and tell her you are hurting inside. Talking is doing something about it.

The information we have about menopause comes only from studies of the 20 percent of women who go to their doctors with menopause symptoms. A nationwide study of the normal experiences of menopause (the remaining 80 percent of women) is very much needed and is in progress in Boston.

Sharing Menopause Experiences

Women and health-care providers need more information about menopause. Throughout the country women are forming supportive menopause self-help groups to share their experiences and concerns, to discuss treatments, and to research alternative treatments. Many of the negative effects of menopause result from lack of knowledge, which leads to apprehension and negative expectations. Women are encouraging each other to take the steps necessary to avoid the traumas of midlife and to approach the last third of their lives as a positive, challenging experience. We can all use the energies we no longer need for our reproductive tasks for new learning and socialization. Margaret Meade referred to these years as P.M.Z.—years of postmenopausal zest. For most of us, thirty-five to forty P.M.Z. years remain after menopause.

Hysterectomy

My recent hysterectomy was not nearly as routine as I'd been told. I wasn't prepared about what to expect and therefore found myself discouraged at my long confinement afterward. Usually busy and energetic, I was wiped out for several weeks. I hope other women will ask more questions and undergo this major surgery only after they have consulted with two or three physicians, and only if it's absolutely essential.

Sheila, age 47

A hysterectomy (from the Greek *hystera*—uterus—and *ectomy*—surgical removal) is an operation in which the uterus is removed either through the abdominal wall or through the vagina. Several surgical procedures are commonly referred to as a hysterectomy, including the following:

- Simply hysterectomy: the removal of the uterus and cervix
- Partial hysterectomy: the removal of the uterus, with the cervix remaining
- Oophorectomy: the removal of both ovaries and the fallopian tubes, which connect the ovary to the womb (this causes a "surgical" menopause in younger women)
- Total or complete hysterectomy: the removal of the uterus, cervix, ovaries, and fallopian tubes.

The Decision

The decision to have a hysterectomy is one of the most controversial subjects in medicine today. It is an expensive, irrevocable, painful, and possibly traumatic surgical procedure. Hysterectomy became increasingly popular in this country in the 1970s, and it is now the nation's second most frequently performed gynecological operation, after D&C. The annual incidence has increased 24 percent since 1971. More than 800,000 women have hysterectomies each year. One out of four of those women is younger than

Types of Hysterectomies

Uterus Tube Ovary Cervix Vagina

Subtotal
(body of uterus removed, cervix remains)

Total
(entire uterus)

Total plus tubes and ovaries

50. If the current rates continue, it is projected that more than half of all American women will have had a hysterectomy performed by the time they are 65.

A hysterectomy is major surgery involving a high rate of possible complications and often a long and painful recovery. A hysterectomy should be considered only for such reasons as the following:

- Cancer of the cervix, vagina, uterus, ovaries, or fallopian tubes.

- Extreme endometriosis that doesn't respond to any other treatment.

- Excessive numbers of large fibroids (benign growths attached to the uterus) that cause pressure on the bladder or other disabling symptoms. Large fibroids located on top of the uterus may cause a dangerous bowel obstruction and should be removed. The preferable treatment for this, however, is a myomectomy, which removes only the fibroids and not the uterus.

- Excessive and prolonged hemorrhaging (bleeding) that does not respond to a D&C (a scraping of the uterine lining).

- Disease or infection of the fallopian tubes or ovaries. One ovary (or even a part of an ovary) should be left, if possible, because the ovaries produce estrogen that the body needs. Rapid bone loss is noticed within three years after the loss of a woman's ovaries, often leading to osteoporosis.

Only about 12 percent of all hysterectomies are performed for the above reasons. Studies show that up to 40 percent of all hysterectomies are unnecessary. A common excuse for removing a woman's uterus is that she doesn't need it because it is useless after childbearing and should be removed (diseased or not) to prevent future trouble. This is like saying all breasts should be removed at age 35 because of the rapid increase in breast cancer after that age (as has been suggested by one physician). It has been said that if ovaries were testicles, there would be many fewer hysterectomies. Women themselves often request a hysterectomy as a way to end the "nuisances" of menstruation and birth control. Hysterectomies are also done for unexplained pelvic pain.

Many hysterectomy operations are performed for sterilization purposes. Yet tubal ligation (a simple surgical procedure in which the fallopian tubes are severed and tied, to prevent conception) is less expensive and less dangerous. Poorer women, especially poorer black women, have been subjected to the greatest abuse from unnecessary hysterectomies. Dr. Charles McLaughlin, former president of the American College of Surgeons, has noted, "Hysterectomy for sterilization is like killing a mouse with a cannon." Hysterectomies are performed for such ambiguous complaints as backaches, depression, and migraine headaches. Sometimes they are performed instead of an abortion.

Most hysterectomies are performed a few years after the menopause for a prolapsed uterus. A prolapsed uterus (or a "falling of the womb") occurs when the uterus descends below its normal position in the pelvis. A much simpler surgical repair is possible. It is rarely necessary to have a hysterectomy to correct this condition.

Hysterectomy is often performed to remove smaller fibroids, which may cause menstrual pain or irregularities and pressure on the bladder. These are found in 25 to 30 percent of all women. They are almost always benign and usually shrink after menopause, a fact that physicians rarely tell women. Small fibroids do not usually need to be surgically removed.

> *When my gynecologist said, "We need to operate," after two episodes of prolonged bleeding, I was given no information at all about the hysterectomy except the date of the surgery. My daughter called to ask if my ovaries would be removed. I didn't even know. My doctor said, "While we're there we might as well take everything. They might prove cancerous later in life." Only then did I begin to read several articles contrary to this philosophy and requested that he remove only the uterus. I also was wise enough then to ask him the questions I should have asked in the beginning: why the operation was necessary, what the surgery would encompass, how long recuperation would take, and the potential risk factors.*
>
> Liana, age 59

The Risks

Hysterectomy, like any surgery, entails risk. About 1,200 women die from hysterectomies each year. Postoperative infections, anemia, thrombophlebitis, as well as the need for blood transfusion and antibiotics, are common complications following a hysterectomy. Lengthy hospitalization is sometimes necessary, and the full recovery period can take up to a year. (However, normal recovery takes from six weeks to three months.) A vaginal hysterectomy, in which the uterus is removed through the vagina instead of the abdomen, increases the risks of complications which include fevers, urinary tract infections, and long periods of pain during intercourse. Despite these risks, many women choose vaginal or "bikini" surgery because the incision scar is inside the vagina and, therefore, not visible. Women who have this type of hysterectomy may notice reduced sexual sensation for several months. One woman reported that her gynecologist recommended vaginal surgery so that she "would be able to wear a bikini." She refused, saying she had never worn a bikini and didn't intend to begin wearing one at age 52. This is now her family's favorite joke.

Prevalence of Hysterectomies in America

The National Center for Health Statistics estimates that in 1976 more than 794,000 women in the United States had some form of hysterectomy and an additional 378,000 had their ovaries and fallopian tubes removed. Hysterectomies are performed in the United States two and a half times more often than in England and four times more often than in Sweden. In England and Sweden, medical care is paid for by the state, and doctors stand to gain less financially for performing the operation. Some people theorize that the large number of obstetrician-gynecologists in the United States, faced with the 50 percent decline in the birth rate, are filling the gap with hysterectomies, at an average cost of $1,500 to $2,000. Hysterectomy has been called "hip-pocket surgery" because the benefit is only to the doctor's wallet. Nationally, the number of hysterectomies performed for women with medical insurance is double that for uninsured women. In prepaid health plans, such as those run by unions, where peer review boards actively discourage unjustified surgery, many fewer hysterectomies are performed. Surgery should be considered only when all other medical alternatives have been explored.

What to Do When a Hysterectomy Is Recommended

When your physician recommends a hysterectomy, there is always time to obtain a second opinion. This should be a routine procedure for anyone facing elective surgery. Choose another gynecologist not associated with your own doctor or hospital. If the first two opinions do not agree, or if you yourself are not convinced of the need, seek a third opinion. Blue Cross/Blue Shield in most areas (as well as other private insurance companies) will pay for these consultations. Administrators of the health plan of the United Mine Workers found that hysterectomies decreased 75 percent when a second opinion was obtained. Blue Cross/Blue Shield of Greater New York found that in 28 to 30 percent of the cases, the need for a hysterectomy was *not* confirmed by the second physician. When a hysterectomy is necessary, however, it can save your life.

After you, in collaboration with your physician, have agreed that a hysterectomy is indeed necessary, you should proceed without delay. The surgery will take about two and one half hours and seven to ten days of hospitalization. Total bed rest is required for the first few days at home. Most women need three to four weeks for full recuperation.

Some women after a hysterectomy mourn the loss of their reproductive capacities; others are concerned about having an abdominal scar; others worry about getting the "postmenopausal blues." Studies clearly indicate that women who are not normally depressed will not be so after a hysterectomy.

Some women are concerned about their sexual abilities after a hysterectomy. This fear is most often related to the myth that a woman is "castrated" by such surgery, losing both femininity and sexual desire. The loss of a uterus and cervix will *not* reduce a woman's capacity for orgasm, except for those few women whose orgasm is related to pressure on the cervix. Sexual activity is not advised during the recovery period, but after that most women regain their full range of sexual sensation and response. If either partner is concerned about the sexual effects of hysterectomy, counseling for both is advised. This is especially true as women maintain their sexual lives well into their later years. When recovery from a hysterectomy is complete, most women report feeling healthier, and many report feeling sexier than ever before.

It is hoped, as women become more knowledgeable and assertive, and as their physicians become more aware, that the numbers of unnecessary hysterectomies in this country will sharply decrease.

*R*esources: Menopause

Publications

Boston Women's Health Collective. *Our Bodies, Ourselves: A Book By and For Women.* Rev. ed. New York: Simon & Schuster, 1976.

Butler, Robert, and Myrna Lewis. *Aging and Mental Health.* St. Louis: Mosby, 1977.

Clay, Vidals. *Women: Menopause and Middle Age.* Pittsburgh, PA: Know, Inc., 1977.

Cohen, Joan, Karen Coburn, and Joan Pearlman. *Hitting Our Stride: Good News about Women in Their Middle Years.* New York: Delacorte, 1980.

Lopez, Maria, et al. *Menopause: A Self-Care Manual.* Santa Fe, NM, Health Education Project, 1980. (Paperback in Spanish and English.)

Martin, Leoniden. *Health Care of Women.* Philadelphia: Lippincott, 1978.

Page, Jane. *The Other Awkward Age: Menopause.* Berkeley, CA: Ten Speed Press, 1977.

Reitz, Rosetta. *Menopause: A Positive Approach.* Radnor, PA: Chilton Book Company, 1977.

Riley, Matilda White. "Implications for Middle and Later Years In Women: A Developmental Perspective." U.S. Department of Health and Human Services, April 1982.

Rubin, Lillian. *Women of a Certain Age.* New York: Harper & Row, 1979.

Seaman, Barbara and Gideon. *Women and the Crisis in Sex Hormones.* New York: Rawson, 1977.

Resources: Hysterectomy

Publications

Boston Women's Health Collective Book, *Our Bodies, Ourselves: A Book By and For Women.* Rev. ed. New York: Simon & Schuster, 1976.

Fuchs, Estelle. *The Second Season: Life, Love and Sex for Women in the Middle Years.* New York: Doubleday, 1978.

Lamed, Deborah. "The Epidemic in Unnecessary Hysterectomies." In *Seizing Our Bodies,* ed. Claudia Dreifus. New York: Random House, 1978.

Morgan, Susanne. *Coping with Hysterectomy.* Washington, DC: National Women's Health Network, 1981.

Reitz, Rosetta. *Menopause: A Positive Approach.* Radnor, PA: Chilton Book Company, 1977.

Seaman, Barbara and Gideon. *Women and the Crisis in Sex Hormones.* New York: Rawson, 1977.

Resources: Menopause

Organizations

HERS (Hysterectomy Educational Resources)
501 Woodbrook Lane
Philadelphia, PA 19119
215-247-6232
Publishes newsletter and provides information and services about hysterectomy and ovariectomy

Chapter Nine

Sexuality and Intimacy As We Age

We've been married for fifty years and I feel I've continually grown, not only emotionally, physically, and intellectually, but sexually too. We are always trying new places to visit and new things to do, to bring excitement into our lives. This is also true sexually. I'd say I'm probably enjoying sex more now than at any other time in my life.

Doris, age 70

Sexual Capacity

There is no time limit on female sexuality. We are physiologically capable of full sexual expression until we die. Older women's sexuality can be defined in the broadest sense of the word—including self-image, self-esteem, intimacy with another person, masturbation, intercourse, orgasm, and lesbianism. The well-known Kinsey and Masters and Johnson studies indicate clearly that there is no physical reason why a woman in good health, with a responsive partner, and with a positive attitude toward herself should not enjoy full expression of her sexuality throughout midlife and later life. And yet some women experience a lessening of sexual activity beginning in midlife.

For many of us menopause is tangible evidence that the aging process has begun. Our aging ovaries cause hormonal changes that lead to the cessation of menstruation and reproductive capabilities. These changes are totally unrelated to our ability to continue a sexual relationship, but society's attitudes, the medical literature, and the media have been responsible for many negative sexual myths surrounding menopause. This misinformation has made many of us think that we *should* be less sexually active after menopause and, indeed, that an older woman is no longer sexually attractive. Some of the *myths* that can interfere with sexual satisfaction are the following:

- Menopause means the end of loving and being loved.
- Menopause is a deficiency disease. The loss of estrogen makes a woman the equivalent of a eunuch, suddenly desexed. Her vagina atrophies, her skin wrinkles, and her breasts get flabby.
- After menopause women lose the essence of being a woman.
- Fertility, sex appeal, and femininity end.
- Sexual activity is appropriate only when it leads to procreation.
- Women's hormonal changes cause an emotional imbalance resulting in depression, fatigue, and crankiness.
- Sex doesn't really matter in the later years. Sex is for the young and is abnormal after fifty.

Kinsey has established that women show only a slight decline in sexual capacity throughout life. A woman of 80 has the same capacity for orgasm as she had in her early twenties. It is true that many noticeable physical changes occur with the aging of the body, and some of them affect our sexual activity. Some women report symptoms that are due to the following changes:

- A decrease in the intensity of desire and frequency of sexual activities.
- Slower response to sexual stimulation.
- Shorter duration of orgasm.
- Decrease in vaginal lubrication.
- Reduction in the size of the clitoral hood and the organ itself.
- Thinning of the vaginal walls.

- Loss of elasticity, length, and width of the vagina.
- A decrease in strength of the muscular contractions occurring with orgasm.
- Relaxation of breast ligaments with an accompanying decrease in skin elasticity.

These changes may decrease our ability to respond sexually, but they do not eliminate it. For instance, the clitoris, despite a decrease in size, still remains responsive to stimulation. A greater degree of stimulation may be required, however.

Although our capacity for orgasm may be slowed there is no impairment in our ability to have orgasm—or even multiple orgasms. Indeed, the slower sexual responses of both the female and male aging body give women and men the opportunity to enjoy longer periods of pleasurable foreplay. The quality of these sexual encounters may become even more satisfying to women, especially those whose partners have previously suffered from premature ejaculation. In some women, hormonal changes cause mucosal or vaginal dryness. An unlubricated vagina can produce uncomfortable, even painful, intercourse. This can quite easily be alleviated with some kind of lubrication like saliva, K-Y jelly, or natural oils.

Many physicians suggest estrogen therapy to relieve several of the physical changes that occur during menopause. As discussed in Chapter 8, because of its implications in uterine cancer and breast cancer, women are advised to use estrogen only in extreme cases.

Despite physical changes, there seems to be no appreciable loss in pleasurable sensation as we age. Moreover, women who continue regular sexual stimulation and activity into their adult years experience fewer changes. As Masters and Johnson say, "If you don't use it, you lose it."

Health

Specific health problems may also inhibit sexual desire and performance in some of us as we age.

- *Hysterectomy.* This surgery has no direct physical relationship to a woman's ability to engage in sexual intercourse, but for some women the uterus represents the core of their femininity. Its removal may cause psychological and emotional anxiety, making them feels less attractive and therefore less sexually responsive.

- *Mastectomy.* Breast surgery often results in a lowered self-image and a fear of rejection, which may affect sexual functioning.

- *Drugs.* The indiscriminate dosing of women over 40 with drugs, especially antidepressants and tranquilizers, can lead to a lessening of sexual desire.

- *Alcohol.* Excessive alcohol consumption is a major problem for many women as they grow older. It acts as a depressant and can cause a decrease in sexual performance.

- *Chronic Fatigue.* Caused by depression, diabetes, anemia, or nutritional deficits, chronic fatigue reduces sexual interest and capacity.

- *Arthritis.* This disease can cause joint pain and limitation of motion, leading to sexual inhibition for some women.

- *Heart Disease.* The fear associated with a second heart attack (for a previous victim or her husband) may inhibit a woman's sexual performance. A more restrained type of sexual expression may be necessary. Some physicians recommend that a person who has suffered an earlier heart attack take a drug immediately before intercourse to lower systolic pressure. Any woman faced with heart disease in herself or husband should find a cardiologist willing to discuss openly the question of when sexual activity can safely be resumed after a heart attack and how the couple can find satisfying sexual expression. With such knowledge a modified sex life is possible even with high blood pressure and after a heart attack or cardiac surgery.

New studies at the National Institute of Aging report that older people can, and even should, resume their sexual lives twelve to sixteen weeks after a heart attack. This may actually reduce the risk of a second heart attack.

Too seldom do doctors discuss with both the woman and her partner the effects of health problems on their sexual activities. Arthritis symptoms and emotional tension, for example, may even be reduced because of the cortisone released in the body during intercourse.

Each of us has our own set of sexual values that remain fairly constant throughout our lives. These values result from a lifetime of learned sexual attitudes, taboos, actions, and perceptions that increase or decrease our levels of sexual desire and activity. Today's older women grew up with parents who often passed on rigid, puritanical, and Victorian concepts of sex. We were brought up not knowing much about sex, never talking about it, and viewing it as vaguely sinful. For many of us, sex was for procreation, not for pleasure. Married women were to have as few orgasms and as many children as possible. Enjoyable sex and intercourse was a husband's right, yet sex was merely a duty for wives. Many women faked orgasm throughout their lives out of fear or ignorance. For some women sex was never satisfying or pleasurable, and many chose menopause or a hysterectomy as an excuse to withdraw.

> *If someone told me I could never have sex again, I wouldn't be disturbed. For years the pattern has been that my husband ejaculates before I'm ever aroused. It's all over in three or four minutes. I wouldn't mind if he'd turn over then and hold and cuddle me, but he falls asleep immediately, leaving me feeling empty, rejected, and a little used.*
>
> Missy, age 54

Although our society presents older women with many sexual dilemmas, it also provides some solutions. The women's movement has encouraged women of all ages to explore their own bodies, to recognize their sexual needs as valid, to develop a new consciousness of their sexual potential, to learn to ask for pleasure, and to understand the variety of options possible for their full sexual expression.

Postmenopausal women report new feelings of freedom. The reality is that our sexual capacity peaks in our forties and fifties (much as a man's does in his early twenties). Sex may be better than ever before. The menses have ended and so has the fear of pregnancy. At the same time we are freed from the demands of raising a family, with more time and energy to pursue our own needs.

> *Since menopause I've felt more relaxed in making love. It's a great relief not to worry about getting pregnant, not to have to fear the children opening our bedroom door, and, finally, having enough time to concentrate on each other. I've convinced my husband to enjoy longer periods of foreplay and more tenderness after intercourse. Sex is one thing that's improving with age.*
>
> Jeannine, age 60

Sexual Dysfunction

Sexual dysfunction is a very personal problem—defined only if, or when, an individual woman feels less than satisfied with her own level of response to sexual stimuli. Trained sex counselors or therapists, sensitive to women's needs, can help us overcome most sexual dysfunction. This therapy should be available for single women as well as married, homosexual as well as heterosexual. Partners who are healthy and who have basically sound relationships have been able to increase their sexual functioning through good and sensitive counseling.

We should look for therapists who have been trained to discuss sexual behavior in late life with common sense and knowledgeable openness and without embarrassment. The goal of supportive sex therapy should be to help each partner be as capable as possible of enjoying all sorts of pleasure. This may involve anything from learning more creative coital positions to masturbation. Therapists and their therapies vary—from Masters and Johnson, who use cotherapists (female and male) and who work only with couples for intensive two-week periods to Dr. Helen Kaplan, who routinely works with single people, once a week, for periods of three to six months. Most good therapists will insist on a thorough physical examination first, to rule out physical problems or hormonal imbalances. All women need information about the use of lubricants, outside stimuli such as vibrators, and books on women's sexual fantasies as well as on how to have exciting sexual lives.

Group programs under the leadership of a qualified counselor can create a comfortable environment in which women over 40 can discuss their personal sexual concerns. Often women simply need "permission" to be more sexually active, to experiment with new sexual patterns, such as oral-genital sex or masturbation, to fantasize more, and to tell their partners what "turns them on."

Many women in their later years who have never had orgasm want to achieve that experience. For years they may have felt that they were "frigid," a word used to describe a broad spectrum of problems, from the inability to become excited at all to not becoming lubricated during foreplay to having sexual desire without being able to reach orgasm. Workshops for nonorgasmic women of all ages have successfully helped women to dispel the idea of frigidity and learn to identify what gives them sexual pleasure.

Masturbation

Many of us who live alone or in traditional relationships are becoming more open to masturbation, which some experience as liberating. For a number of women self-pleasuring helps maintain genital readiness and releases tension and anxiety. Masturbation not only gives many women a sense of control over their lives, but it also increases their potential for sexual pleasure. A Sex Information and Education Council of the United States (SIECUS) report in January 1980 states:

> Sexual self-pleasuring or masturbation is today medically accepted as a natural and nonharmful part of sexual behavior for individuals of all ages and both sexes. . . . It is a source of enjoyment and can provide an intense experience of the self as well as preparation for experiencing another. Many persons, however, do not wish to express their sexuality in this way and this also is an individual choice.

Older Women—Younger Men

Our society congratulates the older man who is able to attract a younger woman, but it is unwilling to accept the idea of older women having younger lovers.

For two years I tried to maintain a close and loving relationship with a professional colleague twenty years younger than myself. The strain was too great. Everywhere we went together, people asked me if he was my son (they would never dare do that to a male who came in with young women on his arms). The second major problem was children. I already have three, and that's enough—but he deeply wanted to have a child of his own. And so, despite a very compatible intellectual and sexual relationship, we decided to separate.

Dory, age 48

For only a few older women does a relationship with a younger man become a long-term, satisfying experience. For example, Gloria Swanson, age 80, has a 63-year-old husband; Ruth Gordon, 82, is married to Garson Kanin, 66; and Gloria Steinem, 45, lives with Sam Pottinger, who is 39.

Most women over 40 say that they would prefer a partner close to their own age. However, in the recent Weiner-Starr report on sexuality in the mature years (see Resources section at the end of this chapter), 83 percent of the respondents enthusiastically endorsed older women/younger men pairs, feeling that the standards should be equal. Some felt that such relationships wouldn't work unless the woman was exceptionally young looking and attractive. Maggie Kuhn says, "People are people and making love (and revolution) is good. Age is irrelevant."

Abstinence

Many older women have chosen to abstain from genital sexuality, for a variety of reasons. Those who make that choice and who have then gone on to develop at least one close, nonsexual relationship report being happy.

> *Everything I read nowadays makes me feel there's something wrong with me if I'm not sexually active. Well, I haven't been for many years, by choice, and I'm leading a happy, satisfying life.*
>
> Greta, age 60

Lesbianism

Not all older women look for sexual relationships with men. It is estimated that about 10 percent of older women are lesbian. Although elements of homosexuality are not necessarily acknowledged or expressed, they are probably present in most people. For some women, sexual orientation toward other women is established early in life. They have for years shared intimacy, companionship, love, and sex with other women, and they continue to do so in their later years. For others, identification or expression of bisexuality or lesbianism is delayed by cultural attitudes until later in life. A 43-year-old woman talked about her own experience:

> *I always suspected I was gay and spent many years trying to suppress those feelings and thoughts. Growing older gave me me. At last I'm able to do what I believe right for me. Oh yes, society still said no loud and clear, but now I discovered that I am not alone, not the only one—if only society would listen! My life with my lover is the happiest, strongest love I know—just two beautiful people loving, living, growing, and sharing together.*
>
> Elaine, age 43

Some women who have lived their lives in closely guarded same-sex relationships grow less fearful as they age and finally feel the freedom to live more openly. Women are increasingly turning to each other to explore new ways of intimacy. Some women who were prevented from "coming out" at an early age, because of family and societal pressures, leave (either deliberately or through widowhood or divorce) long-term heterosexual marriages in midlife or late life and join the lesbian community.

It is thought that older lesbians may not have as many problems adjusting to old age as heterosexual women. Because they have already learned to live alone and to cope with their sexual identity in a supportive community of women, they seem less concerned with problems of loneliness and isolation in their later years. On the other hand, many lesbian women have lost contact with disapproving families. As they age, they cannot rely on the network of services many families provide.

Intimacy

Sex is more than intercourse. Having sex and making love are not synonymous. Caressing, companionship, and intimacy are lifelong needs.

> *How long has it been since someone touched me? Twenty years? Twenty years I've been a widow, respected, smiled at, but never touched. Never held so close that loneliness was blotted out. . . . Oh God, I'm so lonely.*
>
> *Minnie Remembers*

These poignant words by writer Donna Swanson[*] reflect one of our deepest fears about aging. No matter what our age, we each need "touching intimacy" in our lives—at least one other person whose life intertwines with ours, with whom we can share both pleasure and pain. We hunger for someone who will accept us as uniquely and delightfully ourselves. This other person can be female or male, young or old.

Research demonstrates that babies who are never held or touched suffer psychologically and may actually wither and die. This is also true as we grow older. And yet, ever-growing numbers of women over 65 live alone, without partners, many of them deprived of any expression of intimacy.

One reality we face as we grow older is that there are more older women than men, and we are very likely to find ourselves without a male partner. Divorce after twenty-five or thirty years of marriage is becoming commonplace, and the average age of widowhood is a very young 56. In addition, men who are

[*]From a poem by Donna Swanson, made into the film *Minnie Remembers* (Mass Media Ministries, Baltimore, Md.).

widowed or divorced in midlife or late life remarry quickly, most often to younger women. There are nine bridegrooms for every bride over the age of 65. Not only is remarriage rare for older women, but there are few social opportunities for close relationships with men.

One thing unites us all—babies, adults, and grandmothers—our need for response from some living creature. Of course, tender loving care would be better, but we can survive without that luxury. What we cannot do without is some kind of reciprocal sharing of life experiences. We can, and many of us do, die of a broken heart. Loneliness can kill.

Mindy, age 82

I know I don't have an empty nest syndrome, but I certainly feel empty. Talk about lonely! Did you ever want to bubble all over about something, and there's no one within miles that you can communicate with?

Barbara, age 46

Are millions of us doomed to loneliness in old age? Of course not, at least if we are willing to plan now for our later years and not just let them happen to us. We need to reshape our thinking, to develop support systems that will offer us nurturing, warmth, and intimacy. And age 40 is not too early to begin. It is important to strengthen and nurture our friendships with women—indeed, to glory in them. Fortunately, as women, we are socialized and encouraged to develop close friendships with women, to share trusts and confidences, and to express our feelings one to the other. Many of us, even many married women, presently share much of our social life with women. The coffee-klatch, PTA sessions have evolved into rap groups, consciousness-raising meetings, and professional networking (the "old girls" club).

There is a prevailing fear of homosexuality among many older heterosexual women, which often prevents them from acknowledging their human need for a "touching intimacy." But increasingly women are realizing how much they enjoy the companionship of other women. Many say they have no desire at all to make the accommodations that would be necessary to form new heterosexual relationships or new marriages. Aging women are enjoying a new sense of independence and freedom.

I am blessed with a few special women friendships. They are nonsexual, greatly sharing, mutually supportive conversational love affairs.

Brooke, age 66

I've a whole circle of supportive, nurturing, loving women friends. I talk over life circumstances, problems and interests with them very openly, receive a great deal of support from them, and give the same. We often have just fun together. I love them and they love me. These friendships have been the most stable thing in my life.

Kathy, age 59

Collective living is another way to counter loneliness in our later years. Small groups of us can join together to share our living space, incomes, companionship, thoughts, and tasks in a supportive social enviroinment. Women are successfully doing this throughout the country. Shared living can take the form of communal city apartments or large surburban or rural homes, which can be converted to provide communal space as well as private quarters. Not only is shared housing economically feasible, but the idea is also ecologically and emotionally very sound.

The seeking of intimacy should be encouraged within nursing homes. My mother, who lived out her last years in a nursing home, developed a close friendship with another woman. They shared all the details of their daily lives, although these two proper women called each other "Mrs." and rarely touched. The friendship was so deep that when one died, the other followed in a few months.

The coming generation of elderly women (the "baby boom" generation, now in their thirties and forties) are more open in exploring the many different lifestyles that can bring them intimacy. Those of us presently in our middle or late years can learn from them. We can make ourselves happier as we grow older by thoughtfully and creatively searching for intimacy, by trusting ourselves enough to take risks, and by exploring and experimenting with living patterns and relationships that bring shared pleasure. Although we have been socialized to seek only one significant other for an intimate relationship, perhaps as older women our search should be for a *few* intimate people in our lives—people to have fun with, to share our pleasure and pain, and to give us the physical comfort we need. Love has the real potential for deepening as we age. We have years of experiences behind us, and now we have the time to develop joyful intimacies. There is no time limit on building new intimate relationships in our lives. Our only real limit may be a weak imagination!

*R*esources: Sexuality

Publications

Ayres, Toni. *The Yes Book of Sex: Masturbation Techniques for Women Getting in Touch.* San Francisco, CA: Multi Media Resource Center, 1972.

Butler, Robert, and Myrna Lewis. *Sex After 60.* New York: Harper & Row, 1976.

Dodson, Betty. *Liberating Masturbation.* Bodysex Designs, 1974.

Hite, Shere. *The Hite Report: A Nationwide Study of Female Sexuality.* New York: Dell, 1977.

Poticha, Joseph, and Art Southwood. *Use It or You'll Lose it.* New York: Marek, 1978.

Seskin, Jane, and Bette Ziegler. *Older Women/Younger Men.* New York: Anchor Press, 1979.

Vida, Ginny, ed. *Our Right to Love: A Lesbian Resource Book.* Englewood Cliffs, N.J.: Prentice-Hall, 1978.

Weiner, Marcella, and Bernard Starr. *On Sex and Sexuality in the Mature Years.* New York, Stein & Day, 1981.

Woods, Nancy Fugate. *Human Sexuality in Health and Illness.* St. Louis: Mosby, 1979.

Organizations

American Association of Sex Educators, Counselors, and Therapists
5010 Wisconsin Ave., N.W., Suite 304
Washington, DC 20016

Eastern Association for Sex Therapy
4 E. 89th St.
New York, NY 10028

Senior Action in a Gay Environment (SAGE)
P.O. Box 115
New York, NY 10023
A positive network of social services for older homosexuals.

Sex Information and Education Council of the United States (SIECUS)
84 Fifth Ave.
New York, NY 10010

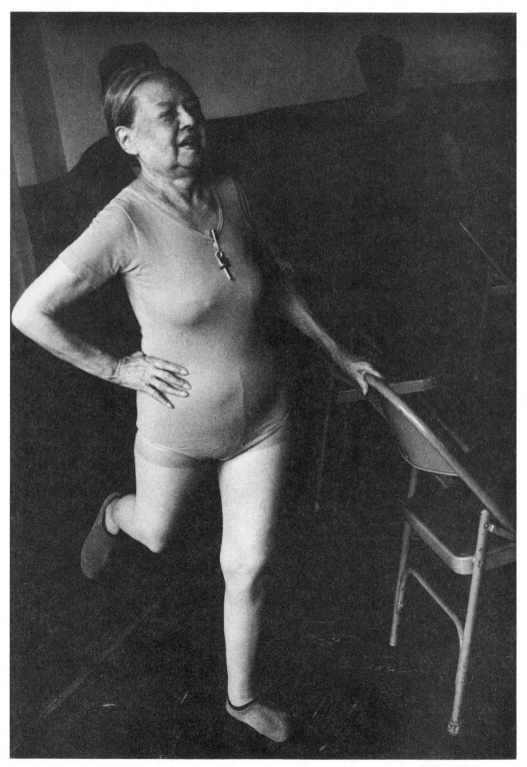

Hilda Bijur

Chapter Ten

Fitness after Forty

You're Never Too Old to Exercise

After recovering from a broken back I began walking daily and doing series of exercises each morning, as soon as I wake up. They only take me fifteen minutes, but they have paid off. The last time I visited my doctor he told me I had the heart of a 25-year-old. He said it's a good thing there are not many people in my condition, or doctors would have no business.

Elizabeth, age 86

Vigorous exercise—daily or several times a week—is essential to growing old gracefully and zestfully. We don't die abruptly of old age: we rust away. Many of us stopped exercising after our high school or college gym classes. We may have exercised when we wanted to lose weight and then stopped, rationalizing our inactivity with the claim that we got plenty of exercise caring for our house and family. Unfortunately, that kind of exercise does not do enough to promote health and keep us in good shape. And regular, cardiovascular exercise isn't easy to begin after a lifetime of neglect of our bodies.

When I first began jogging I could only walk fast for a mile, stopping for breath several times. Gradually I found I could keep pace with some younger friends who jogged two to three miles a day. It was a great accomplishment for me. Now I run a mile a day, five days a week. The beautiful sunrises and fresh air are a delightful bonus.

Sally, age 59

Although there is no proof that exercise extends the life span, there is sufficient evidence that physical fitness improves the quality of life and delays or prevents some of the degenerative changes of age. Dr. Ralph Harris, founder of the Albany Center for the Study of Aging, says that "the risks of not exercising are a greater hazard to an old person's health than exercising."

Exercise provides important benefits to our bodies. It improves the efficiency of the heart, allowing it to pump more blood with less effort. The risk of heart attack decreases with regular exercise. By increasing the amount of HDL (blood protein, associated with protection against heart disease), exercise enhances our body's ability to keep blood vessels clear of those dangerous deposits of cholesterol that can precipitate a heart attack.

Muscle strength increases with exercise, as does energy. We can actually be stronger at age 60 than at 30. When the bones absorb more calcium, they too become stronger and provide a sturdy support system for the body. Exercise promotes this process, which is particularly important to women over 50 who are at high risk of osteoporosis (see Chapter 11).

Arthritic patients benefit from exercise (alternated with rest) because it prevents the muscles from getting weak and the joints stiff. When there is active inflammation from rheumatoid arthritis, exercise should be curtailed. At other times, however, exercises that build muscle tone, such as walking, cycling, and swimming, are all recommended. A woman can be guided by her doctor and physiotherapist in deciding what is harmful and what is helpful. Sometimes she has to find a doctor who understands the benefits of exercise.

I got into exercise at age 55 after a severe bout of arthritis. I went to a specialist . . . and he told me to just sit still and take medication to kill the pain . . . (but) I found that the right exercise could relieve pain by stimulating the nerves and muscles and by increasing blood circulation. . . . I no longer have arthritis, haven't been to the doctor's in years, and don't take any medicine, even aspirin.

Eve, age 78

Exercise aids diabetics by promoting increased insulin production and better use of glucose by the body.

My two aunts, age 78 and 82, are worried about diabetes, which runs in our family. They get up at 6:00 A.M. and drive to a local school track. Here they walk briskly for a mile, joining a group of other oldsters. Then they go home and back to bed for another hour or so.

Cheryl, age 48

Physical fatigue induced by exercise can help combat insomnia. Digestion and elimination are also helped by regular exercise.

Exercising is an excellent way to fight depression and anxiety; try it instead of tranquilizers. And we not only feel and think better after exercising, we look better as well. Dr. James White of the University of California at San Diego reports that women who exercise have fewer facial wrinkles because exercise causes the skin to remain more elastic.

As more and more women of all ages trade in their high heels for sneakers, they have achieved significant rewards in the area of physical fitness.

One of my problems was a high heart rate. I happened upon an article which said running would help. I set a one-mile goal for myself. I was exhausted after the first quarter-mile, but after three months (going out six days a week) I ran my first mile. I lost thirty pounds, my heart rate dropped 40 points. . . . Now I run about twenty miles a week, with a younger woman friend. I've started to race. . . . In my first competition I was the only woman in the 40-plus category, so I won a medal. . . . I really love bringing home the trophies. Runners are so nice . . . there's a special spirit of comradeship. . . . One word of advice to older women who are asking where they can meet older men—start jogging!

Marjorie, age 60

Studies have shown that women, even those who are obese, are likely to benefit as much from a regular exercise program as their male counterparts, and they have no greater risk of injury. A recent *New York Times* article states that those who expend less than 2,000 calories a week in vigorous exercise have a 65 percent higher risk of suffering a heart attack. We can measure these calories in some typical exercises.

To expend 420 to 480 calories per hour you'd need to:

◆ Walk five miles an hour
◆ Cycle eleven miles an hour
◆ Play a game of tennis singles

To expend 480 to 600 calories per hour you'd need to:

◆ Jog five miles an hour
◆ Cycle twelve miles an hour

To expend 600 to 660 calories per hour you'd need to:

◆ Run 5.5 miles per hour

To expend more than 660 calories per hour you'd need to:

◆ Play squash or handball
◆ Run more than 6 miles per hour

If you find yourself complaining of fatigue, breathlessness, tension, backache, insomnia, or muscle aches and pains, it's time to plan an exercise regime. You might want to consult a health professional for some advice on how to begin. A physical exam may be a good idea if you are older and haven't exercised for a long while. It's important to start slowly—don't rush or overdo any exercise. Some hints to help you get started:

- Reserve thirty minutes a day during which you won't be disturbed or distracted.
- Exercise *before* eating.
- Exercise regularly. At first, exercise every other day. Occasional weekend sprees unduly stress the body. Even if you're not feeling top-notch you can exercise (except if you have a fever).
- Choose an exercise you'll look forward to and one that feels good.
- Wear comfortable, loose-fitting clothes.
- Wear a bra for support.
- Try exercising with a friend for greater enjoyment and motivation.
- Exercise to music.
- Always begin with a warm-up and a taper-off period of five minutes each, to avoid undue stress on the heart. (For example, joggers might want to begin and end with walking a quarter of a mile).
- Begin your day by slowly stretching your muscles before you get out of bed—like a cat does upon awakening.
- A hot bath relaxes joints and muscles after vigorous exercise.
- If you experience pain from exercise, go slowly. If the pain lasts longer than two hours, cut back (don't stop!). However, for exercise to be effective, you should try to challenge yourself.
- Breathe deep and rhythmically, to ensure an adequate supply of oxygen to the muscles. Inhale slowly, through your nose, and hold as you count to five. Exhale slowly, through your mouth, for five counts. Do this breathing forty to fifty times a day.

Three basic types of exercise are stretching (to increase joint mobility); strengthening or isometric (use of muscles without movement of joints); and endurance (swimming, cycling, jogging, dancing, cross-country skiing, which promote cardiovascular fitness). The latter are often called aerobic exercises because they cause the heart to beat faster, the lungs to expand, and blood vessels to swell, thus improving the circulation of oxygen. Any exercise that quickens your heartbeat for twenty minutes or more is aerobic.

Swimming is close to being the perfect exercise for people of all ages. It exercises all the major muscles of the back, stomach, arms, and legs. As it tones flabby muscles it helps the body shed excess pounds and it relieves tension, helps control varicose veins, and conditions your cardiovascular system. Women who find exercising on dry land difficult should try swimming, since water may make them more mobile and relaxed. Arthritis, for instance, is a condition that can make any exercise but swimming uncomfortable; water exercise enables you to move all muscles and joints in nontaxing ways. Overweight and asthmatic women might also choose swimming. Swimming lessons are usually available at low cost at local YMCAs and YWCAs. You should try to swim at least a half-hour three times a week, vigorously enough to raise your heartbeat. Swimming can burn up from 300 to over 1,000 calories an hour, depending on your speed and skill.

Walking briskly, two to five miles daily, is an excellent form of exercise. It is not particularly risky, and you don't need special equipment or clothing. Walking aids circulation, exercises the heart, and sends more oxygen and nutrients to your tissues. Walk quickly, swinging your arms, whenever you can—on your way to work, to the store, or during your lunch hour. Walk up the stairs instead of using an elevator.

Jogging uses all of your body systems and is especially good for your legs. Regular jogging not only makes you feel more fit, it also makes you feel better because it increases production of morphinelike substances in the body called endorphins. Endorphins can numb pain and produce a feeling of well-being. These substances may be responsible for the "joggers' high"—the euphoria of long-distance runners, as well as the depression and withdrawal they experience when they cannot run regularly. In one study, women who had not exercised strenuously for at least six months were put on a training program including running, cycling, and calisthenics, and the result was increased levels of endorphins in the blood.

Hatha yoga is a noncompetitive exercise that requires attention to breathing as well as muscle flexibility. The emphasis is on slow stretching. It can be an easy way to begin an exercise program, especially within a supportive class environment.

Tai-chi is an exercise program that has been used extensively throughout China for centuries, by people of all ages. It uses dancelike, slow, rhythmic body movements and is frequently done in a class or group situation. It is an excellent choice for women who experience problems with balance.

Other exercise includes cross-country skiing, aerobic dancing (which uses a mixture of jazz, ballet, and ballroom music), ice-skating, roller-skating, and jumping rope.

One Christmas, when my family of nine had assembled with their mates, someone suggested roller-skating. I was afraid I'd look foolish—I hadn't roller-skated for forty years or so! After a few shaky turns around the rink, my body began to remember how. I can still hear my kids's surprised reaction: "Wow, Mom, you're really good!"

Melanie, age 59

I've just celebrated my big sixtieth birthday. My two daughters, ages 21 and 25, and I registered in an adult education program for an aerobic dance and exercise class. It should be fun!

Susan, age 60

There are fitness classes for older people in nearly every major American city. Not only are the classes physically therapeutic, but they are an enjoyable social activity as well.

Exercise is the closest thing to an anti-aging pill now available. It acts like a miracle drug and it's free for the doing.

Cardiologist

We could throw away the rocking-chair stereotype and move our older citizens from the rocking chair to the joggers' path or the hikers' trail. When more Americans understand the role of fitness in aging, we'll redefine aging in this country.

Richard Schweiker, Department of Health and Human Services

Unless these [physical fitness] programs are addressed now, the life quality of older adults in the next century will be diminished.

1981 White House Conference on Aging

There's no need to be debilitated, sick, and senile in our old age. We can take responsibility to change the patterns of our lives and spend our later years healthy, lusty, and active.

I feel better about myself when I exercise. It doesn't matter which sport I'm currently into. Just the sheer physical activity gives me a sense of power and control over my own aging process.

Roxanne, age 52

Eating May Be Hazardous To Your Health

As a nutritionist I keep having the urge to grab women over 40 by their shoulders and give them a loving shake—wake them up to the joys of the second half of life. I want to tell them to emphasize the importance of good nutrition and exercise in their lives.

Ann, age 42

Adequate nutrition is seen as the most important factor in improving the health status of the elderly in the 1980s. The older shoppers may be the least informed about food values, the most unaware of nutrition information on labels. What is needed is a well-designed nutrition education program.

1981 White House Conference on Aging

Women over 40 are eager for more nutritional information for themselves and their families. As young homemakers we may have been vaguely aware of the relationship between a good diet, preventing disease, and maintaining health, but with little nutrition information available many of us became confused about nutrition. As we grow older, we face the danger that we may neglect or ignore that vital aspect of our lives.

The American diet has changed drastically in the past few decades. At the beginning of this century the average American consumed 60 pounds of fresh apples a year. Today we each consume less than 16 pounds. Half of our diet consists of processed food rather than fresh agricultural produce. Our consumption of fat and sugar has risen markedly, accounting for 60 percent of our daily food intake. It is also becoming clear that our eating habits must constantly change, to adjust to the most current information linking nutrition, health, and disease.

It is a slow and difficult process to change lifelong habits of eating. But planning individual goals for oneself is just one part of the exciting process of taking responsibility for personal growth and change.

Little is known about the specific nutritional needs, intake, and related factors of women 40 and older. Diet recommendations tend to be based on college-age students, since major nutritional research is often conducted on college campuses. Obviously, such recommendations are not necessarily appropriate for older people, since an old person is not just a young person who has lived more years!

Nutritional research at the National Institute on Aging has increased in the last decade. Some recent findings indicate that

- Calcium intake is generally too low in older people, especially women.
- Older people should eat more nutrient-rich foods and cut down on empty calories.
- Some age-related changes in the stomach could result in decreased absorption of iron, protein, and vitamin B_{12}.
- Some decrease occurs in older people's ability to digest or absorb large amounts of fat.
- Kidney functions slowly decrease with age.
- Fat may be healthier; slightly overweight older persons may live longer than those who are underweight.
- There is a high prevalence of obesity in older people (which is not healthy).

Women over 40 have some special nutritional needs and concerns. Many of the chronic problems we are concerned about, including osteoporosis, some cancer, and diabetes, can be helped or prevented by better eating habits. Many women who live alone fall into the "tea and toast" syndrome. My mother, who lived alone for ten years, was slowly starving to death from malnutrition in her late sixties and seventies. Her diet consisted of tea, toast, hot cereal, baked potatoes, and an occasional lamb chop. It was only when a heart condition brought her to a health-related facility near our home that we realized how limited her diet had become. Her health and appearance improved during the first month as she ate nutritious meals in a social setting.

A Department of Agriculture survey of ten states shows that more older women than older men suffer from poor nutrition, since many more women live alone and below or near poverty level. The survey concluded that the poor nutritional rating for women was caused by the high carbohydrate content of convenience foods, insufficient fluids, loss of teeth, and a growing disinterest in other people and surroundings, all of which lead to a decrease in proper food intake. Another factor contributing to the malnutrition of the elderly is lack of mobility. Many women have neither food stores nearby nor the transportation to supermarkets to shop adequately.

Malnutrition leads not only to body shrinkage, fragile bones, reversible symptoms of senility, and chronic constipation, but also to a loss of interest in caring for oneself. People feel tired and confused and prone to apathy and accidents—all attributes that are often used to describe older people. Some signs of poor nutrition in older women include cracked lips, beefy red tongue, excessively dry skin, anemia, and obesity.

Many of us found we shared common problems in food purchasing and preparation, such as keeping nutritional standards up and costs down, without sacrificing the pleasures derived from good food. It's not as easy as it once was to scurry from store to store. Most of us live on fixed incomes and find our pocketbooks aren't as plump as they used to be—so we need to be especially wise in the selection and preparation of our food, but we still all want to eat well. Many of us believe the adage that we are what we eat. . . . Eating well is one of the most important sources of vitality for body and soul.

Good Age Cookbook: Recipes from the Institute for Creative Aging, Boston: Houghton Mifflin Co., 1979.

Government aid has helped relieve some of the nutritional problems of older people. In 1972 Congress passed a nutrition bill for the elderly, allocating $100 million for 1973 and another $150 million in 1974 to improve their nutrition. In 1977 the food stamp program admitted some elderly. In 1978 the Older Americans Act authorized funding for a home-delivered meal program for those who aren't able to cook for themselves. In 1979, these national nutrition programs provided an estimated 160 million meals. Poor eating habits and malnutrition can be induced by living alone and being unwilling or unable to cook nutritious meals. Congregate eating sites in nursing homes and elsewhere provide not only a well-balanced meal five days a week but also an opportunity to interact socially with one's peers.

Nutrition Information

To eat well and to be energetic, each of the following need to be present in our diet: carbohydrates, fats, proteins, vitamins and minerals, water, and fiber. Calories measure the energy in foods and the amount of energy we need to live and grow. The idea is to strike a balance by taking in about the same number of calories as you use up—otherwise, you'll gain weight.

The number of calories you need decreases as you age. Women over 50 require an average of 1,800 calories a day, and women over 65 require about 1,600 calories daily, compared to an active 12-year-old who needs 2,600 calories. Less than 1,500 calories, however, is insufficient to maintain good health.

Carbohydrates

Carbohydrates are the most important source of energy for our body. The 1980 Federal Dietary Goals recommend that our carbohydrate consumption should make up 55 to 60 percent of our total caloric intake.

Carbohydrates are present in foods containing starches, sugars, and cellulose (found in the skins of fruits and vegetables). These starches and sugars are converted to glucose (blood sugar) and used as fuel by our muscles, brain tissues, and nervous system. Cellulose provides bulk for good intestinal functions. Since our ability to process sugar declines with age, it's important to eat carbohydrate-rich food that also contains vitamins, minerals, or proteins (dessert foods should be eliminated). Foods rich in carbohydrates include whole-grain foods (whole wheat breads and cereals, oatmeal, whole wheat or rye crackers, barley, brown rice, and cornmeal), fruits, vegetables, and honey.

Fats

Fats are the most concentrated source of energy in our diet. They provide insulation for our body. Most of us consume more fats than we need, however. Excess amounts of cholesterol, a fatlike substance found in all animal fats, cannot be absorbed properly. It is deposited on the arterial walls, making them thicker, less resilient, and more vulnerable to atherosclerosis and heart disease. Therefore, eating less fats (and thus less cholesterol) can reduce the chances of heart attack, a very real concern for women after menopause. Check with your physician periodically to make sure your cholesterol count is less than 200. Fats should make up only 30 percent of our daily caloric intake, and sources of fat should be divided equally among the three types: saturated fats (from animal sources), which remain hard at room temperature and increase the amount of cholesterol in our bodies; polyunsaturated fats, which remain liquid at room temperature and are essential because they lower body serum cholesterol; and monounsaturated fats (from plant sources), found in lard, margarine, and some vegetable oils. Good sources of fats are whole milk, vegetables, and nuts; corn, safflower, and sunflower seeds; and olives, eggs, and cheese.

> *My life changed drastically due to my increased energy and mind power when I changed to a low-fat diet.*
>
> Réné, age 52

Protein

Proteins provide the major source of building materials for muscles, blood, skin, hair, nails, and internal organs. They help the growth and repair of cells and are necessary to the repair of fractures and wounds as well as to our resistance to infection. Protein should make up 12 percent of our daily caloric intake, and it's important to renew our body protein daily. However, a recent Surgeon General's report advises Americans to consume less red meat, a primary source of protein, so it is essential that we begin to consume other protein-rich foods. Complete proteins are found in most meats and dairy products, dried beans, fish, and eggs. Incomplete proteins are found in whole grains, most vegetables, fruits, and nuts. If beans and grains are combined at one meal, however, they constitute a complete protein. The National Institute on Aging recommends two servings of protein-rich foods a day. One serving might include two to three ounces of red meat, chicken, or fish; two eggs, one cup of cooked dry beans; four tablespoons of peanut butter; or one-half cup of nuts. Since they are low in fats and high in fiber, proteins are an excellent food for older people.

I've discovered there are low-stress foods and high-stress foods for me. After a meal of meats and cheese I get really sleepy—not so after grains and vegetables.

Tammy, age 61

Minerals

Minerals (all seventeen of them) are essential for our physical and mental well-being. Minerals are integral parts of our bones, teeth, soft tissue, muscle, blood, and nerve cells.

Calcium is essential for strong bones and teeth. It aids in blood clotting and regulation of the heart muscle. Calcium absorption in our body is not very efficient, and there is a danger that women over 40 do not get enough calcium. Only 20 to 30 percent of the calcium we take into our body is absorbed. The rest is excreted. A Department of Agriculture study indicates that most women over 40 consume only three-quarters of the calcium they need. Consequently, one out of four postmenopausal women is afflicted with osteoporosis (see Chapter 11). Although the federal recommended daily allowance (RDA)—the Food and Drug Administration's standards defining the essential amounts of nutrients needed daily to meet the physical needs of a healthy person—is 800 mg of calcium, researchers at Long Island's Brookhaven National Laboratories suggest 1,500 mg for women over 50. Foods rich in calcium include milk (one quart of skim or whole milk provides 1,200 mg), yogurt, hard cheese, egg yolks, tofu, sardines, dark leafy greens (such as kale, collard, turnip and mustard greens), sesame seeds, and almonds.

Sodium (salt) is present in virtually everything we eat, from eggs to frozen apple pies. It is found in aspirin, apples, raisins, candy, and even in our drinking water. It is estimated that our average daily sodium consumption is one to three teaspoons; three-quarters of a teaspoon is the recommended daily amount. Restricting our salt intake is very difficult. Read product labels carefully, and if salt is near the top of the ingredient list avoid the product. Cut out salty snack foods (for example, popcorn and potato chips), canned vegetables, and use *no* salt in your cooking. High levels of sodium are unhealthy for all of us, but sodium can be disastrous for those with hypertension (high blood pressure) or those retaining excessive fluid. It is also a possible cause of congestive heart problems, cirrhosis of the liver, and impaired kidney functioning. For seasoning, try substituting more benign but flavorful substances such as garlic, onion, or lemon juice.

Potassium affects the condition of our thyroid glands, hair, and skin. It is found in all vegetables and fruits especially bananas, whole grains, sunflower seeds, and potato skins. The RDA is about 2,500 mg. Iodine is essential to thyroid gland functioning. It is found in iodized salt, kelp, dulse, and seafoods (both plant and animal). Phosphorus aids in building healthy bones, teeth, and skin. It is important to keep an equal ratio between calcium and phosphorus in your diet. Diets containing enough protein and calcium will be adequate in phosphorus. Most of us consume more phosphorus than we need because it is present in large quantities in processed foods, soft drinks, and cheeses. Good sources of phosphorus are milk and milk products, egg yolk, whole-grain cereal, fish, meat, nuts, poultry, and legumes.

Iron is important in building red blood cells and bringing oxygen from the blood to our tissues. Most women do not get enough iron in their diet, and anemia is often the result. Good sources of iron are liver, tongue, leafy green vegetables, and yeast. The RDA is 10 mg. Zinc is important to the absorption and action of vitamins and the healing of wounds and burns. Diets high in protein are usually high in zinc. Rich sources of zinc are shellfish and meat. The FDA is 15 mg. Magnesium builds lung tissue and strong bones and converts blood sugar into energy. It helps the body absorb other minerals. Magnesium is found in fresh green vegetables, nuts, and whole grains.

Water

Water is essential for digestion, circulation, excretion, respiration, and the transportation of nutrients throughout our body. It helps remove waste products through urine and feces and cools the body through perspiration. The average adult body contains approximately 45 quarts of water. We lose an average of 3 quarts a day through perspiration and excretion. Water is the most important nutrient in our diet. We should drink six to eight glasses of fluid a day (fruit juice, tea, and the like) and eat foods with high water content, such as fresh fruits and vegetables. Water can provide much relief from gouty arthritis and constipation.

Fiber

Fiber helps control constipation and hemorrhoids, and it helps prevent bowel cancer, atherosclerosis, and varicose veins. Fiber is roughage that provides the necessary bulk to allow the digestive system to absorb water into the intestinal tract and to move the bowels. The refining process has removed bran, an important source of fiber in our diet, from many foods. New research links low fiber with heart disease, diverticulosis, large-bowel cancer, diabetes, obesity, and gallbladder disease. Good sources of fiber are fruits and vegetables with the skins on, nuts, bran, unprocessed cereals, whole grains, breads, and oatmeal.

Vitamins

Vitamins are chemical substances needed in small amounts for new cell growth, proper digestion, nerve function, and conversion of food into energy. They work in the absorption and utilization of the nutrients in food. Lack of certain vitamins can result in disease. There are two groups of vitamins: fat-soluble (A, D, E, and K) and water-soluble (C and B-complex).

The use of vitamin supplements is controversial. If we eat a well-balanced diet, do we need to take vitamins? Does current food processing take most of the vitamins out of our food? Doctors say no to both of these questions, and nutritionists say yes. The debate has raged since 1956 when scientists indicated that the wide variety of biochemical makeup and nutritional needs of different people was a reason for giving extra vitamins to some people. Megavitamin therapy, which uses large doses of certain vitamins to prevent certain illnesses became popular. Others, physicians in particular, who have had little training in nutrition feel that a good diet gives everyone all the vitamins they need, and therefore no vitamin supplement is necessary.

Vitamins today are big business. Forty-four percent of the American population add at least one vitamin to their daily diet, and vitamin sales have reached $1.5 billion annually (and are expected to more than double in the next six years). Are vitamins necessary for women over 40? Older women in reasonably good health should be able to get all the vitamins they need in their diet, if it includes dark green and yellow vegetables, fruits, whole grains, dairy products, meat, shellfish, and beans. As we age, however, we don't absorb vitamins and minerals as we once did, so we need to take in more. Moreover, we need a very varied diet. Many women living alone find it too troublesome or expensive to stock a large supply of food, and vitamin supplements can help us maintain a nutritional balance.

A 1978 survey of the diet of almost 38,000 Americans revealed that large numbers, particularly adolescent girls and adult women, were consuming considerably less than the recommended daily allowances of vitamins A, C, and B_{16}, calcium, iron, and magnesium. This means two things: we should be planning more wholesome, nutritious diets including the basic four food groups (four servings daily of whole grains, fruits, and vegetables and two servings each of meat or meat substitutes and milk and dairy products); and we should add at least one multivitamin supplement daily, as a precaution. Nutritional needs are significantly increased for women who are on the birth-control pill, those undergoing major surgery or afflicted with a serious illness, or women who have suffered such emotional traumas as divorce, widowhood, or loss of a job. To meet the nutritional needs of such women, extra vitamin supplements may be necessary. The accompanying chart will assist you in determining how you can meet your nutritional needs. The RDAs listed are not specific for women over 40; they are simply guidelines.

Obesity and Related Problems

Fat is not about self-control or will power. . . . Fat is about protection, sex, nurturance, . . . mothering, . . . assertion and rage. . . . Fat is a social disease and a feminist issue, . . . a response to the inequality of the sexes.

Susie Orbach, *Fat is a Feminist Issue*

Obesity is a major health problem for women in midlife and late life. Obesity is overwhelmingly a woman's problem (50 percent of all American women are overweight) and therefore must have something to do with being female in a society that prizes slim and young beauty. The weight reduction industry is big business—an $11-billion-a-year industry.

A person is considered obese when she (or he) is 20 percent heavier than her ideal weight for her sex, age, and height. Compulsive eating (feeling out of control around food, eating when you're not hungry, and feeling awful about yourself because of this) is a symptom of distress. Being fat is a very painful experience for

Vitamin	Function	Best Sources	Symptoms of Deficiency	Recommended Daily Allowance (RDA) (1980, females 23–50)	Comments
A	Needed for normal vision Protects against night-blindness Keeps skin soft and free of skin disease Keeps hair healthy Protects the mucous membranes of the mouth and nose Promotes nail growth Helps fight infection	Fish-liver oils Liver Whole milk Whole-milk cheeses Egg yolk Dark green leafy and yellow vegetables Yellow fruits	Night-blindness Dry, rough, and spotty skin Lowered resistance to infection Poor digestion Loss of sense of smell Loss of appetite Fatigue Diarrhea	800 RE (retinol equivalents)	Signs of an overdose: headache nausea diarrhea dry, cracked skin loss of appetite hair loss blurred vision
B Complex (includes 14 vitamins)	Relieves nervous irritability Promotes growth Aids appetite and digestion Develops healthy eyes and skin	Brewer's yeast (richest natural source of the B complex) Dried beans and peas Oatmeal Whole wheat bread Wheat germ Nuts and seeds Egg yolk Rice Liver	Depression Nervousness Mental confusion Changes in emotional and intellectual behavior Poor appetite Constipation Loss of coordination and sense of balance Graying hair and baldness Slow heartbeat	Niacin: 13 mg Riboflavin (B_2): 1.2 mg Thiamine (B_1): 1.0 mg B_6: 2.0 mg B_{12}: 3.0 micrograms	Older women and men often deficient in vitamin B_{12} and folic acid Study suggests older women (and men) need more vitamin B_6 than younger people Ability to absorb vitamin B_{12} (in milk, eggs, and meats) seems to decrease with age Sugar and alcohol destroy B-complex vitamins
Folic Acid	Promotes formation of red blood cells Aids in the metabolism of proteins Increases appetite Helps senile dementia patients	Yeast Fresh fruit Green leafy vegetables Liver, kidney Oysters, salmon	Anemia Tongue abnormalities Symptoms mimicking senility May be a contributing factor in mental illness Graying hair	400 micrograms	

Vitamin	Function	Best Sources	Symptoms of Deficiency	Recommended Daily Allowance (RDA) (1980, females 23–50)	Comments
C (Ascorbic Acid)	Maintains the cementing material that holds body cells together Needed for formation of collagen (a connective tissue that keeps skin supple and elastic) Heals wounds Promotes resistance to infection and bacteria Increases capillary strength Aids adrenal gland functioning	Citrus fruits and juices Berries, cantaloupe, apricots, peaches Green vegetables (especially broccoli, cabbage, peppers, asparagus, sprouts) Tomatoes Potatoes	Bleeding gums Easy bruising Physical weakness Rapid heartbeat Headaches Blood vessel rupture and strokes A wearing down of the taste buds of the tongue Scurvy	60 mg	The body does not store vitamin C, so it must be replenished daily. Potatoes are an inexpensive source of vitamin C. Doubling the RDA reportedly reduces cold symptoms. Dr. Linus Pauling, Nobel Laureate, says the optimum daily intake of vitamin C is 2,300–9,000 mg; take frequent small doses daily rather than a single large dose up to 5,000 mg; the body discharges whatever it can't use. Smokers require more vitamin C; approximately 25 mg are destroyed with each cigarette smoked. Signs of overdose: diarrhea, cramps, kidney stones
D (The Sunshine Vitamin)	Helps absorb and utilize the calcium and phosphorus required for strong bones and teeth Helps maintain a stable nervous system and normal heart action Promotes good muscle tone Relieves acne	Fish-liver oil Fortified milk Yogurt Yeast Green vegetables (cabbage, spinach, asparagus) Salmon, sardines Sunshine	Soft, fragile bones (osteoporosis) Muscle cramps Twitching	5 micrograms	Vitamin D can be acquired by ingestion or exposure to sunlight. If your exposure to sunlight is limited and you don't drink milk regularly, it makes sense to take a vitamin D supplement. Vitamin D deficiency occurs most frequently among the elderly. Signs of overdose: nausea, stiffness, aches, kidney stones

Vitamin	Function	Best Sources	Symptoms of Deficiency	Recommended Daily Allowance (RDA) (1980, females 23–50)	Comments
E	Helps transport oxygen to the cells, preventing cell aging Protects red blood cells Helps leg cramps and "restless legs" Aids arthritic and circulatory disorders Relieves itchiness in aging skin Keeps skin smoother Especially important for menopause symptoms, particularly hot flashes	Whole grains Wheat germ and bran Seeds Nuts Eggs Sweet potatoes Leafy vegetables	Gastrointestinal disease Rupture of red blood cells Loss of hair A severe deficiency would cause damage to the liver and kidneys	60 mg	Vitamin E is stored in fat and muscles and must be replenished regularly. Women with high blood pressure or with rheumatic heart disease should use small doses. Dr. A. A. Albanese, Burke Rehabilitation Center, White Plains, N.Y., recommends 800–1200 mg daily for women over 40. Can be toxic in large doses. An overdose might produce flulike symptoms.
F (Unsaturated and Fatty Acids)	Lubricates cells Aids in oxygen transportation throughout the body Aids respiration of vital organs Aids glandular function	Wheat germ Vegetable oils Butter Sunflower seeds	Brittle, lusterless hair, dandruff Varicose veins Underweight Allergic conditions Nail problems Diarrhea	1% of total daily calories	No known toxic effect.
K	Permits blood clotting Helps maintain normal liver function Increases vitality and longevity	Dark green leafy vegetables Cauliflower Soybeans Milk, yogurt Egg yolks Safflower oil Fish-liver oil	Colitis Intestinal malabsorption Prolonged blood-clotting time Hemorrhaging Nosebleeds Diarrhea	300–500 micrograms	Essential before surgery to help blood clot. Toxic in large doses Symptoms of overdose: flushing, sweating, chest constrictions.

the woman involved. Most often women who are fat have feelings of fear, shame, and humiliation. They are out of step with society and isolated even by other women. Obesity can symbolize a woman's fear of success on the job or as a sexual partner; it can be a rebellion against powerlessness. But one thing it is not: a "character defect." The popular conception is that weight is a matter of personal choice; fat women could control their size if they would just exert some willpower ("you're really a slim woman in a fat body"). Because of such societal attitudes, fat women constitute one of the most oppressed groups in society.

Although obesity is often caused by a cycle of alternating undereating and overeating, we are learning that some overweight people may be in the grip of metabolic factors that are hard to control. Some obese women may be the victims of biochemical problems such as lack of the appetite-depressant hormone that helps regulate food intake. Heavier women may also have too many enzymes that promote fat storage (typically, women have more body fat than men and gain weight more easily).

There are two types of obesity: mild to moderate (which can be successfully controlled by changing diet and lifestyle) and morbid (involving one hundred pounds or more of overweight, which interferes with the woman's social and work life and seriously threatens her health).

When our body takes in more calories than it expends, fat is formed. Just 100 extra calories a day will add twelve pounds to your body in one year. A decrease of 1,000 calories each day results in about two pounds of weight loss a week.

Many of us turn to crash diets, which seldom work. Often they produce a rapid weight loss owing only to loss of fluid. Usually, the weight is regained quickly. This leads to a frustrating cycle of abusive food intake and deprivation. If the hundreds of fad diets available really worked, why would new ones be proposed every month? Examples of fad diets are high-protein, low-protein, liquid-protein, and high-carbohydrate diets. Few such diets encourage the fundamental necessary change in eating habits. Fortunately, few of us stay long enough on such a diet to induce malnutrition. The Weight Watchers program is an example of one that offers a practical long-term diet that is workable for many women over 40. It also offers group support as we grow slimmer, as does another effective organization, Overeaters Anonymous.

Some obese women turn to surgical solutions. For morbidly obese people, procedures such as gastric stapling may be an option. This surgery consists of inserting staples into the patient's stomach to reduce the capacity for solid food. Any large intake causes great pain and the risk of tearing the staples open.

For most women seeking a safe, gradual program to lose weight and keep it off, a high-protein, low-carbohydrate, low-fat diet of about 1,200 calories daily generally proves effective. New, intriguing evidence indicates that a good meal in the morning will produce less weight gain than a large meal in the evening, and several small meals have been found to be less fattening than a single big meal with the same total calorie count. Exercise is a valuable part of any weight-loss program. Women are working on the issue of overweight in self-help groups that explore how each individual feels about fatness and thinness and that suggest new ways to approach food.

Weight control is important for healthy bodies. The extremely fat and the very thin have an increased mortality rate and are at greater risk to the diseases of old age. Being overweight places unnecessary stress on our joints. Fat layers separate tendons and ligaments, resulting in an increased need for energy to accomplish activities. Despite the fact that fat women are notoriously unfit, gyms, jogging in the streets, yoga classes, and other forms of exercise are rarely available without fat women encountering hurtful stares and comments. Some of the health problems associated with obesity include the following:

Backache can be an especially crippling ailment for many women past reproductive age. It can send us to bed for weeks at a time or to drugs and muscle relaxants. Poor posture, arthritic changes, chronic exhaustion, psychological stress, and sedentary living all may contribute to back problems. Obesity is also a factor; three-quarters of all women with chronic back pain are obese. Overweight increases the weight the spine must support as well as pressure on the spinal disks. To alleviate an aching back:

- Try some form of regular exercise, such as walking, swimming, jogging, cycling, or cross-country skiing.
- Sit on a chair with a hard back so that your feet can rest firmly on the floor.

- At work or on a car trip, stop every hour to stretch and walk about. In the car, a rolled towel behind your lower back may increase comfort.

- Always sleep on a firm mattress. Toughen yours with a one-half-inch-thick sheet of plywood under it. Sleep on your side with your knees bent.

- While reading or watching TV, lie down whenever possible, keeping your arms at your sides, raising your knees. Breathe deeply while letting go of any muscle tension.

- Combine fewer calories with exercise for maximum back protection.

Diabetes is much less likely to occur in women who are slim. Often diet alone can control the onset of diabetes in the mature woman. Diabetics do not have enough effective insulin to handle the amount of glucose-producing foods being consumed by an obese person; therefore the food intake needs to be reduced to match the available insulin.

Hypertension affects more women than men in their late thirties to early fifties. Coffee, tobacco, drugs, emotional disturbances, and obesity seem to play a role. Diet therapy includes reducing salt intake and bringing your weight to an ideal level and maintaining it even after your blood pressure returns to normal.

Gallbladder disease is also often a problem for obese middle-aged women, especially those who are constantly gaining and losing weight. Inflammation, gallstones, constipation, or obesity cause the gallbladder to malfunction, preventing bile from flowing to the intestine, with resulting pain. The pain is generally sharp and comes in waves, radiating from the upper abdomen to the back, shoulders, and pelvis. Other symptoms include mild jaundice, nausea, belching, and rapid heartbeat. When the bile duct is infected additional symptoms may be fever, chills, dark-colored urine, and clay-colored stools.

Other medical problems in which nutrition plays a role include:

Osteoporosis affects one in four women over the age of 50. Researchers believe that an increase in calcium, up to 1,200 mg per day (compared to our usual daily intake of 400–800 mg), combined with vitamin D for absorption will decrease the risk of this devastating disease.

Cancer that is affected by nutritional factors include stomach, liver, large- and small-intestine, breast, and colon cancer. Some researchers feel that as many as 60 percent of the cancers in women are diet-related. Japanese women, for example, who eat little fat, have a low incidence of breast cancer—until they migrate to the United States and begin to consume foods high in fat and calories. Lack of proper fiber seems implicated in the rising incidence of colon cancer.

Cardiovascular disease is an increased risk for women after menopause. High cholesterol and saturated fats increase our risk of developing cardiovascular disease. Dietary changes should include fewer calories; less fat, sugar, and salt; more fiber and starch; and more exercise. Americans now consume about half their calories as fat. This should be moderated to less than 35 percent of our caloric intake for weight reduction.

Leg cramps are a common problem for older women. They frequently occur at night, following a day of unusual exertion or tension. Repeated leg or foot cramps are often associated with atherosclerosis, sodium loss (due to heavy perspiration or diarrhea), or lack of calcium and vitamin C. Increased vitamin intake may be helpful. Consult your physician or nutritionist for amounts.

Anemia is caused by a low iron intake. Older women should eat more iron-rich foods—meat (especially liver), egg yolk, whole-grain products, green vegetables, raisins, figs, prunes, and apricots—or take iron supplements prescribed by a doctor. Vitamin C facilitates the absorption of iron.

Chronic constipation can be caused by changes in the gastrointestinal tract due to aging. Food is digested more slowly as we age, and the products of food digestion (waste) do not move as rapidly through the body. A high-fiber diet, as well as adequate consumption of water, will help digestion.

Nutrition Advice

Recently issued federal dietary guidelines offer seven helpful points worth remembering:

- Eat a variety of foods.
- Maintain your ideal weight.
- Avoid too much fat (saturated fats and cholesterol).
- Eat foods with adequate sugar and starch content.
- Avoid too much sugar.

- Avoid too much sodium.
- If you drink alcohol, do so in moderation.

A few other basic rules to remember include the following:

- Eat less. Scientists feel older people need a diet containing all the required nutrients, but about one-third fewer calories to maintain normal body weight.
- Drink lots of water, particularly between meals.
- Eat fresh foods—cook as little as possible.
- Include lots of roughage (fiber) in your diet.
- Eliminate any foods that you feel cause you distress.
- Slow down, chew carefully, taste what you eat.
- Avoid food additives. Despite scientific uncertainty, they may be carcinogenic (cancer-causing).
- Eat only when hungry. Listen to your body.
- Be a wise consumer. Don't be fooled by claims of "fortified" or "enriched" or "all-natural." These may be sales pitches for nonnutritious or highly sweetened foods.
- Try eating your main meal early in the day. Also try a small amount of wine with meals (it may increase your appetite for good food).

If you feel you need more information about nutrition and would like to consult a nutritionist, remember that a qualified nutritionist should have a minimum of a bachelor of science (B.S.) degree in science or nutrition from an accredited college or a master's degree (M.S.) (requiring several years of study beyond the B.S.) or a doctorate (Ph.D.) (requiring more years of study plus research). Most will have professional certification from the Society of Nutrition Educators, the American Society of Clinical Nutrition, or the American Institute of Clinical Nutrition.

A registered dietitian (RD) will also have a B.S. degree in dietetics or nutrition, including a three-year specialized internship or an M.S. in nutrition, with six additional months of specialized experience. Most are members of the American Dietetic Association and must pass an exam to be registered.

Altan Ochsner notes, in an article on aging in the *Journal of the American Geriatric Society*:

Any product of high quality, if cared for well, will last and function well for a long time. Even a product of inferior quality, if not abused, will last and function satisfactorily relatively long. . . . No matter how good a product, if it is abused and not sufficiently maintained, will deteriorate rapidly, age more rapidly and become obsolescent early. There is no difference between inanimate objects and the human body.

It is obvious that the food we consume in midlife can bring us greater vigor and vitality as we age. We can achieve not only a longer but a healthier life. Proper nutrition and a regular regime of exercise can prevent or eliminate many problems of older women. We are products of high quality. Let's keep it that way!

Resources: Exercise

Publications

Boutelle, Jane, and Sam Baker. *Jane Boutelle's Lifetime Fitness for Women.* New York: Simon & Schuster, 1978.

Cooper, Mildred and Kenneth. *Aerobics for Women.* New York: Bantam, 1973.

Frankel, Lawrence, and Betty Byrd. *Be Alive as Long as You Live: The Older Person's Complete Guide to Exercise for Joyful Living.* New York: Lippincott and Crowell, 1980.

Golden, Ruth. "Top to Toe Exercise." Free from Sports for the People, 391 E. 149th St., Bronx, NY 10455.

Higdon, Hal. *Fitness over Forty.* Mountain View, CA, World Publications.

Lorig, Kate, and James F. Fries. *The Arthritis Helpbook.* Reading, MA: Addison-Wesley, 1980.

Luce, Gay Gaer. *Your Second Life: Vitality and Growth in Middle and Later Years.* New York: Delacorte, 1979.

Rosenberg, Magda. *Sixty-Plus and Fit Again: Exercise for Older Men and Women.* New York: Evans, 1977.

Resources: Nutrition

Publications

Ballentine, Rudolph. *Diet and Nutrition.* Honesdale, PA: The Himalayan Institute, 1978.

Brody, Jane. *Jane Brody's Nutrition Book: A Lifetime Guide to Good Eating for Better Health and Weight Control.* New York: Norton, 1981.

Environmental Nutrition, Environmental Nutrition, Inc., 52 Riverside Drive, Suite 15-A, New York, NY 10024 (published ten times yearly, eighteen dollars a year)

Fat Liberation Publications. P.O. Box 72321, Minneapolis, MN 55407.

Harlow, Jean, Irene Ligett, and Evelyn Mandel. *The Good Age Cookbook: Recipes from the Institute for Creative Aging.* Boston: Houghton Mifflin, 1979.

Kirschman, John D. *Nutrition Almanac.* Revised ed., New York: McGraw-Hill, 1979.

Nutrition and Health. Institute of Human Nutrition, Columbia University College of Physicians and Surgeons, 701 W. 168th St., New York, NY 10032. (Six times a year, $10.00 per year.)

Nutrition and Your Health: The 1980 Dietary Guidelines. Office of Governmental and Public Affairs, U.S. Department of Agriculture, Washington, DC 20250 (free).

Orbach, Susie. *Fat Is a Feminist Issue.* London: Paddington Press, 1978.

The Sodium Content of Your Food. FDA Consumer Inquiries, HFE-88-5600. Fishers Lane, Rockville, MD 20857 (free).

Organizations

Consulting Nutritionist
P.O. Box 315
Cold Spring, NY 10516
or
5018 Indigo
Houston, TX 77097
To contact a Registered Dietitian in your area.

The National Association to Aid Fat Americans, Inc. (NAAFA)
P.O. Box 43
Bellerose, NY 11426
516-352-3120

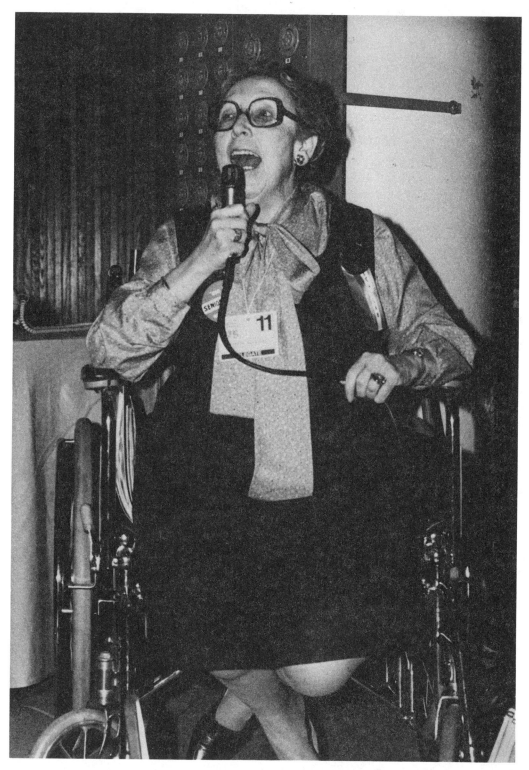

Twin Lens Photography

Chapter Eleven

Osteoporosis

I began having lower back pains in my middle years, which my doctor attributed to an earlier accident. Even when I started to develop a round-shouldered appearance, he merely suggested that I quit slouching and wear a shoulder brace.

At age 60 I decided to seek another opinion and had my first thorough physical in many years. These tests revealed that I had lost nearly three inches in height and that my bones were deteriorating. Vitamin D was recommended.

As I approached 65, my back pains became more bothersome, and one of my "health nut" friends suggested calcium and tennis. A daily dose of approximately 600 mg of calcium and 300 mg of magnesium seems adequate for me, except on stressful days, or when I neglect to exercise.

Now approaching my 69th year, I am mostly pain free but have a pronounced "dowager's hump" which I know now could have been prevented by sound medical advice in my earlier years.

Miranda, age 68

Osteoporosis is a preventable disease. . . . Cut down on alcohol, cut down on caffeine intake, stop smoking, and take plenty of exercise. Beyond that, take an adequate amount of calcium in *your diet, either as diet or as extra calcium. . . . There is no doubt that people who don't get it [osteoporosis] are those who do all these clever things.*

Robert Lindsey, M.D., Director,
Regional Bone Center,
West Havestraw, N.Y.

Osteoporosis is one of the most severe, crippling disorders that affect older women, but many older people are unaware of the disease or its symptoms. The word *osteoporosis* means "porous bone" (*osteo*, bone; *porosis*, porous) and indicates the characteristic softening, weakening, or loss of bone. Although it is a very common condition, women are not condemned to developing it as they age.

Osteoporosis is a poverty of bone tissue or reduced bone mass. Women who have this disease lose bone tissue at a higher rate than their body manufactures it. Their bones become increasingly porous, fragile, and susceptible to painful fracture. Hip, spine and forearm are the most typical sites of fracture. One out of four white postmenopausal women over 50 will suffer from some degree of osteoporosis and one out of ten will be severely afflicted with pain and immobility. Less than half that number of older men will suffer from osteoporosis, and usually not until they are over 65. There are an estimated two million hip fractures each year in the United States, with osteoporosis the major contributing factor. Hip fracture rates rise after age 50, doubling in incidence with every ten-year increase in age. The financial cost is enormous. It costs approximately $10,000 per hip (nationally $1.4 billion a year) for the hospitalization, anesthesia, and surgery required to treat fractures). Even more devastating is the effect on the quality of life of each woman afflicted. Such fractures cause considerable discomfort and deformity. Orthopedic wards are filled with women in their sixties, seventies, and eighties who were leading active lives until a fall hospitalized them with a broken hip or fracture of the wrist. This often means a permanent loss of freedom and mobility. The mortality rate of hip fractures is approximately 15 percent, and 15,000 to 20,000 women die every year after fracturing a hip. Once a woman has had a fracture, she has a very high chance of recurrence.

Black females (and men) start out life with higher bone density than Oriental or white women, and so they are less susceptible to the effects of osteoporosis. All women reach their maximum bone growth around age 30 or 35. There is a decline of bone growth until about age 70, when there is no further loss of bone. This decline can mean a 30 to 35 percent loss of bone mineral content by old age. Small, delicately built women, who have less than normal bone mass, are especially prone to this disease, as are women who have a family history of the disease or are high caffeine users or heavy smokers. Those who have taken cortisone drugs for other diseases are also at risk. By age 50, 26 percent of all white women have had osteoporotic vertebral fractures. By age 75, the figure increases to 50 percent.

Causes of Osteoporosis

Our understanding of the causes of osteoporosis has not improved much in the past ten years. Many factors are involved: Changes in hormones, nutrition, and intrinsic cellular stress have all been implicated. One theory suggests that bones widen as we age, making them weaker and more fragile. Many physicians feel that osteoporosis is caused by hormonal changes—that is, an estrogen deficiency. Others feel the deficiency is of the hormone calcitonin, which decreases with age.

Another widely accepted theory is that accelerated bone loss is due to an insufficient amount of calcium, along with a lessened ability to absorb the calcium the body takes in. After about the age of 30, everyone starts to lose some calcium. After menopause, women with osteoporosis have 30 percent less calcium in their bones than they had before. The rate of loss is more rapid in white women. The only way to measure the amount of calcium lost is an expensive procedure developed at Brookhaven National Laboratory on Long Island. There, researchers measure the amount of calcium in a patient's body by making the calcium temporarily radioactive and measuring the radiation with an instrument (whole-body counter) that reveals the calcium content and its distribution throughout the skeleton. Because of its expense, this diagnostic test is available to only a tiny number of postmenopausal women. We need a method of measuring the amount of calcium in our bones that is inexpensive and available in every community. Some information is offered by X-rays.

Two factors that might contribute to the loss of calcium in women are childbearing and breast-feeding. A fetus requires 400 mg of calcium per day for normal growth. A nursing mother requires between 400 and 800 mg daily, and yet she loses about 300 mg per day while breastfeeding her baby. Therefore, it is important for physicians to recommend calcium supplements to meet the needs of both mother and child. The old expression "a tooth for each child" may indeed be accurate. In fact, the loosening of the alveolar bone, which supports the teeth, may be one of the first signs of bone loss. Another cause of calcium loss is excess phosphorus in the diet, which causes calcium to be drawn out of the bones. The strength of one's bones depends largely on an equal or better ratio of calcium to phosphorus in the diet. Yet the average woman's diet contains at least three times more phosphorus than calcium. A lack of magnesium also causes calcium to be secreted from the bone.

Forced inactivity may contribute to osteoporosis. This was discovered on an eighty-four-day space mission by astronauts, who had almost no physical activity. Long periods of time in bed constitute typical inactivity for older women. Diet is thought to be implicated. Women of all ages are more likely than men to go on diets. When weight is lost, bone is also lost. Exercising will reduce this loss. High intakes of protein may also be a cause of bone loss. Interestingly enough, obese women are less susceptible to osteoporosis.

Bone loss occurs rapidly following menopause. In fact, a bone loss of 30 to 35 percent occurs in all women between the ages of 40 and 80. This loss may be related to a diminished estrogen level. Osteoporosis also occurs much more rapidly after a "complete" hysterectomy in which the ovaries have been removed. The ultraviolet light from the sun converts a form of cholesterol in the body, which is essential for absorbing calcium, to vitamin D. Postmenopausal women with osteoporosis have 30 percent less vitamin D than normal. Diabetics seem to have greater than normal bone loss. Recent evidence shows that alcoholic women have a greater tendency to develop osteoporosis.

Diagnosis

Osteoporosis is difficult to diagnose. Conventional X-rays will not pick up decreasing bone density until a significant amount (30 to 40 percent of the bone mass) has disappeared. Many women have no symptoms. The disease is present in our bodies for a considerable length of time before it manifests itself, and often it is not discovered until the painful fracture of brittle bones occurs.

> *I was standing at the curb waiting for my husband to pick me up. For no explainable reason, I fell and found myself in the hospital with a broken hip. My doctor said I had severe osteoporosis. The bone was so fragile that it broke inside me, as I stood, causing my fall.*
>
> Nina, age 60

Some of the early signs of osteoporosis are the following:

- *Periodontal disease.* This disease, accompanied by gum inflammation and loosening of teeth, is often a forerunner of osteoporosis. It is indicated by dental X-rays.

- *Backaches.* Acute pain in the lower back is often associated with osteoporosis. The pain can also be caused by a trivial incident (turning over in bed), from lifting heavy objects, or from too much physical exertion. It is important to find out whether low back pain is due to lack of activity, muscle strain, or osteoporosis.

- *Gradual loss of height.* Dowager's or widow's hump (rounded shoulders) was quite common in older women in earlier eras. It is rarely seen today, perhaps because women exercise more and have better diets. One simple way to assess any possible loss of height is to measure the length of your two outstretched arms (from fingertip to fingertip). This should equal your height.

Treatment

Physicians disagree about how to treat osteoporosis. Although no single treatment has been proved totally effective, most researchers feel that no therapy is effective once the disease makes itself known, and that early preventive measures are essential. The following are some suggested treatments:

- *Exercise.* Women who have been diagnosed osteoporotic should seek professional rehabilitative therapy. Physical exercise is known to slow the rate of bone loss and even to build new bone tissue. Exercises to strengthen the spinal and abdominal muscles are essential for women over 40—indeed, for all women. Brisk walking for a half-hour to an hour each day, cycling, and swimming are recommended. Swimming is the preferred exercise since it uses all your back muscles, and women of any age can learn to swim. Calisthenics, according to one's physical condition, are helpful.

◆ *Increasing calcium intake.* Robert Lindsay, M.D., Director of the Regional Bone Center, West Havestraw, N.Y., is doing a longitudinal study of osteoporotic women, now in its tenth year. He estimates that the daily average calcium intake of premenopausal women is 600 to 800 mg, which maintains the calcium balance and prevents bone loss. He recommends 1,500 mg daily for postmenopausal women. He believes increased calcium intake is as effective as taking estrogen to slow bone loss. The facing table lists the important natural sources of calcium. It is difficult to obtain the required amount of calcium in diet alone. Therefore, supplemental tablets combining calcium and vitamin D are advised. Those who are worried about the risks of taking too much calcium may be reassured to know that the body seems to adapt by absorbing less calcium from your diet if necessary.

◆ *Drinking plenty of water.* Six to eight 12-ounce glasses a day is a proper amount of water intake. Since bones contain 50 percent water, 20 percent calcium, 10 percent phosphorus, and 20 percent other elements, it is important to take in a generous amount of water every day.

◆ *Vitamin D.* Researchers at Brookhaven National Laboratory and Nassau Hospital on Long Island (along with the University of Washington in Seattle and Creighton University in Omaha) are treating postmenopausal osteoporosis with a new derivative of vitamin D, rocaltrol. They feel this drug will be helpful for two reasons: First, the injuries associated with osteoporosis all seem to be related to decreased levels of calcium absorption; second, vitamin D is known to be important in the absorption of calcium from the diet and in the mineralization of the bone. This treatment is not expected to initiate a reversal of osteoporosis, but it may cause the bones to take up more calcium and get stronger so that patients will sustain fewer fractures. Vitamin D is recommended for persons past middle age who have little exposure to the sun. In the winter, women living in northern areas might drink a quart of milk enriched with vitamin D daily. Again, vitamin supplements are recommended. Products such as Os-Cal combine both calcium and vitamin D. Foods containing vitamin D include: fish-liver oil, egg yolk, liver and other organ meats, salmon, sardines, herring, bone meal, and vitamin D-fortified milk and milk products.

◆ *Reducing animal protein in the diet.* It is suspected that a diet high in animal protein draws calcium from the bones that is excreted in the urine. This leaves a negative calcium balance.

◆ *Balancing the intake of calcium and phosphorus.* Early studies have indicated that the calcium/phosphorus ratio is implicated in osteoporosis. (See the accompanying table.) However, more research and data are needed for conclusive evidence of a relationship between this ratio and osteoporosis, but it is probably wise to make sure your calcium intake equals your phosphorus intake. Foods containing phosphorus include:

Foods Containing Calcium and Phosphorus

	Amount	Amount of calcium (mg)	Amount of phosphorus (mg)
Milk: Skim	1 cup	296	233
Whole	1 cup	288	227
Yogurt (skim-milk)	1 cup	294	230
Cheeses: Parmesan	1 oz.	323	221
Swiss	1 oz.	226	160
Processed American	1 oz.	198	219
Green vegetables (steamed)			
Collard greens	1 cup	357	99
Broccoli	1 cup	136	96
Swiss chard	1 cup	100	35

Also high in calcium are molasses, shellfish, sardines, canned salmon (with the bones), bone meal, sesame seeds, and seaweed.

meat, fish, poultry, eggs, nuts, legumes, bread and whole grain cereals, bone meal, and snack foods such as crackers and chips. Food excessively high in phosphorus include processed foods and cola drinks. Many processed foods have phosphorus-containing food additives. For example, processed cheese contains more phosphorus than calcium. Natural cheese and milk contain almost as much phosphorus as calcium. There is little incidence of osteoporosis in vegetarian societies as compared with meat-eating cultures like our own, for instance. Protein foods such as meat, are high in phosphorus. Eating more fruits and vegetables helps neutralize the effects of excess phosphorus.

- *Increasing magnesium intake.* Make sure that your diet includes at least half as much magnesium (400 to 600 mg) as calcium. (Dolomite supplements contain both.)

- *Increasing vitamin K.* Vitamin K, long known for its role in blood coagulation, is now believed to be vital to calcium "turnover" in bone, so that a deficiency of vitamin K could be a cause of osteoporosis. Mineral oil laxatives seriously interfere with absorption of vitamin K. Foods containing vitamin K are green vegetables, cauliflower, potatoes, and liver.

- *Total hip replacement.* This procedure has been successful for women immobilized by a fractured hip caused by osteoporosis.

- *Experimental treatments.* Several therapies for osteoporosis are still in the experimental stage. They include using parathyroid hormone (vitamin

D) for short periods of time followed by the injection of the hormone calcitonin; using phosphates to activate cells, followed by calcitonin therapy; using a low dose of synthetic parathyroid hormone fragments; and treatment with a combination of estrogen, calcium, and fluoride.

Treatments Not Recommended

There are two treatments currently in use for osteoporosis that involve serious risks. The first is estrogen therapy. Studies show that small doses of estrogen prevent bone loss in postmenopausal women, but as soon as the estrogen is stopped the rate of bone loss increases beyond normal loss for women who never took estrogen. In addition, some studies have shown that estrogen leaves us at high risk of endometrial and other cancers (see Chapter 8).

The second nonrecommended treatment is the use of sodium fluoride to stimulate bone growth. Fluoride is one of the few substances known to increase bone mineral content. Less osteoporosis is found in geographic areas with high fluoride content in the water supply. However, to be effective it is required in such large amounts (50 mg daily) that it has many dangerous side effects, including gastrointestinal bleeding and arthritis.

Since osteoporosis affects one-fourth of all white women over 50, it is shocking that there is so little known about prevention, cause, and treatment. Adequate public education is essential. Women and their physicians have a right to all the information currently available so that they can take the proper steps to prevent this disease. More research is also essential so physicians know how to diagnose bone loss before it becomes traumatic and to treat it when it appears. Since proper diet and daily vigorous exercise seem to be the most effective therapy, osteoporosis is a disease we *can* prevent. We all want to assure strong bones and a healthy body throughout our lives, and we have it within our power to do so.

Resources: Osteoporosis

Lindsay, Robert. "Osteoporosis." In *Health Issues of Older Women: A Projection to the Year 2000*, ed. Jane Porcino, Elaine Friedman, and Margaret Bruhn. Stony Brook, NY: Health Sciences Center, SUNY, 1981.

Dr. Stanton Cohn
Brookhaven National Laboratory
35 Brookhaven Ave.
Upton, NY 11973
For information on osteoporosis research.

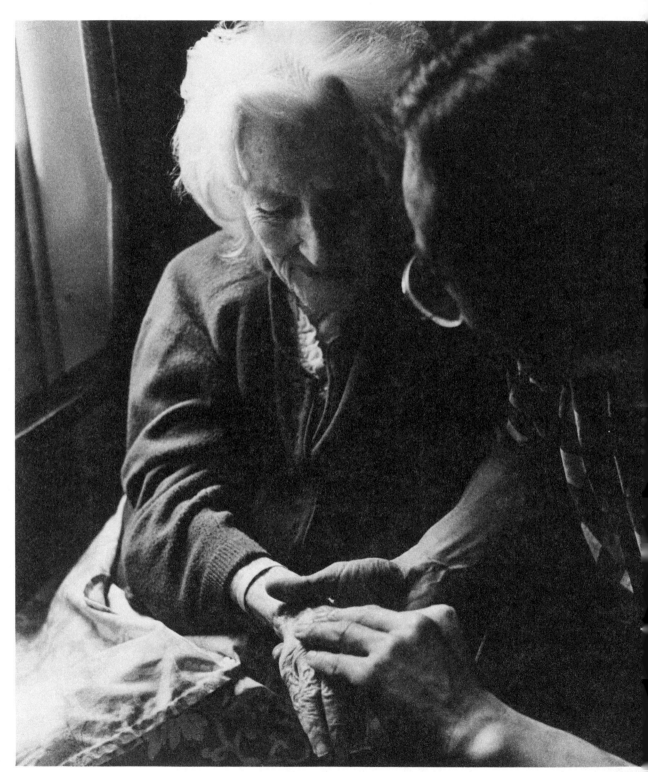

Chapter Twelve

Common Afflictions of Older Women

If this many people were coming down with typhoid, we'd be horrified. But heart disease is not contagious. It is a socially acceptable disease. And so we take a ho-hum attitude about it, instead of waking up to the fact that the disease is destroying millions of lives.

William Castelli, M.D., Director of the Framingham Heart Study, Framingham, Mass.

Cardiovascular Disease

Each day more than 4,000 Americans suffer heart attacks. It is estimated that 40 million (one-sixth of the population) have some major form of cardiovascular disease. Years ago, women rarely had heart disease; now nearly one out of every four women does. Cardiovascular diseases—diseases of the heart and blood vessels including coronary heart disease, hypertension, and stroke—are the leading cause of death today among older women. The ratio of male to female heart victims is narrowing. Women account for one-third of all deaths from heart disease (250,000 women in 1981), more than the number of women who died from cancer or accidents.

Coronary Heart Disease

Twice as many men as women aged 45 to 60 suffer coronary heart disease leading to heart attacks. After age 60, however, the incidence is the same. Coronary heart disease is more prevalent among white people than blacks. Scientists do not know why. Coronary heart disorder is caused by atherosclerosis (hardening of the arteries). Atherosclerosis, leading to a stoppage of the flow of blood, is a progressive disease that is thought to begin in childhood. Cholesterol deposits accumulate on the walls of the arteries and narrow the passage of blood needed for the heart. When the arteries are clogged, the blood supply to the heart is shut off and oxygen to the heart is diminished.

Angina, which sometimes precedes a heart attack, is usually an exercise-induced chest pain resulting from an inadequate supply of oxygen to the heart. Coronary thrombosis is clotting in a coronary artery. It is the leading cause of male death in ages 40 to 60 and in women after age 60. Dr. William Castelli, director of the thirty-year Framingham, Mass., Heart Study, says, "Every fifth man and every seventeenth woman develop some form of coronary heart disease *before* they are 60."

Most researchers feel that women are more vulnerable to heart attacks after menopause because of a loss of protection from the hormone estrogen. Dr. Estelle Ramey of Georgetown University in Washington, D.C., believes estrogen is not necessarily protective. She feels that the male hormone testosterone causes more rapid aging, leading to earlier incidences of heart disease among men. There is no evidence that estrogen therapy as a treatment protects postmenopausal women from increased heart attack. What we do know is that estrogen therapy increases the risk of cervical, uterine, and possibly breast cancer. Even a group of midlife men who were given estrogen had more heart attacks than the control group.

The consequences of a heart attack may be worse for women:

Plaque Formation in Atherosclerosis

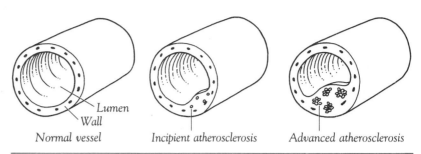

Normal vessel — Lumen / Wall   Incipient atherosclerosis   Advanced atherosclerosis

- Women's chances of a second heart attack over a five-year period is two to three times greater than for men.

- More women suffer from angina (chest pains).

- Women undergoing bypass surgery are at greater risk than men. Bypass surgery is not as successful for women because they have smaller blood vessels than men.

Risk Factors

Women and men share many of the known risk factors for coronary heart disease: cigarette smoking, elevated cholesterol and blood pressure levels, diabetes, obesity, family history, sedentary living, stress, and the effects of aging on the cardiovascular system. Cigarette smoking seems to be the most serious hazard that we can personally control.

One additional risk factor for women is the use of oral contraceptives, especially after age 35. The risk of death from heart attack seems to be more than four times greater among women who use birth-control pills containing estrogen. A British study reported that women over 35 who used the pill and smoke had a 1 in 1,000 chance of heart attack (compared with a 1 in 5,000 chance for nonusers). On the basis of those studies, in the late sixties the U.S. Food and Drug Administration warned physicians to stop prescribing oral contraceptives to women over 40. Not until 1976, however, were orders issued that all oral contraceptives be accompanied by a written warning to women of the increased risk of heart attack. Most critical is the combination of being over 40, smoking, and using oral contraceptives. Birth-control pill users of all ages who have high blood pressure or diabetes, have a strong family history of cardiac disease, or are overweight are at a special risk of heart attack.

A certain type of personality and a certain type of stress are likely to bring on a heart attack. The most vulnerable people are the following types:

- People with drive, ambition, a sense of urgency, and involvement in deadlines.
- People who change jobs a lot, live in cities, or are recently bereaved.

One study of 133 white, middle-aged women who had been hospitalized with their first heart attack revealed that many of them also suffered from hypertension, angina, and diabetes. Many were living in stressful, crowded conditions. Blue-collar workers (women and men) are at special risk, perhaps because many of them work at sedentary jobs.

Prevention

- Don't smoke.
- Have your blood pressure checked regularly.
- Avoid a rich, fatty diet.
- Learn to handle your reaction to stress; learn to slow down and take it easy.
- Watch your weight.
- Exercise regularly.

Symptoms: How to Know If You're Having a Heart Attack

The chest pain (often confused with indigestion or heartburn) is a heavy, uncomfortable pressure nearly always centered under the breastbone. Its intensity varies from oppressive pain to a feeling of fullness or squeezing. (Sharp, stabbing twinges are not usually the signs of a heart attack.) The pain may radiate to your arms, shoulders, neck, jaw, or stomach. Dizziness, fainting, sweating, nausea, or shortness of breath may occur. Sometimes these feelings go away and then recur.

What to Do

- Don't delay. If symptoms last more than two minutes, get help immediately. Go to a hospital emergency room right away (even before calling your physician). Call a local ambulance service (in most areas, just dial 911) if you have no driver immediately available.
- Loosen any restrictive clothing (open shirt, belt, etc.).

- Sit with your head lowered (sitting is the most effective position for the heart).
- Try to breathe regularly.

Treatment

- *High technology.* Coronary heart units of hospitals have succeeded in cutting hospital heart deaths from 30 to 15 percent.
- *Regular exercise.* Exercise has a host of benefits. Aerobic exercises (calisthenics, exercise bikes, cycling, swimming, walking, jogging) increase cardiovascular strength. Although the evidence is not conclusive, it is believed that jogging promotes the growth of new auxiliary channels between coronary arteries, which help nourish the heart. This enables a person to tolerate fatigue better. Sex is good exercise for the heart, under proper conditions.
- *Diet.* Small amounts of saturated fat and refined carbohydrates and large amounts of vegetables, grains, and fruits are essential.
- *Surgery.* Surgery can be used to insert a cardiac pacemaker to regulate irregular heartbeats (arrhythmias) that occur after a heart attack. Open-heart surgery is also often performed to head off a heart attack in patients with dangerously irregular heartbeats.
- *Drugs.* The use of sulfinpyrazone, a drug with anticlotting effects, has caused a dramatic 74 percent reduction of the death rate after heart attacks (*New England Journal of Medicine*, 31 January 1980). Calcium blockers are used to prevent "coronary spasms" and to enlarge coronary arteries. Until recently, physicians have been able only to observe a heart attack once it has occurred and to treat the complications. A new drug has been approved by the Food and Drug Administration for use in treating victims early in the course of a heart attack (three to six hours after onset). The drug is a clot-dissolving enzyme called streptokinase, which appears to stop heart attacks while they are under way. This is the first treatment that can salvage the heart muscles, which usually die in a heart attack. (Whether a heart attack victim lives or dies depends on how much heart muscle is destroyed.) The treatment is called reperfusion therapy, and it combines an angiogram (a procedure in which a flexible tube is injected into a leg or arm and fed all the way to the heart, injecting a radio-opaque substance into the coronary arteries so they can be seen on X-rays) and the drug steptokinase. Because the success of this treatment depends on its administration very early in the course of a heart attack, it is imperative for people to recognize the symptoms of a heart attack and to call for help immediately. Nitroglycerin is the drug usually used to treat angina.
- *Heart transplant.* At Stanford University Medical Center in California, 50 percent of the transplant patients survive five years after surgery. After that period most transplant patients are free of serious complica-

tions. In the future, surgeons will be able to implant a permanent artificial heart in humans.

The death rate from heart disease has been reduced 25 percent in the last decade. Preventive measures that people themselves have taken have helped turn the table on cardiovascular disease. Dr. Henry Blackburn of the University of Minnesota said in a *New York Times* article on heart disease (1 March 1981), "If you don't have a high fat diet—one that gets more than 10 to 15 percent of calories from saturated fat—heart disease is extremely rare in your culture, no matter how much smoking and high blood pressure there is."

Hypertension

Hypertension, or high blood pressure, is commonly called the silent killer because it has few recognizable symptoms. A person is unaware of her condition unless it is discovered by a blood pressure test. Hypertension affects one out of every four Americans, an estimated 60 million. The incidence of hypertension rises steadily with age. It is twice as high for blacks as for whites at all ages up to 80. High blood pressure affects black women between the ages of 34 and 44 with great severity.

As blood flows through the heart and out of the blood vessels, it creates pressure against the blood vessel walls. Your blood pressure reading is a way of measuring this pressure. Hypertension is a major cause of heart attack deaths and stroke. It is also implicated in kidney impairment, renal failure, and serious changes in the retina of the eye (hypertensive retinopathy).

Cause

In at least 90 percent of the cases of all cardiovascular disease, the cause is unknown; heredity, obesity, high salt consumption, hardening of the arteries, smoking, and stress are suspected contributors. Even calm, relaxed people can have high blood pressure; it is a physical condition, not an emotional one. One theory about why black people have higher rates of hypertension is that earlier generations of blacks in America had a diet heavy in salt, i.e., ham, bacon, and salt pork. Five to 10 percent of hypertension is caused by other illnesses. This is called "secondary hypertension."

Symptoms

You can look and feel great and still have high blood pressure. Dizziness, pounding headaches in the back of the head (often worse in the morning and relieved by vomiting), facial flushes, fatigue, shortness of breath, or vague feelings of tension and anxiety may be symptoms.

Preventive Measures

A yearly blood pressure test will catch any early signs of hypertension. Other preventive measures are dietary: decreasing or limiting cholesterol and eliminating salt. Salt absorbs water. The more salt you consume, the more excess liquid is maintained in your body, and this raises your blood pressure.

Measuring Blood Pressure

The blood pressure test is painless. Blood pressure is measured with an inflatable cuff wrapped around the upper arm and pumped up with air. This simple procedure can be performed by a nurse, physician, or other health professional, as well as by any individual. New coin-operated electronic blood pressure machines are available in drugstores and other public places. Measuring instruments that are easy to use can also be purchased at any drugstore.

There are two pressure levels taken in a blood pressure measurement. *Systolic* pressure is the pressure in the arteries when the heart is contracting and pumping blood into them. *Diastolic* pressure (which is lower than systolic pressure) is the pressure in the arteries between heartbeats, when the heart is relaxing. Blood pressure is read as systolic over diastolic pressure. A reading of 120/80 is considered average for adults. Many experts feel that readings as high as 140/90 are acceptable for older people. Anything over this level requires some form of treatment. Your doctor should take several readings on different days before deciding that your blood pressure is too high, because it can be affected by many factors.

Treatment

High blood pressure can be controlled but usually not cured. Once you have hypertension you have to continue treatment even if you feel great; misconceptions about this by doctors and patients have been major obstacles to blood pressure control. Twenty-five million Americans have borderline high blood pressure (between 140/90 and 160/95) that is often left untreated. The latest studies, however, show that this group can cut their risk of death by 20 percent if they undergo vigorous treatment.

Persons with hypertension who are trained in blood pressure biofeedback have learned to decrease their blood pressure. Biofeedback is a technique involving the use of an instrument that picks up information about the physiology of the body. Relaxation techniques have proved equally effective in treating hypertension.

Medication. High blood pressure can be medically controlled with drugs, including antihypertensive agents and diuretics. These are not without risk, however. Antihypertensive drugs may cause fatigue, depression, visual impairment, and repressed sexual drive. At least one of these drugs, reserpine, is known to increase a woman's risk of contracting breast cancer. Diuretics may cause heart-rhythm abnormalities and possibly diabetes. If these side effects are present, ask your physician to review your medication. Hypertensives must stay on antihypertension medication for life, although some people incorrectly believe that once blood pressure is brought to normal levels the medicine is no longer needed. Diet is sometimes enough. After medication is started, you should see your physician in about a month for a blood pressure level test.

Diet. High blood pressure is controllable by lowering weight, eliminating salt, increasing potassium (see Chapter 10), and eliminating caffeine. Increased intake of garlic has been found useful.

Exercise. Aerobic exercise such as swimming, cycling, and jogging is recommended.

Relaxation technique. Emotional stress raises blood pressure, so relaxation techniques can be beneficial (see Chapter 7).

Stroke

Every year nearly 400,000 people in the United States suffer a cerebral vascular accident, commonly called CVA or a stroke. Approximately 40 percent die within a month and at least two-thirds of those who survive have some degree of permanent disability.

A stroke is a sudden disruption of the blood supply to a part of the brain, which in turn disrupts the body function controlled by that brain area. Its onset is sudden or rapid and the stroke persists for more than twenty-four hours. Without a source of fresh blood, the cells are deprived of oxygen, and that can temporarily disable or kill them.

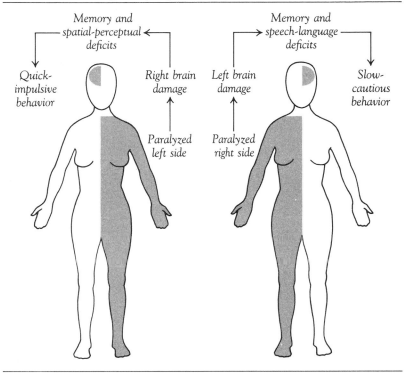

Effects of Right- and Left-Sided Stroke

The most common type of stroke is thrombotic (called ischemic), which results from clogged arteries (closed by the fatty deposits of atherosclerosis). The blood supply to the brain literally stops, causing parts of the brain to die of starvation. Although the stroke itself occurs suddenly, it is usually the result of a gradual buildup of fats in the arteries. In hemorrhagic stroke, a more serious type, blood leaks into the brain tissue.

There are often warnings that can alert a victim and her physician to the need for treatment. As the lining of the arteries begins to thicken, small warning strokes may occur. The person may awaken paralyzed and have slight difficulty speaking, walking, writing, or recalling recent events. She may experience numbness or paralysis on one side of her body or be temporarily blind. These transient strokes last anywhere from minutes to hours, and the symptoms clear up completely. These are warnings, and preventive measures should be taken to avoid a full-scale stroke.

A major stroke becomes progressively worse over a twenty-four-hour period. Loss of consciousness, rapid pulse, labored breathing, elevated blood pressure, and/or vomiting may occur. One side of the body may appear limp. If a person survives the first few days, she may begin to regain consciousness, and some of the paralysis may disappear. If partial speech is present at the time of return to consciousness, speech is likely to improve.

Stroke-related depression is a common occurrence between six months and two years after a stroke and lasts eight to nine months. This causes substantial suffering to the individual patient and her family and often limits the patient's return to normal activity. A recent study at Johns Hopkins School of Medicine indicates that this depression is more severe with left-sided stroke victims. It is caused by biochemical changes and is not only a psychological reaction, which was previously believed. The Johns Hopkins research team found that following a stroke, neurotransmitters (which carry messages to the brain) turn their attention to healing the injured area, a change that can alter mood and behavior.

Risk Factors

- A history of previous strokes
- Diabetes
- Hypertension
- Certain forms of heart disease
- A history of small strokes (transient ischemic attacks)
- Smoking

Preventive Measures

Women with hypertension are two to four times more apt to have a stroke as other women. The most important preventive measure is the identification and successful treatment of persons with hypertension. Treatment should include a low-sodium diet, weight control, and medications. Despite the controversy about cholesterol, women at high risk for stroke would be wise to eat less fat and less cholesterol-rich animal food.

A stroke is often caused by hypertension, which may be caused by sudden or prolonged stress. We can prevent some strokes by learning to handle high-stress situations with various relaxation techniques (see Chapter 7).

My 83-year-old mother suffered a thrombotic stroke less than twenty-four hours after her best friend was rushed to the hospital with a heart attack. The friend recovered; my mother did not.

Lena, age 59

Treatment

A CAT scan (computerized axial tomography, a 360-degree X-ray image) should be done, if possible, in the first hours following a progressive stroke. This test is capable of distinguishing between an ischemic and hemorrhagic stroke; it can determine the extent of permanent tissue damage.

Anticoagulant therapy (small daily doses of aspirin) is a common treatment. This therapy is more effective for men than for women. A Canadian study showed that men who had experienced minor strokes were helped by taking plain aspirin four times a day. In fact, this simple treatment seemed to cut in half their risk of a second fatal or crippling stroke. Aspirin did not help the women in that same study. The researchers discovered that even in rabbits, aspirin helped clear clogged arteries in the male but not the female animal. It is theorized that the reason for this variance is hormonal differences between women and men.

Surgery. Cerebral artery bypass surgery is being performed on selected groups of patients. If the artery obstruction (which cuts off the supply of blood) is in the brain, a hole the size of a silver dollar is drilled, and one nearby artery is hooked to another, bypassing the obstruction. This operation has proven very effective in preventing a crippling stroke and should reduce the terrible affliction of a major stroke.

Rehabilitative Treatment. Much can be done to treat stroke-induced disabilities. Rehabilitation centers for stroke patients are showing remarkable results. An article in *Stroke* (May–June 1981) described a study in which 248 patients with severe stroke deficits (average age 67) were admitted to a rehabilitation center in White Plains, N.Y. (instead of the usual admission to a nursing home). Eighty percent were able to return home after an average stay of only forty-three days (85 percent ambulatory, fifty-six people able to care for themselves without assistance). Unfortunately, older persons are rarely considered good candidates for rehabilitation, and thus Medicare will not cover even short-duration physical therapy.

Stroke clubs for families of stroke victims are becoming common. Families attend meetings to learn practical information, to share experiences, and to support each other in their difficult and often isolating task of caring for a stroke victim. The after-effects of stroke can virtually destroy the lifestyle of a family, with a spouse often becoming progressively debilitated by the patient's behavior and the additional responsibilities it creates. Clemmie Barry, the wife of a stroke victim, formed the first support group for other such wives as well as a day-care respite program for stroke victims. This idea has successfully spread to many parts of the country.

Rheumatic Disease

Many of us associate arthritis with long-term pain, encroaching old age or hopelessness. . . . However, both arthritis and deformity can be prevented by use of present medicine and surgery, together with hard work.

James F. Fries, M.D.

By age 65 to 70 about 80 percent of all women have some rheumatic complaint. The most common of these are osteoarthritis, rheumatoid arthritis, and lupus.

Arthritis

Arthritis literally means inflammation of a joint involving swelling, warmth, and redness. It is one of the oldest known diseases. It is so common in older people, and its symptoms are so closely identified with the normal process of aging, that it is often accepted as an inevitable accompaniment of a long life. Yet it need not be.

Osteoarthritis
The most common type of arthritis is osteoarthritis, which has been called the "wear-and-tear arthritis" or "degenerative joint disease." It is a gradual wearing away of the joint cartilage. Osteoarthritis occurs in 40 million persons, most frequently between the ages of 55 and 64. The incidence is highest among women over 55 (and men under 65). It affects one-third of the older

population. Obesity, poor posture, and occupational stress of the joints are possible contributing factors.

Many women have no symptoms of osteoarthritis, although 25 percent show nodes (lumps under the skin) in the major weight-bearing joints of the knees, hips, and back. Nodes in the finger joints may be the first sign of osteoarthritis. Pain is the major symptom, not impairment of motion or joint damage. Early-morning stiffness is usually relieved by activity but recurs during periods of rest.

Rheumatoid Arthritis

Rheumatoid arthritis is inflammation in the membranes that form the lining of the joints and tendons. It is the most severe of the arthritic diseases, crippling 25 percent of those women affected. It attacks mainly the joints but can also affect the lungs, skin, blood vessels, muscles, spleen, heart, and even the eyes. Rheumatoid arthritis is two to three times more common in women than in men. At least half of the three and a half million Americans who have the disease are over 50. The cause is unknown, although a virus or a change in the body's immune system seems to be involved. It is a chronic disease that has no cure. If it is not diagnosed and treated early, joints eventually will become immobilized.

Rheumatoid arthritis begins with general fatigue (commonly caused by anemia, which is almost always found with this type of arthritis), soreness, and stiffness of the joints upon awakening (persisting for an hour or more); weight loss; hot, red, and swollen joints; and occasionally a low-grade fever. Pain often occurs first in the non-weight-bearing joints (such as the wrists and fingers) and may move around the joints in a migratory fashion. Women with preexisting arthritis should not take oral contraceptives. If women already taking oral contraceptives experience swollen and painful joints, they should discontinue using them. Estrogen replacement therapy may be harmful as well.

Lupus Erythematous

Although lupus in its two forms, systemic (involving the whole body) and discoid (skin involvement only), afflicts mainly women between the ages of 20 and 40 (1 in 500), many older women also suffer from its effects. Lupus derives its name from the Latin word for wolf (*lupus*) because the butterfly-shaped rash that crosses the bridge of the nose and the cheeks of a few patients resembles the bite of a wolf. Some 50,000 new cases are diagnosed each year, and an estimated million Americans are afflicted. Lupus is a chronic disorder of the immune system in which damage is done to the connective tissues of the cells; a woman in effect becomes allergic to her own cells. The beginnings of lupus often seem like a flu bug that hangs on for a long time, with fever and arthritic-like pains.

Systemic Lupus Erythematous (commonly called S.L.E.) is difficult to diagnose because no two people have exactly the same symptoms. It also mimics many other serious diseases, such as gastrointestinal conditions, cardiac disorders, arthritis, and pneumonia. It appears to be genetically transmitted, but it is not a contagious disease. The American Rheumatism Association has listed several criteria for diagnosis, among them facial reddening (the butterfly rash) and loss of hair—both characteristic of the discoid type—as well as sores in the vagina or mouth, sensitivity to sunlight, arthritis with severe deformity, lack of energy, appetite and weight loss, and change of color in the fingers and toes when they are exposed to cold (Raynaud's Disease).

My diagnosis of lupus was made when I was 21 years old. Since that time, I've been married to a wonderful man. Through sheer determination, faith and hope, I had three marvelous children who have brought much joy, pain, and growth to my life. With the same determination and family cooperation, I returned to college. My goals since diagnosis have always been short-term: to live my life as fully as possible, day by day. That's not always easy to do, but my illness has taught me what my life is all about. It is to live and love as deeply as possible; to understand and accept myself and others; and to put clearly into perspective what is important in my life. Living with lupus has taught me how to live, and especially how to love. I thank God for the time He has given me.

Marissa, age 42

Lupus can cause inflammation of the membranes around the heart, lungs, or abdomen. It may attack the nerves, the gastrointestinal tract, or the kidneys. It is no longer a rare disease, nor is the incidence of fatality as frequent as scientists once suspected.

Although there is no known cure for lupus, rheumatologists know how to disagnose it earlier than ever before and how to detect early flare-ups before damage is done to the connective tissues. The disease can be contained and inflammation reduced with the use of drugs such as aspirin, anti-inflammatory drugs, and immune suppressants; however, women should be aware of the potential side effects of such medications.

Many cases of lupus are mild, with infrequent or no flare-ups after the first attack. Women can continue to lead normal lives as long as they get at least eight hours of sleep a night (a daily nap is recommended) and avoid overwork, unnecessary emotional stress, and infections. Protection from the sunlight with clothing and sunscreens is important.

Associated with rheumatoid arthritis and lupus is a condition women commonly encounter, a dryness of the eyes and mouth causing sore eyes and difficulty in chewing and swallowing food (Sjogren's Syndrome). This is not curable but it is treatable by using a type of eyedrops that replace tears and by drinking a lot of water.

Treatments for Arthritis

Self-management groups. One very successful treatment method for arthritis seems to be self-help mutual aid groups. The Stanford University Arthritis Center in Palo Alto, Calif., studied one hundred arthritis self-management groups and found that the participants knew more about their problem, required less medical care, and experienced less pain than other arthritics. People experimented with various exercises, relaxation techniques, and nutritional therapies and then chose the ones that best suited their needs. Arthritis cannot be cured, but by changing their lifestyles many women can successfully adapt to it.

Exercise is the most important therapy and should be done regularly, seven days a week if possible. It should be supervised by a knowledgeable physician or physical therapist. If a joint is not used, it loses its function. Each joint affected with arthritis should be moved daily by stretching (just past the point of pain), using isometric or strengthening exercises (which move the joint against some resistance), and endurance exercises such as swimming, walking, or cycling (which keep the heart in good condition). It's a good idea to extend and flex the joints before getting out of bed in the morning. If a joint is red and hot, limited movement is recommended. Cut back on your exercise regime if your pain persists for more than two hours.

Relaxation techniques. The pain and stress of arthritis is often relieved by daily relaxation exercises such as breathing exercises, yoga, meditation, and transcendental meditation. It's a good idea to keep a daily "stress diary" to record when your joints hurt and which method relieves the stress for you.

Nutritional therapy. Good nutrition will help keep our bones, joints, and muscles healthy, but no scientific evidence has been found to support any particular dietary regime as a cure-all for arthritis. Certain foods seem to precipitate joint pain, and these should be eliminated. *The Arthritic's Cookbook* recommends eliminating alcohol, sugar, chocolate, beef, pork, and milk (see Resources section at the end of the chapter). Fresh fruits and vegetables should be added to the diet. Other studies show that many people with arthritis have low levels of vitamin C in their blood. It may be helpful to add vitamin C or other vitamins to the diet.

My diagnosis was severe rheumatism of the spine which caused me pain and debilitation. My physician offered the usual drugs such as aspirin for relief. I read an article about vitamin E helping arthritic patients. I began a regime of 800 units of vitamin E daily and found immediate relief. The intense pain and daily exhaustion is much reduced. I stopped taking the vitamins for periods of time, as an experiment, and again experienced the acute symptoms. I hope this information can be of some help to others.

Lotye, age 53

Alfalfa tea or alfalfa sprouts relieves some arthritics. Others find that eliminating additives and preservatives from their diet is helpful. It is very important to maintain a lean body weight. Arthritis is less troublesome when people lose weight, which decreases the stress on joints. A diet low in calories and fats can help reduce weight.

Medications. Aspirin is the single most valuable drug in alleviating the painful inflammation of arthritis, when used correctly. Aspirin's activity is based on a chemical from willow bark and other plants, which have been used to relieve rheumatic pain for thousands of years. Today's aspirin is derived from coal tar and petroleum products, not plants. It inhibits a hormonelike substance produced by the cells and found in inflamed red tissues. The main drawback of aspirin use is its tendency to irritate the lining of the stomach and to cause the loss of small amounts of blood. Other drugs, including aspirin-related drugs and gold salts, seem to work, although no one knows quite why.

Surgery has been successfully used to replace or repair arthritic joints, principally the hip but also the knee, ankle, and finger joints.

Other techniques. Heat of any sort relieves arthritic pain. An electric heating pad or blanket, a down comforter, a sleeping bag, or even a warm water bed help. Sexual activity may be therapeutic for an arthritic person. It's important to talk with your partner about comfortable sexual positions. The chemical cortisone, a powerful anti-inflammatory substance that relieves certain types of arthritic pain, is released during lovemaking. Massage is usually helpful, and victims should have no fear about rubbing sore joints. Whirlpool baths and physical therapy relieve the pain of many arthritic women. For women whose hands are handicapped with arthritis, some practical aids for daily living are available—implements for pulling zippers, combing hair, turning on the water, holding playing cards, and manipulating keys.

> *If your arthritis is serious, it may represent the greatest challenge of your life. Meeting that challenge may be your greatest satisfaction. You need a bit more will and determination and self-discipline than others. But the future is still yours.*
>
> James F. Fries, M.D., *Arthritis: A Comprehensive Guide*

Cancer

> *Americans have the power to prevent more than one-half of the major cancers by simply altering behavior patterns already under our control.*
>
> American Cancer Society

Cancer (from the Greek word for crab—a cancer grows by sending out invasive roots and thus resembles the sea crab) is the disease everyone fears most. It is the second greatest killer in the United States and yet it is one of the most curable diseases. Our fear of cancer is often so great that we disregard simple and important preventive measures such as monthly self-examination of our breasts and a yearly Pap smear. Such examinations frequently lead to an early diagnosis that allows us time to consider all possible treatment alternatives. Many of the treatments for cancer, if begun early enough, have a high probability of success. Cancer is *not* inevitable with age.

Breast Cancer

Breast cancer is discovered, on average, at age 42, and it is found most frequently between ages 44 and 55. It is linked to family history, obesity, and high-fat diets. It slows down after menopause, although no one knows why. The incidence rises again in women over 70. Cancer is treatable if discovered early, with 65 percent of its victims still alive five years after treatment.

Risk Factors

Different women have different risks for developing breast cancer. Knowing your personal risk factors will help you make informed decisions about preventive measures you can take. Those in the highest risk category for breast cancer are women in the following categories:

- Over age 40 (including women over 70).
- Family history of cancer in females (mother, grandmother, sister, aunt). Recent studies consider the history of the female members of the father's family important as well. A woman's chance of getting breast cancer is four times greater if her mother had it. If a member of her family had cancer in one breast after age 70 she is not at as great a risk as if her mother had cancer in both breasts at an early age.
- Prior history of benign tumors or other cancer.
- Late or no sexual activity.
- History of early menstruation (before age 12) or a later than normal menopause.
- No pregnancies or a first child born after age 35.

254

- Mothers who did not nurse their babies.
- Long-term estrogen users or oral contraceptive users.
- Unusual obesity or height.
- European Jewish ancestry, non-Jews of northern European background, and affluent black women.
- Living in urban industrialized areas of the U.S. Northeast.

Causes

No one knows what causes breast cancer but there are many current theories. Estrogen is suspected to be a major factor in the incidence of breast cancer (see Chapter 8). Many women over 40 have taken large doses of estrogen in the form of birth-control pills. Scientists originally believed that estrogen protected women against cancer, but just the opposite seems to be true. Postmenopausal women with cancer produce twice as much natural estrone (a type of estrogen) as postmenopausal women without cancer. The dangerous practice of continuing to prescribe premarin (a commonly prescribed estrogen drug containing primarily estrone) to women with cancer leaves them with too much estrogen in their body, and too much estrogen seems to encourage the growth of a malignant tumor.

Environment factors such as pollution, toxic industrial products, and radiation may prove to be significant health hazards for American women. In Japan, female victims of the atomic bomb had an increase in breast cancer.

There is new evidence linking the typical American high-fat diet with breast cancer. Americans consume much meat, eggs, and dairy products. Japanese women today, whose diet is low in animal fat and calories, have the lowest incidence of breast cancer in the world. Studies indicate a link between breast cancer and obesity. Weight reduction and reduced fat in the diet may decrease a woman's chances of getting breast cancer as well as improve the chances of cure after mastectomy, should that be necessary. Caffeine and cigarette smoking are associated with fibrocystic disease (diffuse lumpiness of the breast or a solitary breast lump).

It has been discovered that in rats there is a milk factor, the Bittner virus, which is responsible for the inheritance of breast cancer.

Preventive Measures

The risk factors and theories about causes give us important clues about how to prevent breast cancer. There are several preventive measures for which we can be responsible:

- Do a breast self-examination monthly.

- Have an annual checkup, especially if you are at high risk.

- Avoid estrogen therapy, particularly if you have a family history of cancer.

- Lose excess fat in your body.

- Eat less fat (high-fat diets are associated with other cancers as well as with heart disease).

- Do not smoke.

- Reduce the caffeine in your diet. Caffeine is found in coffee, black tea, chocolate, soft drinks, and many drugs. When women with fibrocysts eliminate caffeine, their cysts often disappear.

- Take vitamin E, which seems to help eliminate fibrocysts.

Breast Self-Examination
Since breast cancer is prevalent in women over 40, we should all learn and practice the techniques of monthly self-examination so that we are familiar with our own breasts and if a symptom shows up we'll recognize it. Lumps that prove to be malignant are most commonly found in the upper section of the breast near the arm. An estimated 90 percent of breast lumps are discovered by women themselves or their lovers.

- Stand in front of a mirror, without a bra.

- Raise your arms. If one breast rises higher than the other it is suspect.

- Look for dimpling, nipple deviation, or a change in skin texture.

- Place your hands on your hips and press down to flex your chest muscles to outline your breast structure more clearly.

- Palpate (feel) each breast with the flat part of the fingers of the opposite hand. Press gently against each breast with small circular motions, to feel the inner part of the breast. Start at the breastbone and move to the nipple. Feel the area around the nipple, gently pressing the nipple for any sign of a discharge.

- Lie down with a small pillow under your right shoulder and your right hand behind your head. Palpate your left breast, as above; then reverse the procedure to examine your right breast.

How to Examine Your Breasts

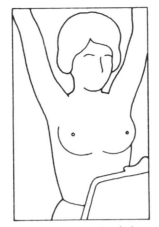

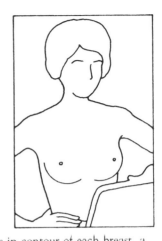

1. **In the shower:** Examine your breasts during bath or shower; hands glide easier over wet skin. Fingers flat, move gently over every part of each breast. Use right hand to examine left breast, left hand for right breast. Check for any lump, hard knot, or thickening.

2. **Before a mirror:** Inspect your breasts with arms at your sides. Next, raise your arms high overhead.

Look for any changes in contour of each breast, a swelling, dimpling of skin, or changes in the nipple. Then, rest palms on hips and press down firmly to flex your chest muscles. Left and right breasts will not exactly match—few women's breasts do. Regular inspection shows what is normal for you and will give you confidence in your examination.

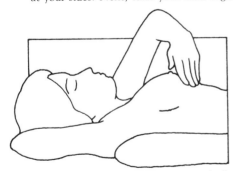

3. **Lying down:** To examine your right breast, put a pillow or folded towel under your right shoulder. Place right hand behind your head—this distributes breast tissue more evenly on the chest. With left hand, fingers flat, press gently in small circular motions around an imaginary clock face. Begin at outermost top of your right breast for 12 o'clock, then move to 1 o'clock, and so on around the circle back to 12. A ridge of firm tissue in the lower curve of each breast is normal. Then move in an inch, toward the nipple, keep circling to examine *every part of your breast*, including nipple. This requires at least three more circles. Now slowly repeat procedure on your left breast with a pillow under your left shoulder and left hand behind head. Notice how your breast structure feels. Finally, squeeze the nipple of each breast gently between thumb and index finger. Any discharge, clear or bloody, should be reported to your doctor immediately.

- Bring your right arm down to your side, and with the left hand feel for any lump under your right armpit. Repeat for the left side.
- Finally, squeeze your nipple gently and look for any sign of discharge or bleeding.

Symptoms of Breast Cancer

- Asymmetry: one breast larger than the other.
- A lump or thickening in the breast; persistent soreness.
- Any change in the skin texture or color of the breast; scaliness (especially around the nipple), redness associated with itching, puckering, or dimpling.
- A discharge from the nipple.
- A lump in the armpit.
- Any "hot spot" in the breast.

These symptoms do not mean you have breast cancer, but they do mean you should have a checkup. A yearly examination by an experienced physician is essential for all women. Women in a high-risk category should be examined more frequently. The lower mortality rate among women who are examined regularly, compared to those who do not see a physician once a year, is impressive.

If You Discover a Lump

Try not to panic; there is only a 15 percent chance of a lump in the breast being malignant. Go directly to an oncologist, a physician with specialized training in the detection and treatment of cancer. There are oncologists in all large cities and in the country's twenty existing cancer centers (see Resource section at the end of this chapter.)

There are several diagnostic procedures that are used to screen women for breast cancer:

Mammography, a breast X-ray, detects tumors too small to feel. Two X-ray pictures are taken of each breast. Since the radiation used in X-ray machines can be a cause of cancer, or could damage the cells of the breast, it is important that you receive a low-dose mammography. You should not receive more than one-quarter rad (the unit used to measure radiation) for each X-ray, or a total of 1 rad for the whole test. Mammography is particularly useful for women with large breasts, where a growth is difficult to find by self-examination. A few years ago there was a massive nationwide drive to add mammography to the routine checkup of all women. Research then showed that this exposed women without cancer unnecessarily to the damaging effects of radiation. The 1980 guidelines of the American Cancer Society suggest that women aged 35 to 40 with no cancer symptoms have just one mammography (to establish a reference point). Women aged 40 to 50 should have a mammography if their mothers or sisters have had breast cancer; after 50, women should have a mammography each year. An annual mammography is particularly important for high-risk postmenopausal women.

Thermography is a diagnostic tool in which infrared scanners pick up breast heat patterns (rapidly growing tumors have a high surface temperature). Although this method is not yet precise, it is recommended for a second or third opinion. Serially taken, thermograms may be a valid approach in identifying women with breast cancer. GST, or graphic stress telethermography, a new form of thermography, uses light probes to examine breast temperature. When this procedure is computerized, it produces the woman's "risk score." If the risk is high, a mammography may be in order.

Ultrasound (still in the experimental stage) projects sound waves into the breasts while they are immersed in water. These sound waves are converted by a computer into a picture of the interior of the breast.

Needle biopsy. Fine-needle biopsy uses a hypodermic needle to remove fluid from a tumor. If upon examination the fluid shows the mass to be a benign cyst, it may be completely drained of fluid, surgically removed, or observed for a period of time. If the fluid contains cancerous cells, the entire tumor will be removed under anesthesia. Wide-needle biopsy (done in a physician's office with anesthesia) is removal of some tissue from a tumor. This is not always successful since it is difficult to find the tumor, and often not enough tissue is withdrawn to make a firm diagnosis. The safety of these methods is now being questioned. More preferable is a *lumpectomy*, the removal of the entire lump for pathological examination. This is one of the most accurate forms of diagnosis.

Diaphragmography uses highly sensitive film that detects protein concentrations in the breast, since cancerous tumors contain more protein than normal breast tissues.

Blood or urine tests. Experiments are under way to use blood or urine tests to increase the chances of early detection of cancer in any part of the body.

When a surgical biopsy (the removal of the whole tumor for examination) is recommended, women are often asked to sign a release form that gives their surgeon legal permission to do a rapid analysis of the tumor while the woman is still anesthetized and to remove her breast immediately if a malignancy is found. This "one-step procedure" is unsound and has been challenged by reputable specialists and women's groups. Most women prefer a two-step procedure in which only the biopsy is performed the first time. Since a quick analysis of tumors has been found inaccurate in many cases, the two-step procedure allows a more thorough and accurate laboratory analysis of the tumor and also allows the woman time to consider which treatment method she prefers. It is important to separate diagnosis from treatment.

I discovered a sizable lump in my breast. My gynecologist sent me to a local surgeon who scheduled a mammography to be followed by surgery. My cousin strongly urged me to get a second opinion with an oncologist who specialized in breast cancer at a major urban cancer center. This physican had a splended reputation as a surgeon, but his manner was authoritarian, abrupt, and abusive. When I told him my father's two sisters had breast cancer, he responded, "How did you happen to be born into such a lousy family?" He said it was too late for a mammogram or other tests and quickly scheduled a biopsy for the following week. I told him I wanted a two-step procedure, but he said he was dead-set against that. I felt devastated and vulnerable but resigned myself to the fact that he was skilled and was affiliated with one of the country's leading cancer centers. I contacted another doctor I'd seen on a TV show about alternative breast cancer treatment, and he gave me a much more thorough and compassionate interview and an extensive examination of my whole body (not only my breasts). He encouraged me to express my fears, my anger (why me?) and my feelings of guilt (I must not have taken good enough care of myself, etc.). I was given a thermogram and later a mammogram, which proved positive. My wish for a two-step procedure was agreed upon. He allayed my worries about time by saying the tumor had been growing for years and that a few days would not make a substantial difference. I am scheduled to enter the hospital after I've spent Easter with my husband and family—but I want other women to know that they can find a physician who is both skilled and compassionate.

Sharon, age 48

Treatment Options

Considerable controversy surrounds breast cancer treatments. The dispute revolves around the advisability of a radical mastectomy, less extensive surgical procedures, or no surgery at all.

- The Halsted radical mastectomy is the surgical removal of the entire breast, the muscle, and the lymph system of the chest wall. Studies show no difference in the rates of survival and cancer recurrence between people who had this radical surgery and those treated more conservatively. This procedure was repudiated in 1979 by the National Institutes of Health.

- Modified radical mastectomy is the removal of the entire breast, leaving the chest muscles in place. This has fewer complications, and leaves the woman a good candidate for breast reconstruction. This procedure is recommended by the National Institutes of Health.

- Lumpectomy is the removal of the tumor only. This is followed by radiation therapy if the malignancy has not invaded the rest of the breast, or chemotherapy if it has. The survival rates with a lumpectomy plus local radiation therapy are as good as those following mastectomy.

Regardless of the type of surgery, every tumor should be tested immediately after its removal to determine its estrogen dependency. The estrogen normally secreted by the body appears to encourage tumor growth. The patient's natural supply of estrogen may be reduced by removal of the ovaries or by use of anti-estrogen drugs. Both methods are often successful in slowing down the progress of the cancer.

In June 1979 the National Cancer Institute at a conference of international experts on breast cancer reached consensus on two important issues about surgical procedures:

1. There should be a time lapse between the biopsy of a suspicious breast lump and any surgical procedure.

2. The Halsted radical mastectomy should not be the treatment of choice; a modified radical mastectomy is preferable.

If you are searching for nonsurgical treatment methods, the following therapies are alternatives:

- *Radiation therapy.* Many women and their doctors are beginning to believe that a microscopically small cancer with no evidence of spread does not require the same extensive surgery as an advanced, very large tumor. They feel that extensive surgery (or any surgery) may not be necessary. The National Cancer Institute is experimenting with a series of radiation treatments for patients with early diagnosis of breast cancer. Researchers at Harvard Medical School report encouraging success using radiation therapy. Their five-year survival rate for stages I and II breast cancer (cancers less than two inches in diameter that have not spread) compare with the survival rate of surgery.

- *Radiation implants.* A treatment in which tiny bits of radium implants are placed around the malignant tumor. After a three-to-five-day period, the implants are removed. The woman returns as an outpatient for a series of radiation treatments. Mutilation of the breast is avoided. Any form of radiation therapy, however, is risky, since we don't yet know the long-term effects of radiation.

- *Chemotherapy.* Chemotherapy is the use of drugs to attack cancer cells. When a breast cancer is being evaluated, a sample is taken of lymph nodes under the arm. If there is any evidence of a tumor in the nodes, chemotherapy is initiated. Women on chemotherapy typically lose their hair, become anemic, and develop intestinal problems.

- *Tanoxifen.* This anti-estrogen drug is becoming the treatment of choice for the very elderly woman who has a solitary hard breast lump. It is taken as a pill, has minimal side effects, and enables most older women to live out their lives without progression of the disease.

- *Holistic cancer treatments.* At holistic health centers, a broad range of traditional and experimental therapies are used such as biofeedback, nutritional therapy, enzyme therapy, psychotherapy, exercise, massage, relaxation, and lots of physical touching.

One such center, the Cancer Counseling and Research Center in Fort Worth, Texas, treats people who have been diagnosed medically incurable. This program has been a model for the whole country and has aided many women to feel a measure of control over their disease.

I am now 45 years old. Six years ago I found a lump in my breast that turned out to be malignant. I had a modified radical mastectomy and radiation treatment. I recovered quickly from surgery and radiation and had to face the issue of living with fear of a recurrence. I had been practicing a form of counseling in which people learn to help each other to free themselves from the effects of past distress experiences through emotional discharge (laughing, crying, shaking). This helped me very much to deal with the anger at what had happened to me. The first two years after a mastectomy are the ones in which most recurrences appear; they were the most difficult for me. After the first two years passed and my good health continued, I started to feel more confident, and in my fourth year I began to feel that the cancer experience was behind me.

During that year I developed a cough that resisted any treatment. X-rays and blood analyses were normal and I was told not to worry. Finally, after a year an X-ray showed liquid in the pleura (a membrane around the lungs), technically known as a "pleural effusion." Liquid was taken from it and it was shown to contain malignant cells. At the same time I found another lump in my remaining breast, which turned out to be malignant also. I found this second lump on my own, when I was already scheduled to have an oophorectomy (removal of the ovaries) for the pleural effusion. Just a few weeks after the oophorectomy I began to notice a change in the sound and frequency of my cough. It looked like the treatment had worked! Next I started reading and learning about nontraditional approaches to cancer treatment. I mobilized all my intellectual and emotional energies to fight the spread of cancer.

My most important decision and a turning point in my recovery was to attend a Simonton workshop led by the Simontons themselves [founders of the Cancer Counseling and Research Center in Fort Worth, Texas] and their staff. This two-and-a-half day workshop was a crucial experience in my developing a new sense of myself in relation to my disease. I started to believe that emotions could play a role in my recovery and that I could step out of a victim role. I became intensely interested in holistic health and started reading and educating myself about mind/body interactions. I adopted a total-person approach to cancer. I had been running for a while; I decided to pay even more attention to physical exercise and slowly trained myself to run three miles at least three times a week. I chose a modified form of the macrobiotic diet and followed it strictly. I started meditating two or three times a day and doing visualization of positive images regarding the outcome of my disease. I started therapy with a woman therapist who had herself been through the Simonton training and had dealt successfully with her own cancer.
I have experienced a shift in the center of power and decision making that extends to all areas of my life. I now consult with the medical profession but see myself as the final source of knowledge. I believe that the views that doctors have about cancer, their own fears, and their sense of frustration play a role in the course of the disease. I believe that as a result of applying an approach that deals with mind, body, and spirit my whole life has been enriched. I know that my emotional well-being is crucial for my health, and I work in therapy to enhance my positive feelings about myself. The experience of living with cancer can be an empowering one. Being confronted with one's mortality is a sobering experience. I have rearranged my priorities and learned to rely more and more on my instincts and my inner resources. I am doing very well, my cough is gone, and so is the liquid in my

pleura. In many ways this has been one of the most intense years of my life and certainly one of the best.

Mary Helen, age 45

None of the currently available treatments for breast cancer is *the* answer. But we do have options, and each individual should be able to chose the option she prefers. If you are not satisfied with a diagnosis or the recommended treatment, seek a second and, if necessary, third opinion. Ask questions and insist on taking part in any decisions concerning your treatments. Remember, it's *your* body and *your* life. Your physician is only your adviser.

We can also be deceived by the "safe-after-five-year" myth. There is always a chance of recurrence, even after five years, but if detected early enough it can be successfully treated. Any woman who has been treated for breast cancer should plan to return to her physician for frequent examinations for the rest of her life. This follow-up is one of the most important steps you can take.

Breast Reconstruction

Most medical insurance plans will pay for both the fitting of a good prosthesis (an artificial breast replacement) as well as for the reconstruction of the breast (mammaplasty) for a woman whose breast has been removed. Insurance companies are beginning to realize that breast reconstruction after cancer is not simply a cosmetic operation but a matter of psychological health for many women. Almost all Blue Cross/Blue Shield plans now cover breast reconstruction costs. Reconstruction may begin within six months or more after the mastectomy, when the skin on the chest has softened. About 10,000 women each year undergo this surgical treatment. Women should be aware of a slight risk of a tumor recurring behind the silicone implant of the breast reconstruction, and such a tumor would be hard to detect.

Support for Cancer Survivors

Personal support is necessary both before and after surgery. Brookhaven Hospital in New York State offers a five-week program to support women who have had mastectomies. Support groups for family members are also formed as needed. The Reach for Recovery Program of the American Cancer Society is a rehabilitative program for women who have just had breast surgery. In this program, a woman who has successfully adjusted to her own surgery visits a new patient and shares experiences, insights, and positive approaches to recovery.

Cancer Hopefuls United for Mutual Support (CHUMS) was formed in New York City in 1981 by psychologist Sarah Splaver, a cancer survivor. It has several hundred members, led by counselors or psychologists with a history of cancer.

We are an organization of cancer survivors, not victims. Victim means to be conquered. We are not conquered; we are alive.

Dr. Sarah Splaver, CHUMS

Other Types of Cancer

Women over 40 face the dangers of other forms of cancer. Cancer is the leading cause of death among women aged 30 to 54. From 1950 to 1977 the cancer death rate has declined seven percent for black women and nine percent for whites. This is due mainly to a sharp reduction in deaths caused by cancer of the cervix, attributed to regular checkups and the increased use of Pap tests. There was also a decline in stomach cancer. The lung cancer rate for women has tripled in these twenty-seven years, however.

Lung Cancer

More than 100,000 Americans have lung cancer. For a long time it was thought that women were somehow protected from the problems inherent in smoking, but a 1980 HEW report to Congress indicated an epidemic of smoking-related disease among women.

Women represent 43 percent of those who have lung cancer, the second leading cause of cancer deaths among women. Lung cancer may soon replace breast cancer as the number-one cause of cancer death. Although it is largely preventable by not smoking, it is not as easily diagnosed and cured as breast cancer. Only about 10 percent of lung cancer patients are cured.

Many women who began to smoke after World War II are now reaching midlife or late life, when lung cancer strikes. Thus it is not surprising that in the mid-1970s one out of every three women in her middle years smoked an average of nineteen cigarettes a day.

You've come a long way, baby . . . toward a shorter life.
Dr. Daniel Horn, U.S. Public Health Service

Smoking has also been implicated in the increased risk of cardiovascular disease. If you use oral contraceptives or estrogen replacement therapy, this risk becomes even greater.

Smokers who don't stop smoking by age 40 are twice as likely to die prematurely as nonsmokers. If you stop smoking, in fifteen years your chances of living longer will be the same as if you never smoked. The U.S. Public Health Service says that the elimination of cigarette smoking would be the most major health promotion action Americans could take.

Mortality for the Five Leading Cancer Sites by Age

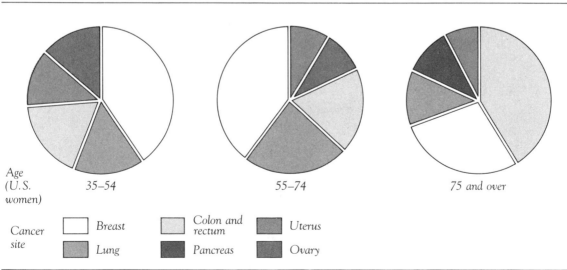

Age (U.S. women)   35–54   55–74   75 and over

Cancer site
Breast   Colon and rectum   Uterus
Lung   Pancreas   Ovary

Colon and Rectal Cancer

Colon and rectal cancer ranks third in the causes of cancer deaths for women. Ninety percent of all cases occur in people over 40.

In older women colon-rectum cancer, a disease that has not been written about enough, nor talked about enough, strikes frequently. An estimated 58,000 American women will develop this cancer in 1979. Most of them will be older women.

National Cancer Society

Despite its high mortality rate (almost half of all those diagnosed die), the potential for saving lives from this disease is greater than for most other types of cancer. Two out of three patients can be saved with early diagnosis and prompt treatment. Digital rectal exams and stool tests should be part of your annual checkup.

Symptoms

- Blood in the stools
- Weight loss and anemia from unknown causes
- Constipation or diarrhea

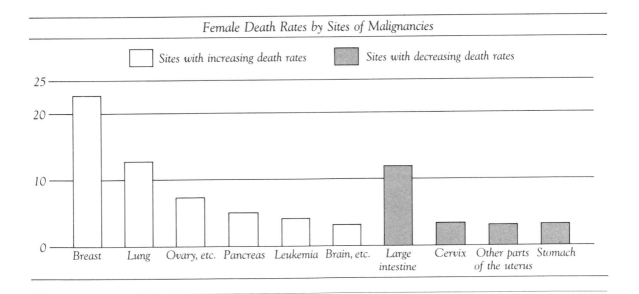

Female Death Rates by Sites of Malignancies

☐ Sites with increasing death rates   ▨ Sites with decreasing death rates

Breast · Lung · Ovary, etc. · Pancreas · Leukemia · Brain, etc. · Large intestine · Cervix · Other parts of the uterus · Stomach

- Tenseness, feeling the need to have a bowel movement with no success
- Abdominal pain or an increase in intestinal pain

Discuss any of the above symptoms promptly with a physician. Women who have ulcerative colitis for ten years or more are at high risk for contracting colon or rectal cancer.

Diagnosis

Diagnosis can be accomplished in the following ways:

- *Digital rectal examination.* By inserting a gloved finger into the rectum, your physician can inspect your anal area.
- *Guaiac testing for occult blood.* Stool samples from three consecutive bowel movements are tested for blood in the feces. This is usually done in the physician's office, but a kit is available for use at home.
- *Proctosigmoidoscopy.* A lighted tube is passed into the rectum and lower colon through which the physician can inspect the wall visually. Fifty to 60 percent of all colon and rectal cancers are within reach of this instrument.
- *Other tests.* A physician may recommend a barium X-ray exam or a colonoscopy, a technique for viewing the entire colon with a flexible lighted tube.

Treatment

Surgery is the most effective treatment. Depending on the type and stage of the disease, surgery consists of removing the part of the bowel containing the tumor. The American Cancer Society says that about 70 percent of patients undergoing surgery for early colon-rectal cancer survive the crucial first five years after treatment, after which the chances of a cure are good. Radiation therapy (not usually very effective) and chemotherapy, in combination with surgery, are being used in some cases.

To reduce the risk of colon cancer, include generous amounts of fiber in your daily diet. Whole-grain breads, cereals, and raw fruits and vegetables (cooking significantly destroys the fiber content) are all good sources of fiber. High-fat diets have been implicated in colon cancer.

Uterine Cancers

Uterine cancers (including both endometrial and cervical) have the fourth highest cancer death rate in women. This could be reduced dramatically if every women over 35 had a Pap test during her regular checkup and reported any abnormal bleeding promptly to her physician.

Endometrial Cancer

Endometrial cancer (cancer of the body of the uterus) most often occurs in mature women. Of the more than 50 million women over age 35, about 700,000 eventually will develop this cancer. Most cases are diagnosed in the 50 to 64 age group. Incidence of this cancer increased dramatically in the years that estrogen treatment for postmenopausal women was popular. A woman taking estrogen is up to twelve times more likely to be a victim of endometrial cancer than a nonuser. This relative risk does not begin to increase until a woman has been taking estrogen for at least three or four years. One encouraging study indicates that women who discontinue estrogen are almost as risk-free after two or three years as women who have never taken it.

High-risk women are those with a history of infertility, obesity, failure of ovulation, or abnormal uterine bleeding; women who have never become pregnant; or women who have undergone estrogen therapy for more than two or three years.

Symptoms

The most common early sign of endometrial cancer is abnormal spotting or bleeding or a heavy mucous discharge. Bleeding after menopause should always be a concern. Since the Pap smear test is only about 40 percent effective in detecting endometrial cancer, the American Cancer Society recommends that every menopausal age woman have a pelvic exam as well as a Pap test once a year. Women at high risk should have an endometrial tissue sample examined.

Cervical Cancer

Cervical cancer is cancer of the neck of the uterus. If every woman had a Pap test with her regular health checkup, there would be virtually no deaths from cervical cancer because malignant cells detected early can be destroyed by cryosurgery (freezing) or cone biopsy (removal of the diseased part of the cervix). Women over 20 and younger women who have had frequent sexual activity in their early teens are at highest risk. Fifty women out of every 100,000 women aged 45 to 65 get cervical cancer. It is more common in low socioeconomic groups. Cervical cancer occurs in

Puerto Rican immigrant women about four times as often as in mainland U.S. women. Overall, 34 black women per 100,000 get cervical cancer, compared to 15 white women per 100,000.

Symptoms
Abnormal bleeding (especially after intercourse) or an abnormal vaginal discharge are the primary symptoms of cervical cancer.

Treatment
Surgery and/or radiation therapy (in particular the insertion of a radioactive implant) are the usual treatments.

Ovarian Cancer

Ovarian cancer is not a common malignancy. Symptoms include a feeling of recurrent or sudden pain in the pelvis (caused by a twisting of the ovarian tumor on the fallopian tube), abnormal fullness or pressure in the bladder or rectum and gastrointestinal complaints. The average age of occurrence is 50. It is one of the most rapidly fatal of all malignancies, accounting for five percent of cancer deaths in women. If the tumor is small, it may be possible to remove just the tumor and one ovary. Otherwise, the tumor, both ovaries, the uterus, and fallopian tubes have to be removed. During a regular pelvic examination, when the doctor puts his or her fingers inside your vagina and presses your abdomen with the other hand, he or she is checking the ovaries, including the possibility of an ovarian tumor.

Vaginal and Vulval Cancer

Vaginal and vulval cancer are almost exclusively associated with older women, except for DES daughters, with the highest incidence in women over 75. Any unusual sore or prolonged itchiness, discharge, or bleeding from the vulva should be checked. This type of cancer does not respond to radiation treatment. A vulvectomy, simple or radical (extensive removal of skin and lymph glands), is the treatment. A radical vulvectomy is disfiguring, particularly for younger women and those who are sexually active.

Skin Cancer

About 400,000 new cases of skin cancer occur in the United States each year. Since such cases are easily visible, they can be treated early. Most of these are highly curable basal- or squamous-cell cancers. These two cancers are often indistinguishable. They show up on the skin in one of two forms—either as a pale, waxlike, pearly nodule that may eventually ulcerate and crust or as a red, scaly, sharply outlined patch. The vast majority of skin cancers can be prevented by avoiding overexposure to the sun.

One very serious skin cancer is malignant melanoma. A major cause of melanoma is exposure to the sun. It strikes 7,200 women each year with an estimated 2,600 deaths. Melanomas are usually distinguished by a dark brown or black pigmentation. They start as small molelike growths that increase in size, change color, become ulcerated, and bleed easily from even a slight injury. It is important that any such growths not be scratched or bumped. Melanomas occur most frequently in white people, usually on the head, neck, back, or arms. Women are often affected between the knee and ankle. This type of cancer is rare in black people. Melanomas spread rapidly and should be removed as soon as possible.

Symptoms

Watch for any growth in a mole, changes in elevation of a mole (as when a flat mole becomes raised, nodular, thickened, or scaly), changes in sensation (itching or tingling), and changes in color, especially from brown to black. A dermatologist should be consulted immediately.

Treatment

Appropriate therapy consists of removal of the mole and examination for both vertical and horizontal depth of penetration. A wide area around the mole and nearby lymph nodes may need to be removed and chemotherapy begun if the spread is detectable. The development of malignant skin cancer has been tentatively associated with the birth-control pill. Estrogen replacement therapy may increase the risk as well. The overwhelming majority of skin cancers can be cured if treated promptly, except for melanomas.

Stress and Cancer

More than 2,000 years ago the Greek physician Galen observed the connection between cancer and emotional stress, stating that cheerful women were less prone to cancer than were depressed women. This ancient statement seems to hold some element of truth. Stress may seem like an intangible thing, but its effects are real and can be harmful.

Research has shown that it is sometimes possible to predict major illness by the number of stresses in a person's life. Stresses that threaten a central role or relationship are particularly important. Doctors Holmes and Rahe at the University of Washington School of Medicine have designed a scale to measure the stresses in a person's life. They sometimes have been able to accurately predict illness in those with high scores. It seems, however, that it's not the number of stresses you face but the manner in which you cope with them that affects your chances of becoming ill.

Chronic stress tends to suppress the immune system or cause it to function abnormally. A healthy immune system is important in destroying cancer cells. Emotional stress also may lead to hormonal imbalances that could increase the production of abnormal cells at precisely the time the body is least capable of destroying them. Some people feel that our cells "spin out of control" when we haven't learned to cope well with stress and that this may be a leading cause of cancer. Conversely, those who already have cancer can use stress control as a positive therapeutic tool.

Holistic methods of treating cancer (using the intellect, the emotions, and the body) begin with the psychological health of the patient. In the face of death, people seem better able to put their lives into perspective. They can easily be encouraged to discharge long-held-in feelings of depression, fear, anger, and despair. Many individuals are able to change their lifestyles significantly. As these hopeful behaviors occur—and there is a new will and determination to live for many people—the body again mobilizes its defenses against the cancer cells and health is sometimes restored.

The alternative holistic treatments for cancer, including imaging, macrobiotic diets, and megavitamins, remain controversial, especially in the medical world. However, for many cancer victims they are a source of hope and, in a few well-documented cases, the cause for a cure.

Why do some people recover from their cancer with minimal treatment, while others with the same diagnosis do not? Many physicians and psychologists feel that one essential variable may be the patient's attitude toward her disease. A strong will to live and an intense attachment to a particular goal in life may be factors that contribute to recovery. Many people who have remissions are fighters; they are really angry about having cancer and turn their anger into a sincere belief that it can be cured, and they are willing to commit themselves totally to the effort.

Many famous women over 40 have had cancer: Betty Ford, Happy Rockefeller, Shirley Temple Black, Bess Myerson, Virginia Graham, Rose Kuschner, Betty Rollin, and Amanda Blake, to name a few. Their willingness to discuss their personal involvement with this disease has significantly increased the information about cancer and has helped all of us discuss cancer more openly with ourselves and our physicians. As we watch these successful women continue to lead full lives, we are less afraid.

Cancer is not a cause for resignation. Much can be done to prevent it and to cure it if we're willing to alter simple patterns of our behavior.

Diabetes

Sixty percent of all adult diabetics are women. According to the American Diabetes Association, for every 10,000 people in a community, diabetes appears in:

1	over age 20
10	between ages 20 and 40
100	between ages 50 and 60
1,000	over the age of 60

Diabetes develops more frequently in women who have a family history of the disease, who are over 40, obese, Jewish or nonwhite, or who live below the poverty level. Diabetes has many causes. Heredity, virus, the autoimmune system, and obesity are all implicated.

Diabetes mellitus comes from the Greek and Latin words meaning "to pass through" and "honey." Sugar in the urine, or diabetes, was first recorded almost 4,000 years ago. Diabetes is a metabolic disorder characterized by the body's inability to utilize food properly, especially carbohydrates (sugar and starches). Diabetics have difficulty converting carbohydrates into the energy their body needs to function normally. Carbohydrates in our body are converted to a form of sugar called glucose. Insulin is secreted by the beta cells of the pancreas in response to high levels of sugar in the blood. Insulin clears the blood of excess sugar and moves it into the cells. Diabetics release inadequate amounts of insulin, causing large buildups of sugar in their blood. Without insulin, sugar cannot enter certain cells, literally causing them to starve to death. When this occurs, the body begins to break down fats to produce more energy. This improper fat breakdown causes poisons to form in the body, and a vast array of complications occurs.

Only recently, research at the National Institute on Aging pointed out that what physicians refer to as the normal glucose level is the normal level for healthy 20-year-olds and not an accurate measure for older people. New measurement adjustments have been made and promulgated.

Previously, it was thought that the high incidence of diabetes in later years was due to a decline in insulin strength as the body aged or to insufficient insulin. However, recent research by Dr. Jessie Roth of the National Institutes of Health has shown that most diabetics do have an adequate quantity of insulin, but they are simply unable to use it effectively. He believes that in very overweight people an extra amount of insulin is needed to "open the door" of the cells to allow the sugar to pass from the bloodstream into the cell itself. This causes the cells of obese people to work two or three times as hard as those of slender people.

Diabetes and Obesity

Until recently, physicians have believed that diabetes was seldom preventable and rarely curable. Current studies have shown that this is not so. We now know that obesity is a major factor in diabetes. Eighty percent of American diabetics were obese before they developed the disease. Even moderately obese women are five times more likely to develop diabetes than slender women.

Weight loss usually reduces the severity of the disease and the probability of serious complications, even for those who have been diabetic for many years. At the first sign of diabetes, overweight women are advised to return to their optimal body weight as soon as possible.

Diabetes seems to peak in 45-to-60-year-old women and then level off. This is also the age group with the highest incidence of obesity; fat, not age, may be a leading cause.

For the last fifteen years the National Institute of Arthritis, Metabolism, and Digestive Diseases has been studying the close relationship between diabetes and obesity in the Arizona Pina Indian tribe. The overwhelming majority of these Indians are very overweight and more than half the adult population over 35 has diabetes. Such a study hopes to identify warning signs to identify people in danger of developing this metabolic disorder before it occurs.

Insulin injections and medication help control diabetes but rarely reverse or cure it. It is believed that daily exercise and modifications in the diet can do both. These health measures are possible for everyone.

Warning Signs of Diabetes

Many people have diabetes but are unaware of its presence. According to the American Diabetes Association, among the most common signs are the sudden appearance of any of the following:

C onstant urination
A bnormal thirst
U nusual hunger
T he rapid loss of weight
I rritability
O bvious weakness and fatigue
N ausea and vomiting

D rowsiness
I tching
A family history of diabetes
B lurred vision
E xcessive weight
T ingling, numbness, pain in the extremities
E asy fatigue
S kin infections and slow healing of cuts and scratches, especially of the feet

Some diabetics may have only one or two of these symptoms. Others may not show any signs at all. The disease is often discovered by a urine test during a routine physical examination.

If you notice any of the above symptoms, check with your physician. If you have a family history of diabetes (40 percent of all adult-onset cases show a family history), you should be tested at least once a year for diabetes.

My sister noticed that I was urinating frequently and drinking lots of water. She suggested that I have a blood sugar test. It showed that I have borderline diabetes which, thank God, I now control by diet, with no shots or medication.

Dorothy, age 47

Complications of Diabetes

When the hormone insulin was discovered in the 1920s, it was believed that the problem of diabetes would be quickly solved. Sixty years later, it remains a major health problem in the United States, with a diabetic population of ten million or more. It is also a leading cause of death (300,000 people are its victims each year). Diabetes and its complications can decrease life expectancy by one-third. According to the National Commission on Diabetes it is the leading cause of coronary heart disease. Diabetics are twice as prone to stroke and coronary heart disease. It is also the leading cause of blindness. Eighty percent of all diabetics will suffer some loss of vision due to retinopathy and 25 percent more diabetics will suffer blindness. This problem is closely related to high blood pressure. It is thought that the hypoglycemia connected with diabetes may be the cause of an acute senility.

> *What scared me most with my diabetes is that I might go blind. I woke up several times in the middle of the night recently and saw light. An eye doctor is now examining me for retinopathy (a disorder of the blood vessels in the eye). I'm losing weight and feel I'm making progress, but my biggest worry about the whole disease is blindness.*
>
> Anita, age 52

Diabetics are seventeen times more prone to kidney disease than other people, forty times more likely to suffer from gangrene (caused by poor circulation) leading to amputation, and predisposed to periodontal disease. These problems usually take twelve to fifteen years to appear. The longer one has diabetes, the more likely such life-threatening complications will occur.

Special Problems for Older Women

Among the problems specific to diabetic women over 40 are the following:

- Cystitis, an inflammation and/or infection of the bladder.
- Complications related to oral medications for diabetes. Some diabetic drugs can trigger heart disease and even death.
- Osteoporosis. Diabetic women are at high risk for this disease.
- Menopause. The diabetic menopausal woman not only suffers the discomforts other women suffer, but she is often confused by the symp-

toms, i.e., is the profuse sweating, vaginal itching, and fatigue due to menopause or to an insulin reaction?

- Employment. Older women diabetics may attempt to keep their condition secret, for fear of losing their jobs. A study of 127 firms in Minnesota showed that 31 percent did not hire diabetics, even though surveys have proven that diabetics have high-quality job performance.
- Oral contraceptives (birth-control pills) cause significant changes in the body's glucose tolerance level and should be avoided by all diabetics. Women presently taking such pills should be tested for diabetes yearly. There is some evidence that birth-control pills even contribute to diabetes, as may other forms of estrogen.

Treatments

Insulin therapy: Insulin is a hormone produced from the pancreas glands of animals, mostly pigs and cows, although it has been made from sheep, whales, and even tuna. Recently, researchers at the City of Hope National Medical Center in California induced bacteria to produce insulin identical to human insulin, although it is not yet commercially available. It is usually necessary for a newly diagnosed diabetic to be hospitalized while physicians ascertain the type and amount of insulin she needs.

> *My sugar wasn't going down despite my following my diet to a "T" and taking my daily insulin shot. My doctor kept insisting that I must be cheating. He finally put me in the hospital for a second time. They found that my body wasn't building up antibodies against the insulin. After a process of elimination to find the proper type of insulin, they discovered that pure pork insulin was necessary to make my pancreas work.*
>
> Joan, age 45

More than two million persons take insulin injections daily (another two million use oral insulin medication). This amount of insulin lasts in the body for twenty-four to thirty-six hours. The need for insulin is most acute after meals, when the blood sugar level rises. One problem with long-acting insulin in the daily injection is that it maintains a normal insulin level continuously but cannot peak at necessary specific times, like mealtimes. It is believed that the secret of preventing diabetic complications lies in maintaining normal blood sugar levels at all times. To do this researchers are experimenting with some exciting new types of therapy:

- The insulin pump. A small needle is implanted just beneath the skin and a portable pump the size of a hand-held calculator is attached to the person's belt, providing a continuous infusion of insulin with larger amounts at mealtimes. Experiments are under way to implant a miniature pump in the muscles of the abdomen.

- Transplanting pancreas tissue from a healthy animal has proved quite successful and might be a valuable treatment for humans in the future.

- Chemical approaches such as implanting the plant protein lectin into the tissue of a diabetic are being perfected in the laboratories.

Diabetics are frightened that they will overdose on insulin and cause an insulin reaction. Such a reaction is characterized by intense trembling, sweating, disorientation, and even loss of consciousness.

Other Treatment

- If you are obese, begin immediately to lose weight. A loss of twenty-five to fifty pounds can significantly improve diabetes and may even correct it.

- Regulate your blood pressure. Diabetic retinopathy, which causes blindness, seems to be related to high blood pressure.

- Control your blood sugar with diet. About seven million diabetics control their condition with diet alone.

- Exercise. Exercise has been called the economical and invisible insulin. It acts as a booster to insulin, and allows the body to function effectively with a smaller dose.

- Laser treatment has been successful in restoring proper blood flow to the eyes of diabetics with retinopathy. While this treatment does not increase vision, it can prevent further loss of vision. Current statistics show that only six to seven percent of patients treated with laser therapy suffered severe visual loss.

My mother is a diabetic and is insulin-dependent. She has been under the care of the "best specialists," although her insulin dose is set at the same amount whether or not she exercises (this would never happen with a young patient; it is assumed that older women don't exercise). We, her family, had to insist that they reduce her insulin on the days she exercises—and she's been much better since then. The role of exercise in diabetes is under-emphasized. The amount of insulin required is definitely reduced with exercise.

Stephanie, age 42

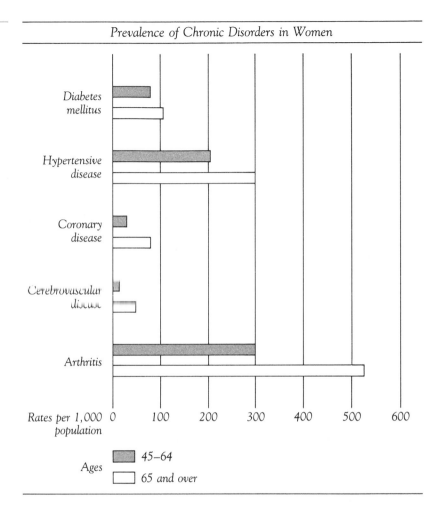

Women have written to us about some practical treatments that lessened their diabetic symptoms.

- Eliminate diuretics (water pills). They are unsafe for diabetics. Prolonged use may even be a cause of the disease.
- Add a tablespoon of brewer's yeast to your daily diet.
- Take adequate C, E, and B-complex vitamins. B-complex and magnesium help the body digest protein.
- Never miss a meal or forget your medication. This can send your blood sugar level up.

279

 ♦ Avoid overwork.

 ♦ Look for a diabetes class in your local hospital where you can talk out your fears and learn as much as you can about this controllable disorder.

 ♦ Have a yearly glucose tolerance test if you are in a high-risk category. A urinalysis is able to diagnose only relatively advanced cases of the disease.

 ♦ Keep your family and friends informed about the changes necessary in your lifestyle. You will need their support.

Although the solutions to diabetes are still to come, the future seems to hold promise for women diabetics. Until other solutions are found, the healing potential of diet and exercise should be vigorously utilized.

Resources: Cardiovascular Disease

Publications

Alpert, Joseph. *The Heart Attack Handbook: A Commonsense Guide to Treatment, Recovery and Prevention.* Boston: Little, Brown, 1978.

American Heart Association. *The Heart Book.* New York: Dutton, 1980.

American Medical Association. *Heart Care.* New York: Random House, 1982.

Wolff, Hanns. *Speaking of High Blood Pressure.* New York: Consolidated, 1978.

Zinman, David. "Heart Disease: Updating the Battle." Newsday, 1 March 1981.

Organizations

American Heart Association (National Office)
7320 Greenville Ave.
Dallas, TX 75231

Biofeedback Society of America
University of Colorado Medical Center
4200 E. 9th Ave.
Denver, CO 80220

Consumer Information Bureau
Pueblo, CO 81009
For information on heart disease.

National High Blood Pressure Information Center
Landlow Building, Suite 1300
7910 Woodmont Ave.
Bethesda, MD 20014

Wifes' Respite Project
c/o Clemmie Barry
Mental Health Association of Marin
1368 Lincoln Ave., Suite 204
San Rafael, CA 94901

Resources: Rheumatic Disease

Publications

Benson, Herbert. *The Relaxation Response*. New York: Avon, 1975.

Blau, Sheldon, and Dodi Schultz. *Lupus: The Body Against Itself*. New York: Doubleday, 1977.

Dong, Collin, and Jane Banks. *The Arthritic's Cookbook*. New York: Harper & Row, 1973.

Downing, George. *The Massage Book*. New York: Random House, 1972.

Fries, James. *Arthritis: A Comprehensive Guide*. Reading, Mass.: Addison-Wesley, 1979.

Lorig, Kate, and James Fries. *The Arthritis Helpbook*. Reading, Mass.: Addison-Wesley, 1980.

New York Arthritis Foundation, *Sex Can Help Arthritis*. 221 Park Avenue South, New York, NY (Free.)

Organizations

American Lupus Society
23751 Madison St.
Torrance, CA 90505
One hundred chapters provide patient services and information.

Arthritis Information Clearinghouse
P.O. Box 344271
Bethesda, MD 20034

Independence Factory
P.O. Box 597
Middletown, OH 45042
Nonprofit organization that makes practical aids for arthritics.

Lupus Foundation
11673 Holly Springs Dr.
St. Louis, MO 63141
Seventy chapters provide medical referrals, educational materials, and counseling.

National Arthritis Foundation
Room 1101, 3400 Peachtree Rd., N.E.
Atlanta, GA 30327
See your phone book for your local chapter.

National Institute of Arthritis, Metabolism, and Digestive Diseases
National Institutes of Health
Building 31, Room 9A04
Bethesda, MD 20205

Stanford Arthritis Center
Stanford Medical Center, S-102
Stanford, CA 94305

Resources: Cancer

Publications

Cherry, S. *For Women of All Ages: A Gynecologist's Guide to Modern Female Health Care.* New York: Macmillan, 1979.

Cope, Oliver. *The Breast: Its Problems—Benign and Malignant—and How to Deal with Them.* Boston: Houghton Mifflin, 1977.

Kuschner, Rose. *What Do You Do If You Find Something That Suggests Breast Cancer.* New York: The American Cancer Society, 1979.

Kuschner, Rose. *Why Me? What Every Woman Should Know about Breast Cancer to Save Her Life.* Rev. ed. New York: Signet, 1977.

LeShan, Lawrence. *You Can Fight for Your Life: Emotional Factors in the Causation of Cancer.* New York: M. Evans & Co., 1977.

National Council of Jewish Women. *Women Helping Women: A Guide to Organizing a Post-Mastectomy Program in Your Community.* 15 E. 26th St., New York, NY 10010. $2.50.

Office of Cancer Communications. *The Breast Cancer Digest.* National Cancer Institute, Building 31, Room 4B39, Bethesda, MD 20205. Free.

Porcino, Jane, Elaine Friedman, and Peggy Bruhn, eds. *Health Issues of Older Women: A Projection to the Year 2000.* School of Allied Health Professions, State University of New York, Stony Brook, NY 11794.

Sattilaro, Anthony J., M.D. *Recalled by Life: The Story of My Recovery from Cancer.* Boston: Houghton Mifflin, 1982.

Simonton, O. Carl, Stephany Matthews-Simonton, and James Creightor. *Getting Well Again: A Step-by-Step, Self-Help Guide to Overcoming Cancer for Patients and Their Families.* Los Angeles: Tarcher, 1978.

U.S. Public Health Service. *The Health Consequences of Smoking for Women: A Report of the Surgeon General.* Washington, DC: U.S. Government Printing Office, 1980.

Wasco, James. *Not for Doctors Only: Breakthrough Reports from the Medical Front.* Reading, Mass.: Addison-Wesley, 1980.

Organizations

American Cancer Society
777 3rd Ave.
New York, NY 10017
212-371-2900

American Holistic Medical Association
Tr. 2 Welsh Coulee
La Crosse, WI 54601
For names of physicians who practice holistic medicine.

American Society of Plastic and Reconstructive
Surgeons
29 E. Madison St., Suite 800
Chicago, IL 60602
For names of qualified surgeons in your area and three
free booklets on breast reconstruction.

Cancer Hopefuls United for Mutual Support (CHUMS)
3310 Rochanbeau Ave.
Bronx, NY 10467

Cancer Information Service
(Sponsored by the National Cancer Institute)
Toll free number: 1-800-4-CANCER
Trained staff provide up-to-date information about
cancer. In New York City, dial 212-794-7982; in
Washington, DC and suburbs in Maryland and Virginia
dial 202-636-5700; in Alaska and Hawaii dial
1-800-638-6070.

Foundation for Alternative Cancer Therapies
Box H.H.
Old Chelsea Station
New York, NY 10011
212-741-2790

Rose Kuschner's Breast Cancer Advisory Center
P.O. Box 422
Kensington, MD 20795

Comprehensive Cancer Centers

Alabama
Comprehensive Cancer Center
University of Alabama in Birmingham
University Station
Birmingham, AL 35294
205-934-5077

California
Los Angeles County–University of
Southern California Comprehensive
Cancer Center
2025 Zonal Ave.
Los Angeles, CA 90033
213-226-2008

UCLA Comprehensive Cancer Center
UCLA School of Medicine
924 Westwood Blvd., Suite 650
Los Angeles, CA 90024
213-825-2532
213-825-5268

Colorado
Colorado Regional Cancer Center, Inc.
165 Cook St.
Denver, CO 80206
303-320-5921

Connecticut
Yale University Comprehensive
Cancer Center
333 Cedar St.
New Haven, CT 06510
203-432-4122

District of Columbia
Georgetown University/Howard University
Comprehensive Cancer Center
Vincent T. Lombardi Cancer Research Center
Georgetown University Medical Center
3800 Reservoir Rd., N.W.
Washington, DC 20007
202-625-7066

Howard University Cancer Research Center
College of Medicine
Washington, DC 20059
202-745-1406

Florida
Comprehensive Cancer Center for
the State of Florida
University of Miami School of
Medicine/Jackson Memorial Medical
Center
P.O. Box 520875, Biscayne Annex
Miami, FL 33134
305-547-6758

Illinois
Illinois Cancer Council
37 S. Wabash Ave.
Chicago, IL 60603
312-346-9813

Maryland
Johns Hopkins Oncology Center
601 North Broadway
Baltimore, MD 21205
301-955-8822

Massachusetts
Sidney Farber Cancer Institute
44 Binney St.
Boston, MA 02115
617-732-3555

Michigan
Cancer Center of Metropolitan Detroit
110 East Warren Ave.
Detroit, MI 48201
313-833-0710

Minnesota
Mayo Comprehensive Cancer Center
200 First St., S.W.
Rochester, MN 55901
507-282-2511

New York
Memorial Sloan-Kettering Cancer Center
1275 York Ave.
New York, NY 10021
212-794-7585

Roswell Park Memorial Institute
666 Elm St.
Buffalo, NY 14263
716-845-5770

North Carolina
Comprehensive Cancer Center
Duke University Medical Center
P.O. Box 3814
Durham, NC 27710
919-684-2282

Ohio
Ohio State University Comprehensive
Cancer Center
357 McCampbell Dr.
Columbus, OH 43210
614-422-5022

Pennsylvania
Fox Chase/University of Pennsylvania
Comprehensive Cancer Center
The Fox Chase Cancer Center
7701 Burholme Ave.
Philadelphia, PA 19111
215-342-1000

University of Pennsylvania Cancer Center
578 Maloney Building
3400 Spruce St.
Philadelphia, PA 19104
215-662-3910

Texas
The University of Texas System Cancer Center
M. D. Anderson Hospital and Tumor Institute
6723 Bertner Ave.
Houston, TX 77030
713-792-3000

Washington
Fred Hutchinson Cancer Research Center
1124 Columbia St.
Seattle, WA 98104
206-292-2930

Wisconsin
The University of Wisconsin Clinical
Cancer Center
1300 University Ave.
Madison, WI 53706
608-263-2553

Breast Cancer Networks

Alabama Breast Cancer Project
UAB P.O. Box 193, University Station
Birmingham, AL 35294
205-934-3376 or 934-5070

Brooklyn Breast Cancer Demonstration Network
Box 1214, Downstate Medical Center
450 Clarkson Ave.
Brooklyn, NY 11203
212-270-1333

Cancer Center
University of Louisville Foundation, Inc.
Health Sciences Center
Walnut and Preston Sts.
Louisville, KY 40232
502-582-2211, ext. 510

Delaware Breast Cancer Management Program
Wilmington Medical Center
Executive Offices
P.O. Box 1668
Wilmington, DE 19899
302-656-5740

Fox Chase Cancer Center
The American Oncologic Hospital
Central and Shelmire Ave.
Fox Chase
Philadelphia, PA 19111
215-722-1900, ext. 302

Georgia Cancer Management Network, Inc.
Freeway Office Park
1645 Tully Circle, N.E., Suite 126
Atlanta, GA 30329
404-329-7016

Hitchcock Clinic
Hanover, NH 03755
603-643-4000, ext 2467

New England Medical Center Hospital
Box 319
171 Harrison Ave.
Boston, MA 02111
617-956-5000

Oklahoma Hospital's Breast Cancer Control Network
Oklahoma Medical Research Foundation
825 N.E. 13th St.
Oklahoma City, OK 73104
405-235-8331, ext. 460

Regional Breast Cancer Program
(for upper New York and Western Massachusetts)
Albany Medical College
47 New Scotland Ave.
Albany, NY 12208
518-445-5036

University of Vermont
College of Medicine
Burlington, VT 05401
802-656-2563

West Coast Cancer Foundation
50 Francisco St., Suite 200
San Francisco, CA 94133
415-563-5213

Resources: Diabetes

Publications

Covelli, Pat. "New Hope for Diabetics." *New York Times Magazine*, 8 March 1981.

Dolger, Henry, and Bernard Seeman, *How to Live with Diabetes*. 4th ed. New York: Schocken, 1978.

Hunt, Beatrice, and Morton Hunt. *Prime Time: A Guide to the Pleasures and Opportunities of the New Middle Age.* New York: Stein and Day, 1975.

Wasco, James. *Not for Doctors Only: Breakthrough Reports from the Medical Front.* Reading, Mass.; Addison-Wesley, 1980.

Zimmerman, David. "New Hope for Diabetics." *Woman's Day,* 24 April 1979.

Organizations

The American Diabetes Association, Inc.
600 Fifth Ave.
New York, NY 10020
212-541-4310
State and regional offices are listed in the phone book.
Publication: *Diabetes Forecast* (bimonthly, $5.00 per year)

National Diabetes, Information Clearinghouse
805 Fifteenth St., N.W., Suite 500
Washington, DC 20005
202-842-7630

Alice Shafer © 1982 from the Unitarian Universalist Service
Committee *Positive Images of Aging* Slide Tape Show

Chapter Thirteen

Other Health Concerns

Urinary Incontinence

> *All my life I was an activist. My husband and I were Quakers, worked for peace and against racism, sexism, and ageism. At age 78, after a minor operation, I returned home incontinent—an enormous embarrassment. I wouldn't wear those diapers so I stopped going anywhere—even to Sunday meetings. This depression and withdrawal lasted two years. I went to three doctors and the first two said, "What do you expect at 78—incontinence is a part of growing old." The third doctor whisked me into the hospital for minor surgery, which ended the incontinence. I was free again to resume my old activism. When will doctors learn that we're treatable until we die?*
>
> Dora, age 81

Although most healthy women continue to maintain urinary muscle control throughout their lives, there is a natural decrease in bladder control with age, which can lead to incontinence. Urinary incontinence is a major health problem for older women as well as their families and health providers. Its incidence is estimated at 5 to 15 percent of people over age 65 who are living at home and as high as 50 percent among older patients in hospitals. Studies have shown incontinence to be twice as high in women as in men; over half of all women have occasional urinary leakage as they age.

Incontinence means "wanting in self-restraint; unable to hold something in." Urinary incontinence is a loss of urine at any time other than when it is desired. This is a problem, not a disease, and it can range from the nuisance of an occasional slight loss of urine to a severe disability.

Incontinence places women at an increased risk for other significant medical problems. It often leads to psychological reactions such as withdrawal, depression, insecurity, and overdependence. Incontinence is one of three leading reasons for admission to nursing homes. Twenty-five percent of nursing time in nursing homes is spent dealing with incontinence; it therefore costs 2.5 times more to care for such people in long-term care facilities. A more frequent problem, stress incontinence (dribbling), which occurs from coughing, sneezing, laughing, or lifting may be caused by a prolapsed uterus or damage to the pelvic floor (often from a difficult childbirth). There seems to be some association between Parkinson's disease and incontinence.

Temporary incontinence may be caused by:

- An acute illness.
- Cystitis (an inflammation of the wall of the urinary bladder) or other genitourinary infection.
- Diminished or complete loss of muscle control in the bladder resulting in the incomplete emptying of the bladder. Symptoms are a burning sensation while urinating, frequency of urination (especially at night), and sometimes fever.
- Immobility caused by bed or wheel chair confinement, which interferes with normal urination habits.
- Oversedation (bladder control depends on alertness).
- Diuretic therapy.
- A temporary state of confusion interfering with awareness of the need to void.

- Psychological regression resulting from a forced move to a strange environment (such as a hospital or nursing home).
- Inaccessibility to toilet facilities.

Fixed incontinence may be caused by:

- Weakness or defect in the bladder outlet. This can occur after an injury to the bladder or because of an obstruction or anatomical distortion at the neck of the bladder, or because the pelvic floor was overstretched during childbirth.
- A narrowing of the uretha.
- Lack of sensation in perceiving the need to void.
- Neurological damage (such as dementia).

Health care providers and women themselves often have the false assumption that urinary incontinence is inevitable in old age. This assumption is self-defeating; incontinent women should understand this and make every effort to correct the problem.

Treatment

Numerous therapies are used to treat incontinence. Temporary incontinence can usually be remedied; fixed incontinence can be treated, if not cured. Consult your gynecologist or a urologist for the treatment plan most suitable for you.

Limit Fluid
Limit your fluid intake after 6 P.M. (especially coffee and alcohol), place a commode at your bedside at night, and during the day go to the toilet regularly (every two hours is recommended).

Exercise
Perhaps the simplest way to maintain or regain urinary muscle control is through a series of exercises called the Kegel exercises. A large muscle (called PC, or pubococcygeal) surrounds the vagina and covers the whole pelvic floor. This muscle may be lacking tone, especially in women who have had many children. The PC muscle, which helps contain the urine and reduce the spontaneous flow of urine caused by a sneeze or cough, can be strengthened and tightened by exercise. To locate your PC muscle practice stopping the flow of urine. It is the PC muscle you use to do this.

There are four exercises that should be practiced ten times each, at three different periods during the day. The first consists in squeezing the PC muscle for three seconds (as though you were holding back urine), relaxing it for three seconds, and squeezing again. A second exercise is called the "flutter," in which you squeeze the muscle and release as quickly as possible. The next exercise consists of imagining you are sucking a tampon up into your vagina and the last is bearing down (as during a bowel movement) with emphasis on the vaginal area.

Slowly increase the number you perform of each exercise until you reach twenty of each. It will take about six weeks to notice a difference.

Surgery

In the last fifteen years, urethrovesical suspension surgery has had an 87 percent success rate for persons with urinary stress incontinence. This is a short operation in which the urethra (the tube leading from the bladder that discharges urine) is sutured and then connected to the pubic fascia (fibrous tissue that envelops the body beneath the skin), thus changing the urethra's angle and position. The major complication rate is low and no patient's condition was made worse by the surgery. This operation can be combined with other surgery, such as an oophorectomy (removal of the ovaries) or hysterectomy (removal of the uterus).

Surgery will also help an incontinent woman who has a coexisting condition called cystocele (a protrusion of the bladder in the vaginal region).

Research

For the last year and a half, the National Institute on Aging has sponsored an ongoing Geriatric Continence Research Clinic to evaluate methods to teach persons over age 65 how to control their bladder and sphincter muscles. The training is only for a small number of research subjects. The results have been relatively good: Of ten patients treated, five became continent, in three the frequency of incontinence was reduced 75 percent, and two did not benefit.

My 74-year-old wife of forty-one and a quarter years has been hospitalized as a result of a stroke and incontinence. She's now much better and I feel she could come home. The biggest obstacle to that now is a catheter, most annoying to her and impossible

The Female Pelvic Organs

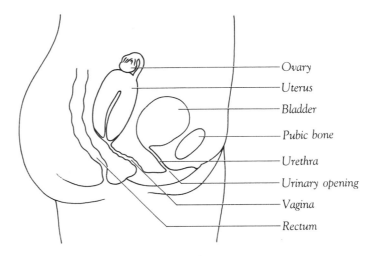

Ovary
Uterus
Bladder
Pubic bone
Urethra
Urinary opening
Vagina
Rectum

for me to manage. If they could treat the incontinence, I feel she could soon return home for the care and happiness she desires.

William, age 78

Sometime later a second letter arrived:

After your letter saying that improvement was possible for my wife's incontinence, her physician ordered the catheter removed. She was placed on a once-every-two-hour bladder training program. She is doing quite well in adapting to this program and we both hope she'll be coming home soon. Thank you.

If one of the causes of incontinence is cystitis, this may be treated by using antibiotics. A high fluid intake is recommended to dilute the urine, which will result in an increase of urine with a beneficial flushing effect. It is important to improve hospital and nursing home practices on incontinence. Protective pads and catheters should be used only when all else fails. Most incontinence can be cured. Women and the health professionals who care for them should actively pursue the range of treatments possible.

An 88-year-old stroke patient of mine in the health-related facility became withdrawn and depressed. One of the aides took her under her wing almost forcing her to respond. She took the time to give her a regular shower and to set her hair. But most important, she insisted she walk to the bathroom with the aid of a walker. She conquered the incontinence in two months and now walks without a walker. She goes out occasionally and now says she'd rather be at the HRF than with her own daughter; she feels more independent. I'm a firm believer that TLC [tender loving care] is a cure-all for most of our illnesses.

Pat, age 46

Hearing Changes

Hearing impairment strikes at the very essence of being human— it hinders communication with other human beings. It restricts our ability to be productive and to engage in social intercourse. It reduces our constructive use of leisure time. Hearing loss often leads to poor self-image, to isolation and to despair.

1981 White House Conference on Aging

When I'm sitting with a group of normal people, I feel like I'm enclosed in glass—like I'm behind a store window, looking in.

Lisa, age 72

Some ten million older Americans suffer some degree of hearing loss. It is usually first noticed around age 50 (one in four over age 65, and one in two over age 75). Hearing impairment, which includes both deaf and hard-of-hearing people, ranks among the three most prevalent chronic conditions among the aging, and yet we know little about its prevention, cure, and care.

Most hearing losses are due to genetic factors, with noise as the second most significant cause. A buildup of ear wax, ear infections, tumors, or drug side effects can cause correctible hearing problems. Sudden hearing loss can simply be due to wax occluding the auditory canal. The loss may be intermittent and recurrent and can be resolved by removal of the wax. The loss of hearing is more gradual than the loss of sight and can be harder for people to adjust to.

Presbycusis, a gradual hearing loss with aging, is the result of damage or changes in the nerves of the inner ear that lead to the brain. For most people there is no cure for nerve-change hearing loss.

Tinnitus is a hearing difficulty in which an older person hears a high-pitched ringing, like a whistle or bell. It is noticed more at night.

A genetic disease more prevalent among women than men is *otosclerosis*. It affects only one percent of the population. The stapes, the doorway to the inner ear, harden and become fixated, preventing the vibrations necessary for sound from passing into the inner ear. The resulting hearing loss can usually be corrected by surgery.

Women who complain of mild dizziness and/or difficulty in discriminating speech sounds may be suffering from an inner-ear disease or a tumor and should receive prompt medical attention by a physician specializing in diseases of the ear.

A distinction needs to be made between women with lifelong impairment and those whose onset of hearing loss occurs later in life. The latter are in double jeopardy and experience a more devastating change, since they have to face the problems of aging and of hearing loss at the same time.

Hearing impairment is seen to a greater degree in men than in women, especially men who have worked in certain industrial environments. Environmental noises in the workplace are an important factor in this difference. The U.S. Environmental Protection Agency estimates that ten percent of all Americans are exposed every day to noise levels that could damage their hearing. A significant number of older women who have returned to the work force and are exposed to noisy environments report some hearing disabilities.

An estimated 90 percent of the residents in nursing homes—more than one million people (mostly women)—have some loss of hearing. They may be there simply because of their hearing impairment. Many are declared incompetent when they are only hearing impaired.

The symptoms of hearing loss, other than diminished hearing, may be dizziness, pain, drainage, or a buzzing in the ear. As early as age 50, you may begin to experience trouble in hearing the higher frequencies. Such consonants as *s, z, t, f,* and *g* are high-frequency sounds. Not hearing them clearly makes it impos-

The Ear

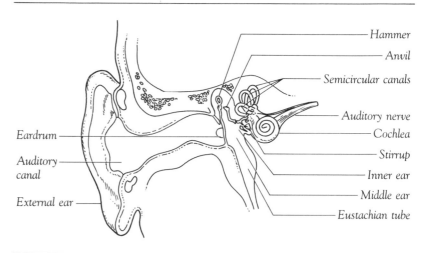

External ear — Auditory canal — Eardrum — Hammer — Anvil — Semicircular canals — Auditory nerve — Cochlea — Stirrup — Inner ear — Middle ear — Eustachian tube

sible to discriminate between words and therefore to understand normal conversations. Men tend to lose higher-frequency sounds earlier than women. High-pitched sounds like fire sirens, telephone bells, and soprano voices may be lost. Losing one's hearing in late life affects the way one is able to communicate with others, and this restricts satisfaction and often leads to isolation and loneliness.

I've been profoundly deaf* for several years. Even though I lip-read, I go home from any gathering of people simply exhausted from trying so hard to follow the conversation. At a luncheon the other day, a stranger next to me began talking rapidly. When I told her I was hard of hearing, she said "Oh" and turned to talk to the woman on the other side of her. I felt all alone, in the midst of many.

Gretchen, age 64

A hearing loss is an "invisible" handicap because it doesn't have an accompanying wheelchair or other noticeable aid. People tend either to ignore it or to become impatient with it. It places us in a new and strange environment, with the familiar sounds of work and play missing. Tensions are created within the

*A profoundly deaf person has less than five percent hearing in both ears.

family. Feelings of personal security, which depend on sound, may be reduced. If no effort is made to counteract hearing loss, social activities may gradually diminish. Older women who already suffer from discrimination in employment are often afraid to reveal their hearing handicap to an employer. In some occupations where acute hearing is necessary (such as among musicians, secretaries and teachers) auditory changes cause enormous personal stress and strain. Women with this handicap should be encouraged to look at their strengths and to seek assistance in changing careers. Women do not have to live in isolation because of hearing loss.

Hearing Rehabilitation

If you have even a slight hearing problem, you should be checked by a hearing specialist (otologist or audiologist). Many women wait until it is too late to correct what might have been only a simple problem. Despite a myth to the contrary, older persons are good candidates for hearing rehabilitation.

- Have a complete otologic examination to rule out significant diseases of the ear. An otologist is a physician specializing in diagnosing and treating medical conditions of the ear.
- For the nonmedical rehabilitative aspects of hearing loss, a woman should then be evaluated by a licensed and/or certified audiologist. Such a specialist will recommend the necessary hearing amplification device (such as a hearing aid), assist the individual in learning to use the aid, offer speech training and auditory training (teaching you to use the hearing you have left to its best advantage), and make referrals for any other nonmedical rehabilitation.
- Any hearing aid should be obtained for a trial period to allow the woman to be sure it will be helpful in her home and work environment.
- Counseling by an audiologist or counselor knowledgeable about hearing loss is strongly advised for both the woman and her family.

Hearing aids today are often sold with little or no professional evaluation. A hearing aid dealer may urge a woman to buy an unsuitable aid or one not properly fitted to the structure of her ear canal. She should have a professional audiological and otological evaluation before making a purchase. The Federal Trade Commission in August 1977 ruled that hearing aids may be sold only to persons who have had a prior medical evaluation (unless the consumer waives such an exam).

When the hearing loss is severe, training in lip-reading can help with communication. It helps to begin lip-reading classes as soon as you suspect you have a hearing loss.

Furnishings and materials that absorb sound, reduce echoes, and muffle irrelevant noises will help alleviate some communication difficulties. Movable furniture allows hard-of-hearing persons to sit close enough to hear others.

The artificial ear for the deaf is in the initial stages of development. In a surgical procedure, some of the bone behind the ear is removed and tiny electrodes are placed along the cochlea (the snail-shaped organ that contains the delicate hair cells that pick up sound and relay it to the auditory nerves and then to the brain). Wires from the electrodes are connected to a small coil amplifier and planted under the skin. A microphone to pick up the sound is concealed in an eyeglass frame.

A new organization, Self-Help for the Hard of Hearing (SHHH), has been formed for those with hearing problems, their relatives, and friends. It educates people about the nature, causes, complications, and remedial aids for hearing loss, and it provides information about alternative communication skills. SHHH counsels members on detection, management, and possible prevention of hearing loss.

Aids

Additional aids help the hearing impaired maintain contact with other people. A captioning device can be added to a television to display captions or subtitles at the bottom of the screen. Only a limited number of programs are currently coded for this service.

The Bell Telephone Company also has many aids for the hearing impaired, such as:

- A sound amplifier that can be installed on your home phone.
- A telephone communications device for the deaf with a typewriterlike keyboard. The device types messages that are transmitted to Bell System operators with similar devices (in four regional locations: Oakland, Omaha, Boston, and Philadelphia).
- By dialing 800-855-1155, users of telephone communications devices for the totally deaf can reach a special operator who will help them with person-to-person, collect, credit-card, and third-number calls.

Classrooms, theaters, auditoriums, and meeting rooms can be equipped with several different communication systems for the hearing impaired:

- *Audio-loops:* a wire (loop) that is installed around the perimeter of a room and enables anyone within that room with a hearing aid or other special equipment with a telephone switch to receive amplified sound.
- *Infrared:* a technique that transfers the audio signal from a microphone into invisible, infrared light that is converted back to sound via a special headset worn by the listener.
- *Amplisound:* the user is provided with an AM radio receiver with earplug, and sound is transmitted through a special station within the building or room.
- *Phonic Ear:* an FM radio broadcast system that is similar to the amplisound; both can be used with or without hearing aids.

Sign-language interpreters are invaluable at all gatherings and TV presentations. They can also be found more frequently at concerts and other public entertainment.

Communicating with the Hard-of-Hearing

Each of us should remember when speaking to someone who is hard of hearing to attract the person's attention first, to talk in a normal voice, not too rapidly, and to stand directly in front of the person facing the light. Gestures make our words easier to comprehend. If the hard-of-hearing person does not understand, rephrase what you have said.

Financing Hearing Health Care

Medicare will pay for a diagnosis or evaluation of hearing loss, if requested by a physician. That is, it will pay you to find out you have a hearing loss, but it will not pay to correct it. Hearing aids and related services are specifically excluded from Medicare. This is an unfortunate regulation that may prove unwise in the foreseeable future when we will need to keep people in the work force for longer periods of time. Twelve million hearing-impaired people are over 45 and their forced retirement because of uncorrected hearing losses will mean a costly reduction in the U.S. labor force and in the individual quality of life for this large population.

How to Preserve Your Hearing

- After age 50 women should have their ears checked every other year at their local speech and hearing center or by an otologist. Any accumulated wax should be removed.

- Avoid exposure to loud sounds. If such exposure is unavoidable, wear ear protectors.

- Treat all ear infections seriously. If untreated, a later hearing disability may result.

- Avoid sticking anything into the ear. Even swabs push waxy accumulations farther into the ear.

Vision Capacity of Women over Forty

So there we are, elderly people at a meeting. The secretary reads the minutes of the last meeting. Then he or she passes around some printed material for consideration.

A stirring bit of business follows. One member pulls his reading glasses from his pocket. A second simply closes one eye and squints at the document. A third person holds the reading matter at arm's length. A fourth pulls out a magnifying glass and peers through it.

Marsha, age 74

Many women maintain near-normal vision well into old age. A surprisingly high number retain adequate vision to age 90 and beyond. However, the eye is subject to various changes and disabilities. Decrease in visual acuity is common to most older people, but most of those over 65 (more than 80 percent) are able to continue normal activities with the help of corrective lenses.

The accommodative power of the lens of the eye is at its peak at about age 10, and gradually decreases until about age 60. Little change in the lens is seen beyond that age. The first subtle changes in the eyes occur earlier for women than for men. Between the ages of 35 and 45, the lens becomes slightly yellow, the tissues thicken, and the area at the center becomes more dense. Less light reaches the retina. These structural changes may result in sensitivity to glare, changes in distance vision or depth perception, and astigmatism (an irregularity in the curvature of a lens, resulting in an indistinct or distorted image). Farsightedness (presbyopia) is a change occurring in middle age in which the lens of the eye loses its ability to focus. It is corrected by glasses (often bifocals or a second pair of reading glasses).

The second series of structural changes begins in the years between 55 and 65. They concern the retina and nervous system and result in changes in the size of the visual field as well as sensitivity to low lighting and to flickering lights. The eye takes on a more wrinkled appearance caused by the loss of elasticity in the skin of the eyelids. Tears are more likely to spill over.

The average 80-year-old woman needs at least three times as much light to see a task with the same clarity as she did at age 20. The tiny muscles that control pupil dilation become more sluggish in old age. An older person requires from six to eight times longer to adapt to changes in lighting levels (going from a dark theater to bright daylight, for example). Older people are also much more vulnerable to glare from shiny surfaces.

Starting at about age 70 there is a loss of color sensitivity that increases to a greater deficiency by age 90. The loss of discrimination occurs over the entire spectrum of colors but particularly in the range of cool colors, blue, green, and violet. Warmer colors, such as yellow, red, and orange, are generally easier to see.

These changes of vision are not related to diseases such as cataract, glaucoma, macular degeneration, and diabetic retinopathy. Females over age 65 constitute 45.6 percent of all people with severe visual impairment, and males over 65 constitute 24.1 percent.

There are three primary degrees of vision loss: legal blindness, severe impairment, and low vision.

Legal Blindness

- Defined as 20/200 vision (or less) in the better eye with the best correction.
- There are almost 500,000 legally blind Americans, over half of them elderly.
- 53 percent (265,950) are older people.
- One percent of the nation's elderly are legally blind.

Severe Visual Impairment

- Defined as the inability to see or to read ordinary newspaper print, even using glasses.

The Eye

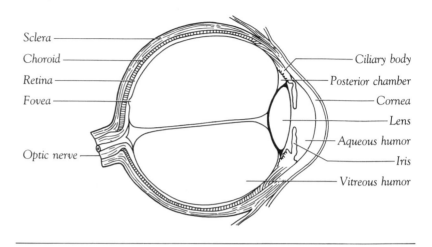

Sclera
Choroid
Retina
Fovea
Optic nerve

Ciliary body
Posterior chamber
Cornea
Lens
Aqueous humor
Iris
Vitreous humor

♦ Four percent (almost 1 million) noninstitutionalized older people have severe visual impairments. Of those in nursing homes, 26 percent are affected and 3 percent are unable to see at all.

Low Vision

♦ Defined as people who are partially sighted. Their imperfect vision cannot be improved by medical or surgical means.
♦ 1,709,000 Americans are partially sighted; 48 percent (824,000) are elderly.

Eye Disorders

Cataracts

The most common disability of the aging eye is cataracts. Anyone who lives long enough will show some evidence of cataract formation. The lens, which normally allows the eyes to focus on near or distant objects, becomes compressed and interferes with the passage of light to the retina. A person needs to hold objects closer to see them and requires brighter light to read. Cataract removal should be requested as soon as a woman notices she is handicapped in her ability to read, write, or sew. It is not necessary to wait until the cataract lens is "ripe" or "mature," as it was once thought.

Cataract surgery, removal of the affected lens, is safe and effective. Ninety-five to ninety-eight percent of surgery is successful in persons of all ages. When the lens is removed, glasses or contact lens are needed to serve as a substitute lens. A relatively new technique (1 percent of the operations performed today) is the intraocular lens implant. There is, however, a 15 to 25 percent complication rate with this surgery (secondary infection and clouding of the cornea). The implant can be removed if this occurs and the woman would be no worse off than if the conventional lens extraction was done first.

Diabetic Retinopathy

This condition is responsible for about half the blindness encountered in older persons. Early diagnosis and treatment can help stabilize the vision of a diabetic woman.

Senile Macular Degeneration

Senile macular degeneration (SMD) is a disease that can cause loss of vision when tiny blood vessels grow into and replace the macula (the small yellow dot in the center of the reddish retina that controls central vision in the retina). Central vision is essential to most tasks like reading, driving, or sewing. SMD is a function of aging and affects about ten million Americans over age fifty; serious vision loss occurs in 5 to 20 percent. This disease is more common in women with blue eyes and light coloring. It is rare among blacks. Of the 500,000 legally blind people in this country, over 100,000 are blind as a result of SMD. Hypertension, diabetes, vascular thrombosis, and central nervous system disorders aggrevate the development of this problem. Indirectly, alcoholism affects central vision.

A new laser procedure is proving very effective in treating this disease; it is expected to save as many as 13,000 people from blindness each year. Early warning symptoms are blurred vision, distortion, and blank spots in the central vision. Early detection is essential. For laser treatment to be effective, the person must be seen within the first few days after the onset of these symptoms. In fact ophthalmologists suggest that older people perform a simple test at home, each day:

- Pick out a straight line (a door frame or telephone pole).

- Cover one eye and see if the line still looks straight.
- Do the same with the other eye.
- If the line appears bent or distorted, of if a blank spot appears, see an eye doctor immediately.

The laser treatment is an outpatient therapy and is relatively comfortable. The eye is anesthetized and the laser beam applied. A patch is put on the eye for a few days. It takes several weeks for the results to be known.

The laser is already being used successfully in treating other eye disorders such as diabetic retinopathy, detached retina, and certain forms of glaucoma.

Glaucoma

Glaucoma, a serious disease of the eye, is excessively high pressure within the eyeball. It is caused by a buildup of a nutrient fluid that forms faster than it can be eliminated. The exact cause of the imbalance is not known, but heredity and farsightedness may be contributing factors. The increased pressure on the eye leads to irreparable damage to the optic nerve and total blindness. This disease is *not* intrinsically related to aging. The incidence of glaucoma rises from age 40 to 65 and levels off after that.

Chronic glaucoma is gradual in onset (usually between age 40 and 65) and is signaled by a loss of side vision. A woman may not be able to see passing cars on a highway or she may bump into things frequently. Warning signs are severe headache, nausea, blurred vision, tearing, dull eye pain, and the appearance of halos around light objects (stars and streetlights). Acute, congestive glaucoma may come on suddenly and run a short course. Nausea, vomiting, eye pain, and redness, along with cloudy vision, are signs of acute glaucoma. It requires immediate emergency medical attention. Pressure should be reduced within 24 hours. Although the damage wrought by glaucoma cannot be repaired, further losses can be prevented. There is no cure for glaucoma, but the disease can be managed with drugs and eyedrops, keeping the ocular pressure at a safe level. In severe cases delicate surgery can be performed.

The importance of early detection cannot be overemphasized, especially in women who have a family history of glaucoma or diabetes. Tonometry testing for glaucoma should be included in all regular eye examinations.

Since vision is one of our most important links to the outside world, visually impaired women suffer a serious communication problem. Not enough attention is paid to methods of preventing vision loss. Many women incorrectly believe that vision can be used up or worn out and unnecessarily begin to curtail their activities to "save their vision." Many limit their exercise because of limited vision. Although most competitive sports (such as tennis and baseball) require visual acuity, other exercises should be continued (walking, swimming) to maintain a healthy body and mind.

Compensating for Vision Losses

Treatment for low-vision victims is developing rapidly. Much can be done to compensate for losses.

In the Home

Since the three most frequent sites of accidents are bathrooms, bedsides, and entryways, better lighting in these areas is important. Fluorescent lights are not the answer for older people because they flicker, causing tearing and headaches. Low-watt bulbs should be replaced, especially where focused activities such as reading, grooming, or table games take place. In most homes a stronger bulb, a better placed lamp, and central lighting are sufficient. Simple improvements to lighting can considerably reduce the prevalence of visual disability.

- Smaller-paned windows with tinted glass and horizontal window coverings (so that light can be controlled) will help. The best visual environment would allow the individual to control her own lighting.

- Fluorescent tape can be put around electric outlets, light switches, keyholes, and door handles.

- Large-print instructions on medicine containers, or different-colored or textured papers to such bottles will alleviate some problems.

Equipment

- Talking books: There are 200,000 volumes available on a wide variety of topics. The tape recorder and tapes of recorded books are free from your local library. Even some professional journals are available on tape, at a modest cost.
- Electronic canes and seeing-eye doors.

- Attachments to glasses for close-up activities such as threading needles, reading, or playing cards.
- Telescopic aids for watching TV.
- Fixtures for reading or dialing the phone.
- Large-print newspapers and books.
- Closed-vision TV in which reading material placed before a TV camera is magnified up to ten times on the screen.
- Low-vision "talking" digital clocks and watches with raised numbers; playing cards; kitchen equipment and a wide variety of aids and appliances.
- Seeing-eye dogs.
- Radio stations that read the newspaper or provide dramatic performances.

Every night I go to bed early with one of my talking books. They are the difference for me between life and sanity.

Beatrice, age 84

Skin

Facial lines and wrinkled skin are devalued in American society. Old people don't have wrinkles, they have expression lines, which come from experience and attitude toward life. Wrinkles are what you remove with an iron. Everything natural ages: leather, wood, and wine. Polyester, of course, doesn't age.

Catherine, age 72

We'd all like to slow down our facial time clock. Women spend millions of dollars a year on cosmetics such as wrinkle creams, skin bleaches to fade "age spots," and oils to keep their skin looking youthful. A new temporary wrinkle-remover product, aimed at women in their forties and fifties, sold 600,000 bottles in its first five weeks on the market. Dermatologists and cosmetic companies are launching into new studies of skin structure and function to meet (or create) the demands of women consumers.

Skin has two main parts: the *dermis,* or underlying, supporting structure, and the *epidermis,* the top layer. Skin cells are constantly renewed as they divide and multiply. As new cells are formed they get pushed up to the outer surface only to dry up and be shed. This process of renewal seems to slow down with age. The skin becomes more fragile. It dries quickly and wounds easier; the wounds take longer to heal. Aging skin is easily damaged by hot water, wind, frigid weather, harsh products, and overexposure to the sun.

Each of us wants to look her best, and in our culture a tanned skin is thought to look not only healthy but attractive. We spend countless hours outdoors tanning our skin. Unfortunately, most of us don't realize that these long periods of exposure to the sun are the major reason our skin wrinkles prematurely. Ultraviolet rays from the sun cause long-term damage to the skin's supporting structure: the collagen, elastic fibers, and the vascular tissues. This damage may not be visible for years. It causes thickened, leathery-looking skin, as well as lines and wrinkles around the eyes, upper lip, neck, and hands. The outer layer of skin begins to thicken even after a mild sunburn.

Sun also results in those dark patches called "liver spots" or "senile freckles." These pigment changes take place with loss of pigment in some areas and increased pigmentation in other areas. There are products on the market that fade brown spots. Check their safety with your doctor. The most dangerous problem, however, is the estimated 300,000 cases of skin cancer a year as a result of long years of overexposure to the sun.

Avoid the sun if you can. It is helpful to wear a straw hat or sun visor to protect the upper portion of your face. The best protection is to use a high potency sunscreen when you must be in the bright sun. These absorb or scatter ultraviolet light. Apply the screen before putting on a moisturizer, so that the skin is well protected at all times and the tanning is gradual. Look for any popular brand name that contains PABA (para-aminobenzoic acid). Note on the container the SPF (sun protection factor). The higher the number the more protection the sunscreen will provide (the range is from 2 to 15). Apply sunscreen liberally, remembering that the nose, top of the ears, lower lip, upper back, and the area over the breastbone get the most radiation when you are standing or sitting in the sun. Lifeguards frequently use zonc oxide, an opaque ointment that is a well-known sun blocker.

Skin which is protected from the sun ages very slowly. We do need limited exposure to the sun, to be provided with vitamin D, which is necessary to maintain strong bones.

Dry Skin

Chronic states of malnutrition, vitamin deficiency, cause skin to age prematurely. Cosmetics should be removed before bedtime.

Dry skin, causing a mild to severe itching, is one of the uncomfortable aspects of aging skin. This is caused by a decrease in the number of functioning sweat glands, which secrete both sweat and oil. Dry skin is produced by the dry air in overheated or air-conditioned rooms and by irritating cleaning products. Avoid strong soaps. The University of Pennsylvania rated eighteen popular basic soaps for irritability (reported in the *Journal of the American Academy of Dermatology,* July 1979). Among the mildest were Dove, Dial, and Fels Naptha. The use of humidifiers and moisturizers and the avoidance of excessive washing help prevent dry skin.

Moisturizers

Dr. Albert Klingman, of the University of Pennsylvania Medical School, has recently opened a clinic for aging skin in Philadelphia. He feels that skin can be preserved by using moisturizers, which have more than a cosmetic effect. He advises women over forty to use moisturizers containing petrolatum, or pure petroleum jelly—such as Vaseline, Eucerin, Albolene, and Nivea Cream. Moisturizers should always be applied over slightly moist skin. Although moisturizers vary greatly in price, the most expensive product is not necessarily the best. Women should know that there is some controversy among dermatologists about how useful moisturizers are for preventing skin aging. Dr. Klingman's clinic is also experimenting with vitamin A acid (a prescription drug), which, applied in low doses, seems to affect skin structure and to speed up cell renewal. It is not yet available for general use.

You can aid your skin's need for moisture by drinking several glasses of water a day. It flushes through your body, eventually coming through the pores. If you're in a dry atmosphere, keep and use a small atomizer filled with water, and spray it on your exposed skin.

Wrinkles

One way to avoid wrinkles is to smile and laugh a lot. People who look unhappy or frown use many more facial muscles than those who laugh—a good reason to avoid unnecessary frowning or squinting! Spontaneous laughter induces blood circulation that nourishes the skin and reduces the tendency to wrinkle. Rapid weight loss causes wrinkles, as does being too thin. Fat helps the skin to stay smooth.

Wrinkles appear when our skin loses its elasticity. They appear in a very definite pattern, starting with the lines on our forehead. Next, crow's-feet appear around the eyes and with time they deepen and set. Wrinkles then go to the nose and move downward to the corners of the mouth. As we begin to age, folds and creases form on the eyelids and small vertical wrinkles appear above the upper lip. These are also caused by loss of teeth. Once wrinkles have set, they cannot be completely removed.

Some physicians (generally dermatologists and plastic surgeons) have begun recently to inject Zyderm, a solution of highly purified collagen protein, under the skin at the site of a wrinkle or scar. Zyderm fills in and smooths out the depressions to make them less noticeable. It seems to work best for age-related wrinkles around the nose and mouth. However, this treatment is temporary, and a touch-up will be required at least once a year. It is also expensive, $300 to $600 per treatment. Some women are allergic to animal collagen and should be tested first. For those women who feel unhappy or insecure with their less-than-youthful appearance, this may be a safe and effective way to eliminate minor wrinkles.

A new and very expensive moisture cream is advertised as an "age-zone controller." The product's ad shows a picture of a baby and claims that she can reach for this lotion when she gets older "to catch new lines before they start." Yet, are women supposed to have baby-smooth skin throughout their lives? The social pressure to maintain unwrinkled skin causes many older women to go to desperate extremes to keep the ageless skin of the baby ad.

Some of us feel that wrinkles can be beautiful.

I look forward to the time when we can merchandise a cosmetic line to make youth look older; a special crow's-foot pencil, the silver bleaches, the stick to make those delicious brown spots on the hands, eyeliner under the eyes for that sexy mature look. Let the young ones eat their hearts out!!

Tish Sommers, Founder of the Older Women's League

H*air*

> *When I was 49 my hair began to gray quite rapidly. The follow-ing year I began supplementing my diet with B-complex vitamins. One pleasant, possibly connected effect was that the graying stopped and some of the gray in my hair even went away.*
>
> Susan, age 57

Our hair, like our skin, is a visible sign of aging. Many healthy women have gray hair in their twenties or thirties. Other women maintain their natural hair coloring far into their seventies. However, for most of us as we age, our head and body hair grow grayer and thinner. The color of your hair and when it turns gray is primarily a family characteristic. If your mother or father grayed prematurely, you are likely to do so. Changes in hair color are also affected by our general health and nutrition. One theory suggests that a marked vitamin D deficiency may hasten the graying process and that vitamin D supplements may slow graying.

With today's cosmetic technology, it is possible to dye your hair any color you choose. It is estimated that some 33 million American women color their hair. There is new evidence that this process involves risk, as some hair dyes contain carcinogens (can-cer-causing chemicals), while other dyes and rinses seem to be relatively harmless. Hair dyes that are carcinogenic are absorbed through the scalp and enter the bloodstream. One study carried out by scientists at New York University found that women over 50 who have used hair dye for ten or more years *may* face an increased risk of breast cancer.

In 1978 the U.S. Food and Drug Administration pro-posed a regulation requiring that certain hair dyes—those contain-ing 4 MMPD or 4 EMPD—include a label warning that they contain an ingredient that has been determined to cause cancer in laboratory animals. Since the FDA announcement, many manu-facturers have altered the composition of their dyes so as to avoid using possible carcinogens. Look at labels to find out what the dyes are made of before you buy a product.

Recommendations for women who use hair dye:

- Use no more than necessary (retouch only at five- or six-week intervals). Leave the dye on the hair no longer than indicated.
- Use reddish or golden blond tones (darker shades contain more coal-tar chemical).
- Rinse your scalp thoroughly with water after using the dye.
- Consider *not* dyeing your hair.

I began to use a rinse in my hair at the first sign of gray. The summer sun, plus saltwater swimming, turned me into a rather garish-looking reddish blonde. One of my colleagues gently prodded me to let my hair return to its natural color again. Now I think I look better than ever—and carry my curly gray hair like a banner of proud aging.

Janet, age 60

Some women, as they age, notice excessive growths of hair on their face, which is a natural age change caused by hormonal shifts. Some cut or shave it, and this does not make hair grow in thicker or more rapidly, as is commonly thought. Others dye the excess hair so that it will be less noticeable. Those with extreme amounts have it removed by electrolysis. If women are concerned about having lost noticeable amounts of hair on their head, they can purchase a natural-looking wig.

Women who suffer from dandruff or seborrheic dermatitis (a scaling disorder at the scalp) will find medicated shampoos helpful in controlling, although not curing, the problem. With these conditions the skin is replacing itself more rapidly than normal, and excess cells are cast off. Ask your physician to prescribe a shampoo with 2.5 percent selenium sulfide, or use an over-the-counter shampoo containing zinc purithion (such as Head and Shoulders), salicylic acid and sulfur (such as Sebulex), tar shampoos (like Zetar), or a regular shampoo containing detergents (surfactants). For best results these should be used every other day.

Dental Health and Dental Problems

The American Dental Association recognizes that poor oral health has a detrimental impact on one's overall health, and contrary to some widely held myths, that poor oral health is not an inevitable characteristic of aging. Optimum oral health can and should be enjoyed for a lifetime. To achieve this goal, regular personal and professional care is required. Preventive dentistry can benefit all age groups, not simply the young.

1981 White House Conference on Aging

A majority of women face dental problems in their later years. In a recent survey, dental problems were second only to depression as the major health concern for women over 40. Despite the fact that chronic dental problems increase with age, more than half the American population over age 65 has either not seen a dentist in the last five years or has never seen a dentist.

Without proper dental care, we will lose our teeth, not from cavities but from gum disease, which causes 90 percent of tooth loss after age 40. For an older woman this creates possible changes in facial appearance, chewing efficiency, speech performance, body image, and, as a result of these, perhaps social acceptance.

Periodontal Disease

Periodontal disease or pyorrhea (gum decay and receding gums) and gingivitis (inflammation of the membrane that surrounds the tooth) are the greatest source of tooth loss in women over 40. Periodontal disease is caused by an accumulation of bacteria deposits, called plaque, under the gum line and along the roots of the teeth. This causes inflammation and bleeding of the gums, which spreads to the bones holding the teeth in place. When the gums, the support system of the teeth, are weakened, the teeth loosen and begin to fall out. A rare form of this disease is periodontosis, which causes the alveolar bone to dissolve and teeth to fall out. It may be corrected; it has the same cause as osteoporosis, the thinning of bone tissue from lack of calcium (see Chapter 11).

Periodontal disease may be prevented by having your dentist periodically remove the plaque. If this is not removed it hardens into calculus, which irritates the gums. Periodontal disease is the primary cause of bad breath in adults. To prevent periodontal disease, we should increase our calcium intake, floss and brush frequently, and rinse our mouths with fluoride after brushing. Emotional stress, oral contraceptives, and smoking are implicated in gum disease; smokers have twice the risk of gum disease as nonsmokers.

Treatment

If periodontal disease is untreated, the membrane around the tooth will be destroyed and the tooth loosened. Some treatment methods include

- A deep scaling or scraping of the pockets of infection.
- The Keyes technique (after Paul Keyes of the National Institute of Dental Research), which involves nonsurgical cleaning of the teeth and gums every two to four months by a dentist. Daily home care includes use of a solution of baking soda, hydrogen peroxide, and salt. The patient is taught to rub an antibacterial paste (a paste of baking soda and peroxide) into the gums around each tooth, brush thoroughly, and use a water irrigating device (such as a water pick) to wash out the infected gums with a salt solution.
- Surgery may be necessary to remove all evidence of infection.

Dentures

Persons without any natural teeth make up 11 percent of the American population, 23 percent of those are ages 45 to 64 and 50 percent are over age 65. These people either have or need dentures. If you need dentures, your dentist should be able to save a few teeth as an anchor. If the residual ridge bone of the mouth is affected by osteoporosis, dental success will be in question. Careful measurements and impressions must be made to assure a good-fitting denture.

New experimental techniques include the use of dental implants, metal pieces implanted into the jawbone, to which false teeth can be anchored. These can be expected to last five years and the risk of complications seems low.

Many women who need dentures cannot afford them. The average set of dentures costs between $600 and $2,000. Medicare, unfortunately, does not cover dental work. In Canada and four states (Maine, Colorado, Arizona, and Oregon) dental technicians, called denturists, are able to work directly, usually under a dentist's supervision, with denture patients. This lowers the average cost of dentures to $250 to $350.

Wearers of full dentures should have them examined by their dentist once a year, for possible refitting or replacement. Because supportive tissues change, dentures need to be relined or replaced about every five years.

Oral Cancer

Although we don't yet know the causes of oral cancer, scientists have identified several significant factors: poor oral hygiene and chronic irritations such as those caused by jagged teeth, projecting fillings, and ill-fitting dentures. Smoking causes four times more deaths from mouth cancer than among nonsmokers. Heavy alcohol use is also implicated.

The incidence of tumors in the mouth increases with age. Twenty-six thousand cases of oral cancer are found annually, causing 9,000 deaths; 90 percent of them occur in individuals over the age of 45, with the average age of occurrence at 60. This problem is found three times more frequently in men than in women. Tumors are found more frequently in people who smoke or drink heavily than in those who do not.

Early stages of oral cancer can usually be detected by a physician or dentist. Malignant tumors are most often found on the side of the tongue and the floor of the mouth. Since oral cancers are relatively easy to detect in the early, curable stages, it's important to request that your dentist check these areas for any suspicious lumps, as well as checking the palate, cheek, lips, throat, and neck during your annual or semi-annual visit. Any sore in the mouth that does not disappear in two weeks should be checked immediately.

Cost of Dental Care

Good dental care, which includes frequent visits to the dentist, is prohibitively expensive for large numbers of older women. Medicare and most private insurance companies do not pay for dental services. Yearly oral screenings are required, however, for Medicare nursing home patients. Medicaid, in thirty-seven out of fifty plans, does provide dental services for low-income adults. Six of these plans offer emergency care only.

Dental benefit plans are a part of the insurance package offered to many employees. In the last few years the auto industry and companies such as AT&T and Eastman Kodak have extended this benefit to their retirees.

Preventive Dental Care

Improved methods of preventive dental care are helping many of us retain our natural teeth throughout our life. These include

- Choosing a dentist who believes in preventive care and in taking all appropriate measures to save your own teeth.
- Visiting your dentist twice a year if tartar frequently forms on your teeth.
- Increasing vitamin C for healthy tissues (especially if you notice any bleeding in your gums).
- Purchasing a toothbrush with soft, flat, multi-row bristles. A toothbrush should be replaced at least every three months.
- Brushing not only your teeth but the roof of your mouth and tongue This is best done before bedtime.
- Brushing with short, circular strokes (not up and down), hitting both sides of each tooth.
- Flossing your teeth daily with unwaxed floss.
- Using a water pik. Especially useful for those with partial or complete dentures.
- Rinsing your mouth. If you notice any bleeding, rinse your mouth with two solutions (1 teaspoon salt to a glass of water followed by a solution of peroxide and hot water, half and half) several times a day.
- Having X-rays as seldom as possible; a full set once every two years is suggested, with single X-rays of individual teeth only as necessary for diagnosis.
- Eliminating or reducing sugar, snacks, and soft, sticky foods from your diet. Increase fresh fruits and vegetables (especially celery, carrots, and apples, which clean your teeth as you chew).

A well-balanced diet, an adequate water intake, and the chewing of firm solids helps all of us, whatever our age, to maintain good dental health.

Resources: Hearing Loss

Organizations

The American Speech, Language, Hearing Association
10801 Rockville Pike
Rockville, MD 20852
Information about speech and hearing centers in your area; information on hearing loss.

Bell Telephone Company
800-342-4181
For hard-of-hearing persons; information on special Bell phone equipment for the hearing impaired.

Bureau of Consumer Protection
Federal Trade Commission
Washington, DC
September 1978 final report on the hearing aid industry.

The New York League for the Hard of Hearing
71 West 23rd St.
New York City, NY 10010
Information about speech and hearing centers near you; information on hearing loss.

Self-Help for the Hard of Hearing (Shhh)
P.O. Box 34889
Bethesda, MD 20033

Resources: Vision

Publications

Hiatt, Lorraine. "Architecture for the Aged: Design for Living." *Inland Architect*, 1978.

Hiatt, L., M. Hagger, et al., eds. *Resource Book on Vision and Aging.* New York: American Foundation for the Blind, 1980.

Report of the Mini-Conference on Vision and Aging, 1981 White House Conference on Aging.

Organizations

Affiliated Leadership League of and for the Blind of America
879 Park Ave.
Baltimore, MD 21201

Committee on Vision
National Academy of Sciences
2101 Constitution Ave., N.W.
Washington, DC 20001

National Accreditation Council for Serving the Blind and Visually Handicapped
79 Madison Ave., New York, NY 11016

American Foundation for the Blind
Unit on Aging
15 W. 16th St.
New York, NY 10011
Director: L. Hiatt
Will respond to all requests for information on visual losses. Updated list and description of nationwide low-vision centers; series of self-help manuals to assist women with sensory losses to continue to function independently; catalogues of low-vision aids.

*R*esources: *Dental Health*

Publications

Denholtz, Melvin. *How to Save Your Teeth and Your Money.* New York: Van Nostrand Reinhold, 1977.

Goldberg, Hyman. *Your Mouth Is Your Business: the Dentists' Guide to Better Health.* New York: Appleton-Century-Crofts, 1980.

McGuire, Thomas. *The Tooth Trip.* New York: Random House, 1972.

Bettye Lane

Chapter Fourteen

Women and Addiction

Alcoholism

I am an alcoholic, now fortunate enough to be able to put the word recovered before the alcoholic. I can never again take even one drink. I have found this to be a very small price to pay for being able to sleep a natural, healthy sleep again. . . . I guess it all began after my divorce. Worries, insecurities, a total loss of self-confidence, financial hardships, and the responsibility of raising my son alone . . . brought sleepless nights and troubled days. . . . I lost all ability to sleep without alcohol. I would wake during the night, reach for the bottle, and go to sleep. This evolved into a round-the-clock episode of drinking-sleeping-waking-drinking and continued for days on end, and I lost all concept of time.

I hid my drinking, hiding bottles in Christmas wrapping and in many places, hiding some so well that I didn't find them until years later. I finally sought the help of three psychiatrists, two of whom were fully aware of the amount and the extent of my drinking. . . . None of them ever told me I was an alcoholic.

One night I telephoned an old friend who realized I needed help and called Alcoholics Anonymous. They came to my house and found me in an alcoholic stupor at the bottom of a flight of stairs. They took me to a detoxification unit. I soon learned that *all of the other people in this center were there with the same problem. I found hands outstretched in friendship . . . through a combination of lectures, group therapy, psychodrama and free time to spend talking with others. I was able to sleep trouble-free and wake up clearheaded and alert.*

I know full well today, seven years later, that I can handle any of life's problems. My son, as well as my friends, have gained a new respect for me. . . . The message I want to share with other women is to seek help from professionals who are specifically trained in dealing with alcoholism.

Linda, age 52

Alcoholism is on the rise among midlife and older women. The breakup of marriages and changing lifestyles and expectations, as women try to be supermom, superwife, super-employee, and superhomemaker all at the same time, have added stress to our lives, and many women turn to alcohol to help ease the strain. Alcoholism is a disease resulting from the excessive and compulsive intake of alcohol and/or a biological intolerance for alcohol. It is the third largest health problem in the United States. The National Institute of Alcohol Abuse and Alcoholism estimates that there are seven million alcoholics in the United States. About half of these are women, primarily aged 35 to 64. About two-thirds of older alcoholics became addicted before age 50, and about one-third became alcoholics later. Women tend to become alcoholics later in life as their children leave home and the realities of old age begin to surface.

The American Medical Association defines alcoholism as "an illness characterized by preoccupation with alcohol and loss of control over its consumption; a type of drug dependence which interferes seriously with the patient's total health and adaptation to their environment." There are three behaviors associated with drinking: alcohol abuse, which is the social use of alcohol for occasionally getting drunk; problem drinking, which indicates a growing dependency on alcohol; and alcoholism, which is the compulsion to drink.

It has been twenty years since the American Medical Society recognized alcoholism as a disease. Yet today most people still cling to the nineteenth-century notion that alcoholism is a problem of self-will and self-discipline and a moral issue. Alcoholism is a family disease. Many of us have had to deal with it as the spouse, parent, child, friend, employer, or employee of an alcoholic. For every one of the millions of alcoholics in this country, it is estimated that another four persons are affected by their behavior. This means that at least forty million of us share alcohol problems secondhand and have a personal stake in helping a loved one cope with life in a more healthy manner.

For women alcoholics, family support is often missing. Although nine out of ten women stay married to their alcoholic husbands, nine out of ten men leave their alcoholic wives. In some families the problem is either overlooked or hidden. Instead of encouragement and support of family members, a conspiracy of silence exists. Compounding the problem is the failure of doctors to recognize alcoholism among their female patients.

> I never took a drink until my late twenties. At first I limited myself to two drinks per party. After my divorce I began taking a drink after work, at home, alone. I became very secretive about my drinking. I would make drinks for my guests and have an extra shot in the kitchen. It's surprising how long you can keep it all hidden.
>
> Cindy, age 42

> I think the scariest thing about the female alcoholic is the family silence. My 60-year-old aunt recently died from acute alcoholism. My mother and her sister knew for years that she was drinking too much. But they kept up this conspiracy of silence, refusing to confront or help her.
>
> Maria, age 35

A Profile of the Older Woman Alcoholic

According to Alcoholics Anonymous (AA), 40 percent of their female clients are housewives, 20 percent are executives, 20 percent are sales or clerical workers, 10 percent are semiskilled workers, and 10 percent are otherwise employed. The number of women seeking help through AA has increased 34 percent in the last three years.

Although some women have used alcohol excessively throughout their lives, women are more likely than men to begin drinking at a later age. They are usually able to point to a specific crisis time in their lives when they began to drink heavily: death of a spouse, divorce, children leaving home, deteriorating health, retirement. These events tend to precipitate feelings of uselessness, and women traditionally have not had strong support as such events occur. Loneliness and depression are two prominent traits of alcoholic women. Women under age 65 are at high risk of alcoholism if they have alcoholism in their family history; are depressed or feel inadequate; have a personal background characterized by disruption and deprivation; are divorced, separated, or widowed (the highest incidence of female alcoholism is among widows). Employed women are more likely to be alcoholic than are housewives. There seems to be a higher incidence of alcoholism among lesbians, perhaps because of the use of gay bars as a place to meet and the social isolation of being gay in a straight world.

> *Problems of women alcoholics reflect the problems of women in general. They have terribly low self-esteem. They're not living their lives for themselves. They are either someone's wife, someone's mother, someone's employee. It's hard for them to see themselves as people—capable, confident people.*
>
> Jeanne Kilpatrick, founder of Women for Sobriety

Identifying Alcoholism

> *For years I thought, "How could I, a nice woman running a house, having raised four sons, holding a part-time job, be an alcoholic?" I drank privately—as I was preparing dinner, then a drink with my husband when he came home, then wine with dinner. I would usually fall asleep right after supper. My husband thought I was just tired from my job. I couldn't understand why I was drinking just a little more each day.*
>
> LizAnne, age 60

If you can answer yes to any of the following questions, alcohol is probably harming your life in some major way and you should consider seeking help:

- Has someone close to you ever told you that they were worried about your drinking?
- If you are having troubles, do you often take a drink to feel better?
- Do you sometimes miss work or find you can't do housework because of your drinking or a hangover?
- Have you ever had problems with the police because of your drinking?
- Have you ever required medical attention as a result of drinking?

♦ Have you ever forgotten what happened while you were drinking?

♦ Have you often broken the promises you have made to yourself about drinking less or not drinking at all?

Symptoms of alcoholism include an increased pulse rate, a high blood sugar level, tremors, insomnia, an early-morning cough, vomiting, heartburn, and tenseness. A spouse or health professional should watch for unexplained bruises or fractures; newly developed problems relating to family, friends, neighbors; depression; frequent, though minor, car or bodily accidents; unexplained absences from work; changes in eating and sleeping habits; inappropriate behavior while drinking; the smell of alcohol on the breath. Early detection is an important factor in helping older women to have a favorable recovery.

It is not the quality or quantity of alcohol consumed that is crucial, but its effects on the individual woman. Women seem to have a lowered tolerance for alcohol; smaller amounts of alcohol may adversely affect us. As we age, our bodies contain less water, leaving less to dilute the alcohol we consume. And because women may sometimes wait longer than men in seeking help (if they are able to deny or hide the problem), the physical damage may be more extensive. With an alcohol content of 15 percent (about six to eight cocktails) in the blood, most women are unable to speak clearly, to walk with coordination, or to control their emotions. It could take up to ten hours for a women intoxicated at this level to become sober. A 40 percent alcohol content can cause a loss of consciousness and even death.

Alcohol tends to shorten our life span and results in higher death rates from cardiovascular disease, pneumonia, and cirrhosis of the liver. Cirrhosis of the liver, an inflammatory disease that hardens the liver so blood cannot pass through it, occurs when the liver enzyme responsible for the breakdown of alcohol is strained by overdrinking. Cancer of the liver and of the larynx have been connected with heavy drinking. Death rates for heavy drinkers are up to four times higher than for nondrinkers.

Alcohol also affects the pituitary gland, which produces hormones. Alcoholism leaves many men impotent or sterile. No studies have been conducted yet to determine the effects heavy drinking has on the sexual functioning of older women. Contrary to the popular belief that alcohol is a stimulent, it actually depresses the nervous system. This can aggravate anxiety; even one drink can make some women hostile and aggressive.

Alcoholism is often accompanied by malnutrition, which can cause memory loss, confusion, and forgetfulness—symptoms often mistakenly diagnosed as senility. The body becomes deficient in minerals like magnesium. This affects nerve function, which may account for a person's lack of emotional control when drunk. Lack of magnesium also affects muscle control, so that it takes longer for the body to react to signals from the brain. The brain itself is believed to age faster with alcohol. CAT scan X-rays show that the brains of heavy drinkers have actually shrunk. Alcoholism is the second most common cause for admission into psychiatric hospitals for older women.

Alcohol is also a major cause of death on the highways. The alcoholic is thus not only a danger to herself but, potentially, to society as well.

Helping the Older Alcoholic Woman

Since the cause of alcoholism in women over 40 is often different from that for men in the same age group, treatment programs addressing the unique needs of women are essential. It is important to remember that although alcoholism is recognizable and treatable, it is generally considered *not* curable, that is, the woman can never return to social drinking. "Controlled drinking" is generally too risky a goal for most women. Abstinence is the usual goal of treatment and therapy. Success rates for women alcoholics are statistically higher than for men, especially when women are helped to feel a sense of productivity and identification with their peer group through continuing support and therapy groups.

In all alcoholism treatment programs, detoxification—removing all alcohol from the system—is the first step. For older persons, this can take twice as long as for younger alcoholics, since recovery from all diseases is slower as we age. Older women often are not treated until they are in an acute stage when they are likely to be suffering also from malnutrition, weight loss, and multiple physical impairments.

The second phase of rehabilitation includes inpatient therapy daily in a hospital. Peer counseling, individual and group therapy, behavior modification techniques, psychodrama and role playing are useful tools for recovery. Daily exercise, such as brisk walking or jogging, is encouraged. Consciousness-raising groups within treatment programs can help women evaluate their role in society. Women are helped to find new ways to express their anger and control their lives. Many need help to change their life situations, not just to cope with their present environment.

> *I think it's important for drinking women to know the despair I once felt; that once I couldn't envision a life without a drink and didn't want to quit. Today, six years later, with the help of AA, I am living a richer, fuller life without alcohol. I've left a very unsatisfying marriage, returned to school, and am devoting my life to counseling other women alcoholics.*
>
> Bobbie, age 42

Most rehabilitation programs encourage women to develop career skills so that they can become self-supporting and social skills so that they can improve and increase their social network.

A major factor in a woman's recovery is the attitude of those closest to her. It is essential for the spouse, a close friend, or a family member who has shared the destructive and dysfunctional aspects of the alcoholic to become involved in the treatment program. Family and close friends are often included in counseling sessions. Since single alcoholic mothers with sole responsibilities for their children often avoid treatment, some rehabilitation programs have begun to encourage both mother and child to live in the center, each receiving the help they need.

An outpatient day program may be the final step in a recovery program. Many health insurance policies cover alcoholism treatment. Treatment is reimbursable under Medicare and Medicaid.

Treatment Programs

> *Older alcohol abusers have received little systematic attention in Federally sponsored alcohol prevention and treatment programs. . . . When older alcoholics do seek professional assistance, often their alcoholic problems remain unattended.*
>
> *Innovative strategies to identify those elderly experiencing difficulties in using alcohol are particularly necessary. Whenever possible, provisions should be made to provide alcohol treatment services in nontraditional settings because older persons are less*

likely to seek services in centers populated by young alcohol abusers.

Mini Conference on Aging and Alcoholism, 1981 White House Conference on Aging

Alcoholics Anonymous is the oldest, best-known, and most effective alcohol treatment program. It was established over forty-five years ago. Its agenda has twelve steps. At large-group meetings fifty to one hundred members admit to being alcoholics, discuss their common experiences, and support each other in breaking destructive drinking patterns. Members also participate in nondenominational prayer, asking God to help them to refrain from alcohol—one day at a time. Basic to the treatment is the AA model of support and discussion.

I was really afraid to attend the local AA meeting . . . I guess I "bought into" the myth that alcoholics, especially women, were people I wouldn't associate with in my regular life. Well, that myth was shattered when I attended my first meeting and found intelligent, well-dressed women cutting across all social lines, including a social worker, college professor, housewives of all ages, nurse, beautician. It's now much easier to admit I have a problem with drinking—and even that first step, I know, puts me on the road to recovery.

Angela, age 58

Al-Anon and Alateen are companion programs within AA. Both reach out to and involve the family and friends of alcoholics, helping them cope with the secondhand effects of alcoholism in their lives. Alateen aids teenagers who live with an alcoholic family member, helping them cope with alcohol-related difficulties at home; Alanon is for spouses or other adult family members. Members of each group are reassured that they have a right to receive help, whether or not their alcoholic family member is actively involved in a treatment program. Here spouses of alcoholics can share fears and feelings of guilt. Common concerns often include financial insecurity (alcohol is an expensive habit) and the possibility of institutionalization for their mate.

Women for Sobriety (WFS) is the only national organization that works solely with alcoholic women. Dr. Jeanne Kilpatrick, a sociologist and an alcoholic for twenty-seven years, developed this self-help program that speaks more directly to women than does AA. WFS differs primarily from AA in its philosophical premise that the alcoholic woman alone is totally responsible for rebuilding her life through positive action. (AA believes that we are all powerless in the face of alcohol and need to seek God's continual help to control it.) Over 8,000 WFS women in the United States and five other countries meet weekly in small groups of six to eight women, led by a woman moderator who is a recovered alcoholic. These all-female sessions are usually a comfortable environment for women to air their feelings and concerns. The goal is to help members develop a sense of self-esteem and a more positive attitude toward life. One of the tenets of WFS is "Life can be ordinary or it can be great." Women are encouraged to be assertive, resourceful, and self-confident.

The stigma against alcoholic women (even by alcoholic men) makes seeking treatment more difficult, and some traditional alcoholism programs have developed women-only treatments. When Joan Kennedy joined AA she became aware that women made more progress at meetings when men weren't around. She formed an AA chapter in Boston for women only. In Brunswick House, one of the largest private facilities for treating alcoholism in New York State, one-third of the beds are occupied by women. Here women are taught how not to rely on drinking: how to live in a community, the basics of nutrition, exercise, and recreational skills. The average length of stay is twenty-eight days, followed by an 11-week after-care program.

There are also programs geared specifically to older alcoholics, both male and female. The Helping Hands program in Long Beach, Calif., is a continuing care support group open without charge to alcholics over age 55. A group of fourteen to twenty-four people, from age 55 to the late eighties meets twice a week. Using a mixture of AA and WFS techniques, the members discuss their common alcoholism and age-related problems. Treatment is focused on replanning lifestyles, setting new goals, and learning new ways to achieve those goals.

The Queen Nursing Home and Treatment Center in Minneapolis admits only older people with drinking problems.

They have found that the confrontational techniques used with younger alcoholic patients aren't always effective with older alcoholics. Here, antidepressant medication and group socialization are also used, as well as family counseling and AA-type support groups.

If you can stop drinking completely for a week, without feeling a craving for liquor and withdrawal symptoms such as nervousness and irritability, you probably don't have a severe drinking problem. In fact, alcohol in moderation has its place in society. The use of small amounts of beer and wine has been found to enhance the lives of older people, increasing their desire for food and decreasing their anxiety. Wine, with its low alcohol content, contains many vitamins and minerals and produces a mild, sedative effect that can relieve aches and pains and aid sleep. Red wines help lower cholesterol levels, control high blood pressure, regulate the heartbeat, and enlarge blood vessels in angina patients. A glass or two of wine offered in the evening in nursing homes seems to foster congenial interpersonal communications and often leads to more positive patterns of behavior.

Nevertheless, current consumption of alcohol and alcohol abuse is rising rapidly. With people living longer, alcoholism can be expected to increase among the aging population. We need to tackle the underlying problems that lead to problem drinking and encourage society to enlarge and maintain treatment programs for alcoholics and education programs for young and old to increase awareness of the causes, symptoms, and treatments of this devastating disease.

Drug Use and Abuse

Mary is one who didn't believe drugs were her problem. . . . She dresses expensively, furs complementing her silver-gray hair . . . at 41 she's been addicted more than 15 years. Her doctor prescribed diet pills when she was 15. Later she was in a traffic accident and another doctor gave her an open prescription for Codeine and Dalmane for neck pain.

The *Los Angeles Times*, 26 February 1982

Although this country is concerned about its 500,000 heroin addicts, there are ten times more women addicted to alcohol and legal drugs than there are heroin addicts. Women in our society tend to be drug-dependent, but they often don't perceive their prescription drug abuse as a problem. Rather they see it as a respectable, legitimate adjunct to their lives.

One out of three women under 30 is given a prescription for a mood-altering drug every year. The number jumps to 75 percent for women over 65. Combined with alcohol and other medications (over-the-counter and prescription) that are frequently given to older women, these drugs often have devastating effects.

- The peak age of medication use for all people is 35 to 65.
- Women constitute 58 percent of those who visit doctors, but they receive 73 percent of prescriptions written.
- Elderly women use 2.65 times more legal medication than elderly men.
- Elderly women who live alone (the majority do) use prescription drugs more heavily than other elderly women.
- Six out of every ten persons who end up in a hospital emergency room with prescription-drug problems are women.
- Those who are 70 to 80 experience twice as many adverse drug reactions as those who are 40 to 50.
- The mean number of prescription drugs administered to those 65 and older annually, is 10.7 per person.
- Two-thirds of all tranquilizers are prescribed for women. Often menopause is depicted as an affliction rather than a process, and tranquilizers and sleeping pills are recommended for normal symptoms.
- Drug companies spend up to $7,000 in advertising for each of the country's 200,000 practicing physicians.
- The bulk of TV advertising for over-the-counter drugs is seen during daytime hours, when the audience is primarily women over 40.

Drugs have been used since ancient times to alter moods and relieve pain. Only recently have scientists realized that the effects of drugs on our bodies change as we grow older. After 60 we run a greater risk of harmful drug effects. Our bodies are less able to absorb, distribute, and eliminate drugs as we grow older. Because the percentage of fat tissue increases as the percentages of water and lean tissue (mainly muscle) decrease, the length of time a drug stays in our body, how it acts, and how it is absorbed and eliminated change. Drugs tend to accumulate in the body because of these changes, as well as because kidney and liver organs (responsible for breaking down and removing drugs from the body) function less efficiently. Consequently drug dosage levels need to be lower for older people.

The issue of drug abuse for women is not drug-specific. It is important to look at the factors that lead women to overmedicate themselves.

Mood-Modifying Drugs

Mood-modifying or psychotherapeutic drugs can be classified as tranquilizers, antidepressants, stimulants, sedatives, and hypnotics. Their use may reduce a patient's symptoms, but they do not treat the underlying cause of the symptoms (as, for instance, antibiotic drugs do). Women consume a great many mood-modifying drugs. In 1978, 36 million women used tranquilizers (mainly Valium and Librium), 16 million women used sedatives (sleeping pills), and 12 million women used stimulants (primarily diet pills).

One might expect that psychiatrists, who are trained in psychopharmacology, write most of the mood-modifying prescriptions. Unfortunately, 80 percent of such prescriptions are written by internists, general practitioners, and obstetrician/gynecologists, who are not trained in diagnosing emotional disorders.

Phyllis Chesler notes that

Women have fewer alternatives as they grow older (having little access to direct political or economic power). They are reacting to the beginning signals of their sexual and maternal expendability. Hospitals provide them with warning therapy (via pills and shock treatment) to make as little protest about this state of affairs as possible.

Many women in their middle years have spent much of their time relying on someone else's time schedule: spouse, children, parents. The boredom and loneliness they begin to feel is often translated into a physical problem, such as headache, backache, digestive problems, and so on, which brings them into the doctor's office. Too often they are given medication to help them cope instead of the help they need in examining the underlying cause of their physical problem. These medications often produce an even greater sense of depression as older women feel that chemicals are being used to keep them down. In nursing homes,

Overdrugged

A study done at the University of Kentucky found that sixty-seven people aged 60 to 90 had been prescribed 221 different drugs for 125 different medical conditions. In a local hospital an 84-year-old woman was recently admitted for depression. A geriatrician asked her husband to bring in all her medications so that he could determine her medical history. Eighty-two prescription medicines were found in her medicine closet, purchased over ten years, prescribed by the twenty or so physcans she had visited in her search for good health.

Older women are often reluctant to ask their doctors about their medications. They feel intimidated by the doctor's lack of time, interest, or availability. If you use two or more physicians or pharmacists, it is essential to ask that they review your current medications before prescribing new ones. This should include vitamins, laxatives, aspirin, and home remedies. Tell your doctor about any drug reactions you've experienced. The incidence of adverse reactions to drugs is greater in older women than in older men.

To help you keep track of your drug intake, write down the name of each drug prescribed, its purpose, the hour and length of time it should be taken, and common side effects. Drug side effects are frequently mistaken for a new problem, for which yet another prescription may be written. Ask whether certain foods or alcohol can be taken with the drug and if the drug should be taken before or after meals.

If you have a complicated medication schedule you might want to set up your daily doses in an egg container or paper cups. If your vision is poor, your pharmacist can provide large-print labels upon request. Today's child-proof containers are difficult for arthritic hands, ask for regular ones. Above all, don't exchange medicines with a friend, even though your symptoms may be similar. Throw away all old medications.

Alcohol and Drugs: Deadly Combination

Betty Ford's frank admission of her own alcohol and drug dependencies exposed a problem common to many women her age. The largest group of accidental or deliberate suicide victims related to misuse of drugs and alcohol is mature women. At least half of the most commonly used drugs can interact negatively with even one alcoholic drink, causing a range of results from sleeplessness to death. The combination of alcohol and sleeping pills (usually not toxic on their own) may cause death in an older person.

One tablet of Valium plus a can of beer is equivalent, in some women, to twelve tranquilizers. Women who drink and then take a birth-control pill and/or an estrogen pill for menopausal complaints put their liver on "overload." If they smoke, the danger increases.

Commonly Used Drugs

Digitalis is prescribed for heart problems. It is a potent source of an adverse drug reaction when it is combined with a diuretic (which reduces water retention). Reports show that doses of digitalis can be reduced for older patients and prescribed for a shorter period of time than is commonly done. In larger doses it can cause fatigue, loss of appetite, vision problems, nausea, and psychological disturbances.

Antihypertensive drugs and diuretics may do more harm than good in older people. Careful regulation is needed, since possible side effects such as sudden low blood pressure, fainting, and abnormally low potassium levels can be dangerous. Reserpine, a drug used to treat hypertension, may be a cause of depression and stomach disturbances.

Sedatives and tranquilizers such as Valium (diazepam) and Librium (chlordiazepoxide) account for half the tranquilizers sold in the United States. In 1978 enough Valium was sold to provide 200 tablets for each American man, woman, and child. In 1980, the most frequently prescribed drug was Valium. Of the 38 million people who received prescriptions, 68 percent were women. Women who take a lot of Valium don't get high on it, but they have to continue to take it just to feel normal. It's easy to get hooked on such a widely prescribed, available, and medically and socially acceptable drug. The only clue that something is wrong may be recurring backaches, migraine headaches, or insomnia. Women may suffer memory loss or lack of appetite.

Withdrawal from Valium can produce the same symptoms it is supposed to control: insomnia, nervousness, trembling, poor appetite, numbness, faintness, weakness, irritability, nausea, lack of energy, headache, and muscle cramps. Sensitivity to tranquilizers increases with age. Older women are more likely than younger women to suffer their unwanted effects. If you need to take a tranquilizer, don't take it for more than three or four weeks.

My doctor prescribed Valium five years ago for a stressful situation in my life. I never took more than was prescribed, and sometimes took none at all. On a recent difficult trip I took three or four a day and found I was tense and couldn't sleep at night. I was ready to go to a psychiatrist but first decided to quit the Valium. I really suffered withdrawal symptoms for over a week—muscle tension, night and day sweats, rapidly beating heart, etc. Valium is destructive. No one should say, "Who me? I just take it once in a while."

Jeanne, age 56

Generic versus Brand-Name Drugs

Generic drugs are identified by their chemical name, not the manufacturer's brand name. Generic drugs are generally less expensive and are equally effective. Ask the physician who prescribes your drugs to sign the "generic" line when writing out a prescription for you. This authorizes your pharmacist to substitute a lower-priced generic drug equivalent if one is available.

Caffeine

Caffeine, unbeknownst to most of us, is a potent psychoactive, nonprescription drug. It is habit-forming and stimulates the central nervous system. Caffeine is suspect in the development of breast cysts and tumors. Therefore, we should be aware of its effects on our body and mind.

Caffeine is found in coffee, tea, cola (and other soft drinks), cocoa, and chocolate. (See table on page 334.) It is absorbed quickly in our bodies, giving us a quick "pickup." We feel more wakeful and alert. Caffeine makes the heart beat faster, enlarges the coronary arteries, stimulates the brain, and relaxes the muscles of the respiratory and digestive systems.

Scientists consider 250 milligrams of caffeine a large daily drug dose, and yet 30 to 40 percent of us get more than double that dose daily. Ten percent of adult Americans go over the 1,000-milligram maximum. When a woman decides to give up coffee "cold turkey" or to cut way back on her caffeine intake, she will probably suffer such withdrawal symptoms as nervousness, irritability, anxiety, insomnia, and occasionally heart palpitations.

Treatment

Many women addicted to legal drugs have been advised by their physicians to quit "cold turkey." This borders on malpractice; it takes many years for a woman to become addicted and will take time for her body to regain independence from drugs. Gradual

333

Caffeine Content of Popular Beverages

Brewed coffee (5 oz.)	85.0 mg
Dr. Pepper (12 oz.)	61.0 mg
Coffee, instant (5 oz.)	60.0 mg
Mountain Dew (12 oz.)	48.0 mg
Tab (12 oz.)	45.0 mg
Coca-Cola (12 oz.)	41.5 mg
Tea, bagged or leaf (5 oz.)	40.0 mg
Pepsi-Cola (12 oz.)	35.0 mg
Tea, instant (5 oz.)	30.0 mg
Cocoa (5 oz.)	13.0 mg
Chocolate (1 oz.)	7.0 mg
Coffee, decaffeinated (5 oz.)	2.8 mg

withdrawal, combined with counseling, daily exercise, and nutritional advice, is essential. This process may take a year or two.

Drug treatment programs for older women have been virtually nonexistent. In fact, the only special drug treatment center for women in the country is the Wingspread Clinic, founded by Dr. Josette Mondanaro, in Santa Cruz, California. It is funded by the National Institute for Drug Abuse and proceeds from clinic operations. There women are offered full-time medical care as well as drug-abuse counseling to fight addiction to doctor-prescribed drugs, and alcohol in combination with drugs. Counselors help women understand the causes of their addictions and the fact that many turned to drugs because of their problems in adapting to ill-fitting societal roles. Dr. Mandanaro says, "The medical care is important. It provides face-saving. When women walk in here, people aren't sure what they are coming for. Addicted women are so ashamed, especially older women."

Although no single approach is effective, a "talking therapy" will allow women as individuals, or in groups, to identify the causes of their anxieties and to find renewed purpose and promise in their lives.

A recent Harvard Medical School letter (March 1981) reports the successful use of beta-blocking drugs (rather than sedatives or tranquilizers, with their undesirable effects) to help people through moments of temporary anxiety and stress. They are widely used now to treat angina, high blood pressure, and migraine headaches and can be obtained only by prescription. Most prescription-drug abusers start out as inadvertent misusers.

Who is at fault for this hidden epidemic of women hooked on drugs? Is it the pharmaceutical industry, which has become one of the most profitable industries in the country? Is it the physicians who welcome a pill as the easy way to satisfy the complaints of their largest patient population, women? Or is it we ourselves—the women who expect to leave our doctors' offices with an instant remedy for our life's problems?

As women, we need support in learning to fully engage ourselves in the stressful, difficult moments of our lives, rather than withdrawing and tuning out with drugs. We should not allow drugs to rob us of the opportunity to live out our years in independence and dignity.

*R*esources: Alcoholism

Publications

Gomberg, Edith. *Alcoholism and Women: State of Knowledge Today.* New York: National Council on Alcoholism, 1975.

Kilpatrick, Jeanne. *The Woman Who Drinks Too Much.* Quakerstown, PA: Women for Sobriety, 1976.

Langone, John, and Dolores Langone. *Women Who Drink.* Reading, MA: Addison-Wesley, 1980.

Sandmailer, Marian. *The Invisible Alcoholics: Women and Alcohol Abuse in America.* New York: McGraw-Hill, 1980.

Youcha, G. *A Dangerous Pleasure: Alcohol from the Woman's Perspective—Its Effect on Body, Mind and Relationships.* New York: Hawthorn, 1978.

Organizations

Alcoholics Anonymous
P.O. Box 459
Grand Central Station
New York, NY 10017

Al-Anon & Alateen Family Groups
115 E. 23rd St.
New York, NY 10010
Local chapters are listed in most telephone directories.

Brunswick House, Alcoholic Rehabilitation Hospital
Brunswick Hospital Center
81 Louden Ave.
Amityville, NY 11701

Helping Hands Program
Alcoholism Treatment and Education Center
Memorial Hospital Medical Center
Long Beach, CA
Coordinator: Janet Ashton Glassock

National Association of Gay Alcoholism Professionals
P.O. Box 376
Oakland, NJ 07436

National Center for Alcohol Education
1601 North Kent St.
Arlington, VA 22209

National Council on Alcoholism, Inc.
733 Third Ave.
New York, NY 10017

National Institute on Alcohol Abuse and Alcoholism
National Clearinghouse for Alcohol Information
P.O. Box 2345
Rockville, MD 20852

Queen Nursing Home and Treatment Center
Queen Street
Minneapolis, MN

Women for Sobriety, Inc.
Dr. Jeanne Kilpatrick
P.O. Box 618
Quakerstown, PA 18951

SENIOR CITIZEN'S JUST DEMANDS: 15% INCREASE IN SOCIAL SECURITY PASS KENNEDY-CORMAN HEALTH BILL

Bettye La

Chapter Fifteen

The Economics of Good Health

Mary Doe is 71 years old and lives alone. About eight years ago she had a mild heart attack, but her doctors told her she could lead a normal, active life as long as she watched her diet and avoided strenuous activity. . . .

Six months ago Mary began feeling a bit of pressure in her chest after doing her housework. She found herself tiring easily, and rather than go to the market regularly she began to skip meals and get along mostly on snacks. She avoided going to the doctor because of the excessive cost of office visits and laboratory procedures, which aren't adequately covered under Medicare.

Then 3 months ago Mary had another heart attack . . . this time a major coronary requiring several weeks' hospitalization and extended after care. The cost to Medicare and to Mary has been enormous. . . . Mary's savings are by now all but wiped out by uncovered medical expenses, even though public funds have paid more than $7,700 toward her bill. . . . Most of that cost could probably have been avoided if someone had given Mary just a little help with her heaviest housework, helped her eat properly—and if she could have visited a community health center periodically to obtain preventive care. She might have been spared the physical and psychological pain, and thousands of tax dollars might have been saved.

Letter from Maggie Kuhn to Gray Panthers, 1979

The high costs of health care and the impact of a rising inflation has created a situation in which many older women cannot afford health care. Despite the availability of Medicare, Medicaid, and private insurance, the elderly pay between 29 percent and 50 percent of their health-care expenses directly out of pocket.

Medicare

Medicare is a federal program providing hospital and medical insurance to persons entitled to social security benefits and their families. It pays 44 percent of total personal health-care costs for the elderly (70 percent of that for inpatient hospital care and 25 percent for physicians' services). Some 25 million persons over age 65 are Medicare beneficiaries (most of the nation's elderly). Medicare consists of two parts: Part A, Hospital Insurance and Part B, Supplementary Medical Insurance.

Part A

For each spell of illness, Medicare pays most of the costs for:

- 90 hospital days
- 100 days of skilled nursing care after you leave the hospital (in your own home or in a skilled nursing facility)
- 60 additional days of hospital care in a lifetime

Beneficiaries must pay a deductible amount ($260 in 1982) that approximates the cost of the first day of hospital care for each spell of illness.

Part B

Supplementary Medical Insurance is a voluntary program that pays 80 percent of physicians' and other health-care providers' bills. It covers "reasonable costs" for such outpatient services as speech and physical therapy, medical equipment, diagnostic tests, ambulance service, and unlimited home visits if prescribed by a physician.

Beneficiaries entitled to Part A can purchase Part B coverage for $12.20 a month (1982 cost). They pay the remaining 20 percent of the "reasonable costs" and about half the time must pay the additional amounts charged by physicians that Medicare does not consider reasonable.

Typical Daily Hospital Costs, 1950 and 1980

	1950	1980
Average cost per hospital day (nominal dollars)	$15	$245
Average cost per hospital day (1967 dollars)	$22	$ 99
Percentage paid out-of-pocket	30%	9%
Out-of-pocket payment per day (1967 dollars)	$ 7	$ 9

Source: U.S. Council on Wage and Price Stability

Medicare, in addition to those services mentioned, covers laboratory and X-ray services, a semiprivate room (two to four beds), drugs furnished by the hospital, physical and speech therapy, rural health clinic services, and durable medical equipment and supplies.

Disadvantages of Medicare for women:

- It does not cover preventive health care (an annual physical), outpatient drugs, eyeglasses, hearing aids, dental or homemaker services, or long-term nursing home care.
- Some one million older persons (most of whom are women) do not qualify for social security benefits and therefore are not entitled to Medicare.
- For those women who do qualify, Medicare covers only 30 to 40 percent of medical expenses; the women themselves are responsible for the remaining 60 to 70 percent.
- Even if a woman is a widow she is not eligible for Medicare under age 60, unless she is totally disabled.
- Medicare focuses on acute illnesses, while most older women have chronic problems that don't require hospitalization.
- Many women are forced by Medicare policy to enter a hospital unnecessarily so they can have their health services paid for.

Medicaid

Medicaid is a joint federal and state program that finances health services for low-income people of all ages. Among the elderly this includes those eligible for SSI (Supplemental Security Income) and AFDC (Aid to Families with Dependent Children). These people are called the "categorically needy." Other persons whose incomes are not high enough to pay for their medical care are designated "medically needy" and are eligible for Medicaid in thirty states. Forty-six states pay the premiums on Part B of Medicare for Medicaid beneficiaries.

This program is administered by the states, and all states except Arizona have Medicaid. Medicaid payments account for 14 percent of the health expenditures of the elderly. Although elderly beneficiaries represent only 15 percent of Medicaid recipients, they account for 37 percent of Medicaid spending.

Each state program must include coverage of hospital, physician, lab and X-ray, skilled nursing, home health, rural health and family planning services. States can choose to provide any other services, and consequently there is a wide variation in benefits offered. Medicaid beneficiaries receive diagnostic, preventive and rehabilitative services. These include drugs, dental care, vision, and hearing services. Unlike Medicare, Medicaid makes payments directly to the service providers, who must accept the reimbursement as full payment.

Older women, who represent 75 percent of nursing home residents and most of the SSI recipients, are the major recipients of Medicaid for the elderly. (Forty-two percent of all Medicaid funding goes to nursing home care.) Women in nursing homes must contribute any income above the eligibility standard to cover Medicaid costs. They are often forced, by this government policy, to enter a nursing home, where Medicaid will pay all their expenses, rather than remain in their homes. It is estimated that 25 percent of these women could remain in their own homes if the one percent of Medicaid monies now covering home health services was increased. This would be cost-effective for the whole country.

Medi-Gap

More than half of all women over 65 purchase private insurance to supplement existing Medicare coverage. This has frequently been duplicative and expensive, and it has not provided protection against extraordinary health expenses. To correct what has become a national scandal, a medi-gap health insurance policy was signed into law in 1980. Private insurance companies are now required to cover some of the health-care costs not covered by Medicare and to meet minimum standards. Criminal penalties are imposed on any companies who fraudulently mislead their elderly policy-holders.

Four Million Women Have No Health Insurance

Despite Medicare, Medicaid, and private insurance policies, some 4 million women between the ages of 45 and 65 are without any health insurance. Health insurance is usually tied to employment and/or marriage, and there is a major insurance gap for women whose marital status changes through widowhood or divorce before they are 65 and eligible for Medicare. In most cases women then lose access to their husbands' group medical insurance policy and many cannot afford the high costs of individual policies. Advocates for older women throughout the country are pressing for legislation that would automatically offer widows and divorced women the right to convert to individual policies at no extra cost and without the need for a new physical examination.

A major problem with many existing health plans is that they don't provide for preventive health care. Many incidences of breast, endometrial, and rectal cancer could be prevented if women had annual checkups. The serious effects of other illnesses like diabetes, hypertension and osteoporosis could be arrested with preventive services. Yet Medicare, Medicaid, and most private insurance plans do not cover adequate preventive care. Health maintenance organizations (HMO's), which stress preventive care, do not generally provide adequate coverage for older people who have retired, since they rely so heavily on funds from employers. However, the Federal government has been experimenting with the use of Medicare funds with selected HMO's and this may one day be an important health resource for the aging.

Recommendations from the 1981 White House Confer-ence on Aging include the need for a comprehensive national health policy that would make health care a right for all individuals regardless of age, sex, race, employment, or marital status. Such a policy would cover a wide range of health-care professionals, both inpatient and outpatient services; home care as well as institutional care; prevention/wellness promotion *and* disease care; mental health care along with physical health care; hospice and respite care; and financial aid to families who act as caretakers to ill older people. If such care was available continuously, over a lifetime, as an individual *entitlement,* women would be healthier and able to take the responsibility necessary to make the second half of their lives productive and independent.

Resources: Women's Health

Publications

Corea, Gena. *The Hidden Malpractice.* New York: Morrow, 1977; paperback HBJ/Jove, 1978.

Organizations

Boston Women's Health Book Collective
Box 192
Somerville, MA 02144
617-924-0271

Coalition for the Medical Rights of Women
1638-B Haight St.
San Francisco, CA 94117
415-621-8030

Consumer Coalition for Health
1751 N St., N.W.
Washington, DC 20036
202-638-5825
CHAN newsletter; trainings.

Gray Panthers Health Task Force
3700 Chestnut St.
Philadelphia, PA 19104
215-382-3300

Health Research Group
#2 2000 P St., N.W.
Washington, DC 20036
202-872-0320
Research, community organizing, advocacy on health and health policy.

Mexican American Women's National Association
P.O. Box 23656
L'Enfant Plaza
Washington, DC 20024

National Council of Negro Women
1346 Connecticut Ave., N.W.
Washington, DC 20036

National Foundation for Women's Health
3300 Heury Ave.
Philadelphia, PA 19129

National Health Law Program, Inc. (NHELP)
2639 S. LaCienega Blvd.
Los Angeles, CA 90034
213-204-6010
Community education on legal services, bulletins; newsletter *Health Advocate.*

National Organization for Women (NOW)
425 13th St., N.W.
Washington, DC 20004
202-347-2279

National Women's Health Network (NWHN)
224 7th St., S.E.
Washington, DC 20003
202-543-9222
Membership newsletter *Network News.*

Physicians for Social Responsibility
P.O. Box 295
Cambridge, MA 02238
617-661-9095
News, information, speaker's bureau from physicians against nuclear power.

Santa Fe Health Education Project
P.O. Box 577
Santa Fe, NM 87501
505-982-3236

Southern Vermont Women's Health Center
187 N. Main
Rutland, VT 05701
802-775-1946

Women's Occupational Health Resource Center
c/o American Health Foundation
320 E. 43rd St.
New York, NY 10017
212-781-5719
Excellent fact sheets.

Twin Lens Photography

Conclusion

As Maggie Kuhn said in the foreword, "We are a new breed of older women." As a group, we are a new phenomenon that has never before existed. We have the dual distinction of being the fastest-growing and most economically disadvantaged age group in this country (and indeed in most of the world). Technological and medical advances have added years to our lives. Our challenge now is to add life to those years.

Many of us are delighting in growing older female. May Sarton, author and poet, said on her sixty-fifth birthday:

> When I was 17, I already began to look forward to being old. Far from a liability, I see it as possibly the most interesting of adventures to come, and in that vision I was not far wrong. My sixty-fifth year, just past, has been the happiest and most fruitful so far. I do not see diminution except in sustained energy, but the lack of energy is more than made up for by my knowing better how to handle myself. I have more fun because I am less compulsive, less driven by time, curiously enough, and more able to take life easy.

More and more we are opening ourselves to new experiences, determined to make our own decisions, to define our own lifestyles and to expand our lives in myriad new directions. Women in their sixth, seventh, and eighth decades are learning to play musical instruments, write poetry, ride bicycles, cross-country ski, enter politics, travel all over the world, and a daring few are even experimenting with hang-gliding. Janice Wetzel of Smith College spoke about older women at the 1982 Mid-American Congress on Aging:

> *Elder women not only have learned how to survive, but how to do it in style. . . . Might it be that elder women are more fully developed human beings . . . retaining their affiliative, nurturing qualities while adding on a sense of mastery and competence? . . . Let their insights shine so that we may all recognize their leadership. These are our role models, our female elders— America's humane strength. Let them show us the way.*

We have many role models of gray-headed women: those who are no longer living, like Susan B. Anthony, Sojourner Truth, Margaret Mead, Dorothy Day, Golda Meir, and Eleanor Roosevelt; and women still living in our midst, like Maggie Kuhn, Mary Calderone, Lillian Carter, Alberta Hunter, and Katharine Hepburn. These famous women have taken risks, made important contributions to society, and worked with a sense of optimism for world change.

Thousands of other women over 40, although less familiar, are models of leadership, stamina, and achievement. In the course of the last five years I have had the privilege of interviewing many such women and want to share just a few of their courageous stories, told in their own words.

> *I was born the fourth child of ten, of a sharecropper's family in North Carolina. It was my job, growing up, to do the laundry and cooking. We all helped each other get an education. At age 18 it was my turn, and I literally hitched a ride on the back of a bus, with just enough money to catch a train east, to pursue what I had hoped would be a nursing education. But first I had to earn money, and I did—as a nurse's aide, manager of a food store, bookkeeper in a life insurance company, proprietor of a beauty salon, supervisor of the county prosecutor's record room, and finally today I am the assistant director of student activities at Farleigh Dickinson University in New Jersey.*

I've been happily married to Mac for twenty-one years. We've not only raised our own four children, but have had seven others living with us for long periods of time. At age 36 I was finally able to return to school, only to discover I was pregnant with our youngest. By then I was determined, so I took only one semester off for Walter's birth and then brought him to class with me each day. I received my B.A. in psychology, M.A. in human development, and this year completed my Ph.D. in adult education and administration. What a thrill it was to teach a class this summer in the all-white college of the town I had ridden out of twenty-seven years ago, clinging to the back of the bus.

As a political activist I was chairperson of Concerned Citizens for Better Education for Black Children, candidate at large for the Hackensack City Council, and the recipient of the Sojourner Truth Award for community involvement. Perhaps my biggest joy has been helping about forty persons over age 30 to return to college to complete their education. I couldn't have handled all of this in my life without my strong faith in God and lots of support from family and friends.

Pargellen McCall, age 45

I work side by side with my husband in the fields, on the tractors, trucks, and combines—along with taking care of cows, pigs, sheep, chickens, and a large garden. I make most of my own clothes, bake bread, put up enough vegetables for the winter, hold office in the county home extension, served eight years as clerk of the local road district, keep our own books, and do income taxes for farmers in our area. I keep alert to all government laws and write letters about farm legislation and funding. I let them all know how we feel, even the President. I attend classes in our junior college whenever I can find one I haven't taken before. I like painting the house, pouring concrete, or mixing mud to lay blocks. I'm not for women's lib, but I'm not helpless either. I don't have time to feel sorry for myself, or lonely, and I've a host of friends everywhere. I take no medication, eat a balanced diet, and walk for at least a half hour each day. I'm very happy here on the farm and believe our years of life experience will be a great help to many others in the years to come.

Lena Ruth Deisher, age 63

I was the second oldest of eight children born to Italian immigrant parents. I married at age 19 and finished my premed studies after marriage. I've now been divorced for fourteen years and have raised my six children (ages 17 to 30) alone. This is the life's work I am most proud of; they are wonderful and unique human beings. My oldest daughter wrote an article about me on my fiftieth birthday which said, "Mom is the professional I most emulate, and the woman after whom I model my life."

I've been a professional writer for twenty-five years — hundreds of national magazine articles and five books, the latest Successful Single Parenting. I was for many years the campus relations director of a large university and am presently the editor of a weekly newspaper in Connecticut. I know that there is one secret for growing old well—that is, to keep a sense of excitement in my life. I see that as my challenge in the years ahead.

Antoinette Bosco, age 51

I am a writer, editor, teacher, and the American-born daughter of Russian Jewish immigrants. I married at 18 but continued working in advertising and took college courses at night. After the birth of my children I wrote for radio and for popular magazines and published my first novel in my forties. I became an editor, was divorced and remarried, and returned to college for my first degree in my fifties. I published another novel, worked at free-lance editing, and taught fiction workshops. In my seventies I have acquired a doctoral degree and completed a third book.

These late years are the most challenging of all. There has been a long process of discovery, testing, and learning what is true for myself—and now I am writing about the difficult, ambiguous facts of married and unmarried life. I don't want this gift of years to be wasted.

Florence Bonime, age 73

I am the wife of a campus minister, mother of four, and grandmother of eleven. When I was 70 I received my B.A. degree from Cheyney State College in Pennsylvania, with a 3.8 grade cum. This year, despite a radical mastectomy and a fractured hip, I was awarded my M.A. in adult education, from the same college to which I had ridden my bike daily for several years. Last year I was chosen as the oldest of eight women, ranging in age from 24, to take part in a grueling two-week-long Outward Bound Wilderness Journey for Women. We took this trip on foot, in a canoe, backpacking, rock climbing, and even taking a thirty-six-hour solo hike. We were televised for a documentary soon to be released. I've sent out several résumés and am confident that one of them will bring me a satisfying job in counseling or organizing. My age shouldn't make a difference; in fact, because of my age I feel I will be uniquely able to counsel and encourage others.

Mary Frances James, age 74

My mother died when I was young. My father remarried and I grew up in a family of ten children. I taught for two years after graduation but at age 24 decided I'd worked long enough. My father helped me transform one of the first Dodge cars into what may well have been the original motor home. In 1923 I set out to drive cross-country with a young woman friend. We slept in the car, camped along the way, went through cow paths where no roads had yet been built, and arrived in Los Angeles with ten cents between us. Those were depression days, with long unemployment lines, but we were able to find work in an experimental school for delinquent girls in the Mobai Desert. I served two years as an army sergeant in the Women's Army Corps. From 1948 until my retirement in 1962, I was superintendent and warden of the Connecticut State Farm and Prison for Women.

For thirty years I worked and lived with a woman friend who recently died. Our life was rich—spending the summers in a small cabin in the woods of rural Massachusetts and winters in our home next to the water in Florida. I am a member of the Appalachian Mountain Association, the Middlefield Grange and Concerned Citizens, the American Legion, the United States Power Squadron Auxiliary, and three Winnebago clubs. I enjoy concerts, the Orange Bowl festivities, the theater, attending church every week, reading, and visits from friends of all ages and many parts of the world. I walk several times a day for exercise and eat everything. Last summer I visited my sister in Tunisia and plan to go to the Orient with another sister this year. My life has been and continues to be a full, healthy, and happy one.

Elisabeth MacKenzie, age 85

These and thousands of other women have rich and varied histories to share with us—full of hope, imagination, and accomplishments. I hope they will be as inspiring to you as they are to me. Because of such role models, older women are beginning to be recognized as a powerful force in the revolution of women throughout the world. This is only possible, however, when we unite with each other and with our younger sisters, forming alliances with women of different ages, races, and classes, and with those men who find ageism and sexism equally disturbing.

Each of us can, and should, assume some responsibility to be a role model for younger women, so that as the next generation enters the second half of their lives, they will know clearly that growing older *really* means getting better. The goal of this book is to help women, no matter what their age, to learn to celebrate age, and to live out their lives in dignity, full growth, and zest.

Older Women—
A Bibliography

Block, Marilyn R.; Davidson, Janice L.; and Grambs, Jean D. *Women over Forty: Visions and Realities*. New York: Springer Publishing Co., Inc., 1981.

Boston Women's Health Book Collective. *Our Bodies, Ourselves* (2nd ed., revised). New York: Simon & Schuster, 1976.

Brody, Jane. *New York Times Guide to Personal Health*. New York: Times Books, 1982.

Cahn, Ann Foote, ed. *Women in Mid-Life: Security and Fulfillment*. Select Committee on Aging, U.S. House of Representatives, 1978.

Cohen, Joan, and Pearlman, Karen. *Hitting Our Stride: Good News About Women in Their Middle Years*. New York: Delacorte Press, 1980.

Cooke, Cynthia, and Dworkin, Susan. *MS Guide to a Woman's Health*. Berkeley, Calif.: Berkeley Publications, 1981.

Curtin, Sharon. *Nobody Ever Died of Old Age*. Boston: Little, Brown, 1972.

Edelstein, Barbara. *The Woman Doctor's Medical Guide for Women*. New York: William Morrow, 1982.

French, Marilyn. *The Women's Room*. New York: Simon & Schuster, 1977.

Fuchs, Estelle. *The Second Season: Life, Love and Sex for Women in the Middle Years.* Garden City, N.Y.: Doubleday, 1979.

Gilman, Charlotte Perkins. *Herland.* New York: Pantheon Press, 1915.

Goodman, Ellen. *Turning Points: How People Change Through Crisis.* Garden City, N.Y.: Doubleday, 1979.

Hailey, Elizabeth. *A Woman of Independent Means.* Boston: G. K. Hall, 1979.

Health Issues of Older Women: A Projection to the Year 2000. Proceedings of a conference held at SUNY Health Science Center, April 1981. School of Allied Health Professions, State University of New York, Stony Brook, N.Y. 11794.

Hot Flash: A Newsletter for Midlife and Older Women (quarterly). Jane Porcino, ed., School of Allied Health Professions, State University of New York, Stony Brook, N.Y. 11794.

Howard, Jane. *A Different Woman.* New York: E. P. Dutton, 1973.

Jacobs, Ruth. *Life After Youth: Female, Forty—What Next?* Boston: Beacon Press, 1979.

Lake, Alice. *Our Own Years: What Women over 35 Should Know About Themselves.* New York: Random House, 1979.

Langone, John, and Langone, Dolores. *Women Who Drink.* Reading, Mass.: Addison-Wesley, 1980.

Laurence, Margaret. *The Stone Angel.* New York: Knopf, 1964.

Lessing, Doris. *The Summer Before the Dark.* New York: Knopf, 1973.

Luce, Gay. *Your Second Life: Vitality and Growth in Middle and Later Age.* New York: Delacorte Press, 1979.

Miller, Jean Barker, M.D. *Toward a New Psychology of Women.* Boston: Beacon Press, 1976.

Preuss, Karen. *Lifelines: A New Image of Aging.* Santa Cruz, Calif.: Unity Press, 1978.

Reitz, Rosetta. *Menopause: A Positive Approach.* Radnor, Pa.: Chilton, 1977.

Robey, Harriet. *There's a Dance in the Old Girl Yet.* Boston: G. K. Hall, 1982.

Rubin, Lillian. *Women of a Certain Age: The Midlife Search for Self.* New York: Harper & Row, 1979.

Scally, Sister M. Anthony. *Medicine, Motherhood and Mercy: The Story of a Black Woman Doctor.* Lafayette, Ind.: Associated Publishers, Inc., 1979.

Scott, Maxwell Florida. *The Measure of My Days.* New York: Knopf, 1968.

Seskin, Jane, and Ziegler, Betty. *Older Women/Younger Men.* Garden City, N.Y.: Doubleday, 1979.

Seskin, Jane. *More than Mere Survival: Conversations with Women over 65.* New York: Newsweek Books, 1980.

Sheehy, Gail. *Passages.* New York: Bantam, 1977.

Shields, Laurie. *Displaced Homemakers: Organizing for a New Life.* New York: McGraw-Hill, 1981.

United States Congress. House Select Committee on Aging. *National Policy Proposals Affecting Midlife Women.* Washington, D.C.: U.S. Government Printing Office, 1979.

  Women in Midlife—Security and Fulfillment. Washington, D.C.: G.P.O., 1978.

  Women and Retirement Income Programs: Current Issues of Equity and Adequacy. Washington, D.C.: G.P.O., 1979.

Vining, Elizabeth. *Being Seventy: The Measure of a Year.* New York: The Viking Press, 1978.

Wax, Judith. *Starting in the Middle.* New York: Holt, Rinehart & Winston, 1979.

Woolf, Virginia. *A Room of One's Own.* New York: Harcourt Brace Jovanovich, 1981.

Yglesias, Helen. *Starting Early, Anew, Over and Late.* New York: Random House, 1978.

Index

AA, 321, 326, 327, 328
AARP, 44, 154
  Women's Division, 154
Abuse
  elder, 94–95
  wife, 92–94
ACLU, 121
  of Georgia, 121
Action groups, 154
Acupressure
  for alleviating hot flashes, 176
Addiction. See Alcoholism; Drug use
    and abuse.
ADEA, 119, 120
AFDC, 341
Age Discrimination Act of 1975, 74
Ageism, 115–122
  in health care, 162–163
Aid to Families with Dependent
    Children, 341
Al-Anon, 326
Alateen, 326
Albany Center for the Study of Aging,
    200
Alcohol
  benefits from, 328
  and drugs, 329, 331–332
  and sex, 188
Alcoholics Anonymous, 321, 326, 327,
    328

Alcoholism, 319–328
  Al-Anon and Alateen, 328
  and cancer, 323
  effect on others, 321, 326
  and heart disease, 323
  incidence, 320–322
    compared with drug abuse, 329
  and malnutrition, 324
  and sexual functioning, 323–324
  symptoms, 320, 322–324
  treatment, 324–328
    Alcoholics Anonymous, 321, 326,
      327, 328
    Brunswick House, 327
    Helping Hands, 327
    peer counseling, 324
    Women for Sobriety (WFS), 327
Alone, being, 9–10
Alzheimer's disease, 149–150. See also
    Senility.
  effect on family, 150
  progress of, 149
  treatment of, 149–150
American Association of Retired Per-
    sons. See AARP.
American Civil Liberties Union. See
    ACLU.
American Diabetes Association, 273, 275
American Institute of Clinical Nutri-
    tion, 222

American Medical Association, 320
American Society of Clinical Nutri-
    tion, 222
Amniocentesis, 65–66
Anemia, 212
  and nutrition, 221
Angina, 238, 335
Anthony, Susan B., 348
Antibiotics, in treating cystitis, 292
Arthritis
  and exercise, 200
  lupus erythematous, 249–251
    discoid, 249
    incidence, 250
    Raynaud's Disease, 250
    systemic, 249, 250
    treatment, 251
  osteoarthritis, 248–249
    incidence, 248
    obesity and, 249
    symptoms, 249
  rheumatoid arthritis, 249
    estrogen, oral contraceptives, and,
      249
    incidence, 249
    symptoms, 249
  and sex, 188, 253
  Sjogren's Syndrome, 251
  treatment, 251–253
    aspirin, 252–253

Arthritis (*cont.*)
    cortisone, 253
    exercise, 251
    massage and physical therapy, 253
    nutritional therapy, 252
    relaxation, 252
    self-management, 251
    sexual activity, 253
    surgery, 253
Aspirin
    and arthritis, 252–253
    dangers of, 253
    and stroke, 247
Assertiveness training, 76, 122
Atherosclerosis, 210
    and cholesterol, 210, 238
    and stroke, 245
Auden, William, 14
Avon, 126

Barry, Clemmi, 88, 248
Battered women. *See* Abuse.
Benson, Dr. Herbert, 142
"Bikini" surgery, 181
Bioenergetics, 146
Biofeedback, 146
    for alleviating hot flashes, 176
Birth defects, 65
Birth-control pills. *See* Contraceptives.
Blackburn, Dr. Henry, 242
Bladder control. *See* Urinary incontinence.
Bleeding, vaginal, 174
Blood pressure. *See* Hypertension.
Blue Cross/Blue Shield, 181–182
Boston Secretarial Network, 125
Breast cancer, 162, 254–265
    breast reconstruction, 264
    caffeine and, 334
    causes, 255
    diagnosis
        blood and urine tests, 259
        diaphragmography, 259
        lumpectomy, 259
        mammography, 258
        needle biopsy, 259
        "one-step" vs "two-step" procedure, 260
        surgical biopsy, 260
        thermography, 259
        ultrasound, 259
    prevention, 256
    risk factors, 254–255
    self-examination, 256–258
    support groups, 264–265
    symptoms, 258

treatment
    chemotherapy, 262
    Halstead radical mastectomy, 261
    holistic therapy, 262
    lumpectomy, 261
    modified radical mastectomy
    radiation implants, 262
    radiation therapy, 261–262
    Tanoxifen, 262
Breast self-examination, 256–258
Brookhaven National Laboratory, 229
Brunswick House, 327
Bulk. *See* Fiber.

CAEL, 75
Caffeine, 333–334
Caine, Lynn, 43
Calcitonin, 229, 234
Calcium, 211
    and osteoporosis, 230, 232
Calderone, Mary, 348
Calories, 209
Cancer Counseling and Research Center, 262
Cancer Hopefuls United for Mutual Support. *See* CHUMS.
Cancer, 253–273
    alcohol and, 323
    breast. *See* Breast cancer.
    colon and rectal, 267–268
        diagnosis, 268
        diet and, 268
        incidence, 267
        symptoms, 267
        treatment, 268
    and estrogen, 172, 174
    larynx, 323
    liver, 323
    lung, 265–266
        incidence, 265
        smoking, 265–266
    and nutrition, 221
    oral, 313
    skin, 270, 306
        malignant melanoma, 271
    stress and, 271–273
    uterine, 172, 174, 268–270
        cervical, 269
        endometrial, 269
        ovarian, 270
        vaginal and vulval, 270
CAPS, 91
Carbohydrates, 209
Cardiovascular disease. *See* Heart disease; Hypertension; Stroke.

Careers
    guidance, 76
    new, 20
    over 40, 126–128
Carter, Lillian, 348
Cataracts, 301–302
Celibacy. *See* Sexuality, abstinence.
Cesarean birth, 65
Chesler, Phyllis, 330
Children leaving home, 16, 18. *See also* Empty nest.
Children of Aging Parents. *See* CAPS.
Chlordiazepoxide (Librium), 332
Cholesterol, 209–210. *See also* Fats.
    and heart disease, 210, 238
CHUMS, 265
Cirrhosis, 323
Civil Rights Act, Title VII, 119
CLEP, 75
Climacteric, 168, 171–172
Colitis, 267
Collective living, 30, 195
College-Level Examination Program. *See* CLEP.
Communes, 30
    intergenerational, 30
Congressional Women's Caucus, 125
Consciousness-raising, 2, 76, 151–153
    guidelines for success, 152–153
Constipation
    and nutrition, 221
Contraceptives, 277
    and alcohol, 332
    and arthritis, 249
    and gum disease, 312
    and heart disease, 239
    possible cause of breast cancer, 255
    and skin cancer, 270
Council for Advancement of Experimental Learning. *See* CAEL.
See Stroke.
Cystic fibrosis, 65
Cystitis, 290, 292

D&C, 178, 179
Dating
    after divorce, 41
Day, Dorothy, 348
Deafness. *See* Hearing loss.
DeCrow, Karen, 37
DeGroot, Mary, 44
Dementia. *See* Alzheimer's disease; Senility.
Dental problems, 312–315
    cancer, 314
    dentures, 313–314

gum disease, 312
  incidence, 312
  insurance, 314–315
  periodontal disease, 312
    periodontosis, 312
  prevention, 315
  smoking and, 314, 315
  treatment, 313
    cost of, 314–315
Department of Labor, 119
  Women's Bureau, 92
Depression, 143–145
  causes, 143
  checklist for, 144–145
  drugs and, 143
  exercise and, 201
  following stroke, 245
  and incontinence, 290
  and menopause, 170
  and sex, 188
  symptoms, 143–144
  treatment, 144–145. *See also* Therapy.
DES, 174–175, 269
Diabetes, 273–280
  complications of, 276
  diabetes mellitus, 273–274
  diabetic retinopathy, 303
  diagnosis, 275
  and exercise, 201, 278
  and nutrition, 220, 279
  and obesity, 274–275, 278
  older women, special problems for, 276–277
  and osteoporosis, 230
  in pregnancy, 65
  symptoms, 275
  treatment, 277–280
    insulin pump, 278
    insulin, 277
    lectin, 278
    pancreas transplant, 278
  warning signs, 275
Diazepam (Valium), 330, 332
Diet. *See* Nutrition.
di-ethyl silbesterol. *See* DES.
Dieting. *See also* Nutrition; Obesity.
  crash diets, 218
  fad diets, 218
Digitalis, 332
Dilation and curettage. *See* D&C.
Disabled spouse, 87–91
  legal intervention, 91
  nursing home, 88–91
Discrimination. *See* Ageism; Sexism; Racism.

Displaced Homemakers Program, 122
Diuretics, 279
  natural, 177
Divorce
  belief in, 14
  celibacy, 41
  dating, 41
    casual sex, 41
  economic concerns, 35–36
    alimony, 40
    child support, 34, 36
    medical insurance, loss of, 36
  emotional issues, 32
    impact on children, 34
  friends
    conflicting loyalties, 35
  lawyer, choosing, 38
  no-fault, 39–40
    alimony and, 40
    property settlement and, 39–40
  of children, 20
  out-of-court settlement, 40
  positive aspects of, 37–38
  recovery from, 32–33
    phases of, 32–33
  second, 63
  and separation, 32
  statistics of, 31–32
  who initiates, 37
  and widowhood, contrasted, 27
Down's syndrome, 65
Drug use and abuse, 328–335
  antidepressants, 330
  antihypertensives, 332
  beta blockers, 334
  caffeine, 333–334
  contraceptives, 332
  digitalis, 332
  diuretics, 332
  drug combinations, 331
  drug-alcohol combinations, 329, 331–332
  estrogen, 332
  generic vs. brand-name, 333
  hypnotics, 330
  incidence of abuse, 329
    compared with alcoholism, 329
  Librium, 330, 332
    withdrawal from, 332
  overdrugging, 331
  sedatives, 330, 332
  and sex, 188
  side effects, 331
  stimulants, 330, 333–334
  tranquilizers, 330, 332
  treatment for abuse, 333–335

Valium, 330, 332
  and alcohol, 332
  withdrawal, 332, 334

Education. *See* Returning to school.
Educational Amendments of 1976, Title I, Part B, 74
EEOC, 119, 120, 121
Elder abuse, 94–95
  incidence of, 94
Elderly, caring for, 83–87
  day care, 84
  legal intervention: joint accounts, trusts, etc., 91
  nursing home, 86
  restrictions on freedom and privacy, 87
  role of women in, 85
  shared housing, 84, 103–106
Electrolysis, 311
Employee Retirement Income Security Act (1974). *See* ERISA.
Empty nest, 20
Endometriosis, 65, 174. *See also* Cancer, uterine.
Environmental Protection Agency, 294
Equal Employment Opportunity Commission. *See* EEOC.
Equal Pay Act, 119
ERISA, 134
Estrogen. *See also* Contraceptives; Menopause.
  and alcohol, 332
  and breast cancer, 255
  creams, 174
  DES, 174–175
  dosage, 175
  estrone, estradiol, and estriol, 172, 255
  and heart attack, 175, 238, 239
  premarin, 172, 255
  and skin cancer, 270
  and uterine cancer, 172, 174
Exercise
  and anxiety, 201
  and arthritis, 200, 251–252
  cardiovascular, 200
  and depression, 201
  and diabetes, 201
  and digestion, 201
  and heart disease, 202
  housework inadequate as, 199
  and incontinence, 291–292
  and insomnia, 201
  and osteoporosis, 200, 230, 231

Exercise (*cont.*)
  as a tranquilizer, 201
  types of, 203–205
Eye problem. *See* Vision, loss of

Fatigue, and sex, 188
Fats
  cholesterol, 209–210
  monosaturated, 210
  polyunsaturated, 210
  saturated, 210
  and heart disease, 242
FDA. *See* Food and Drug Administration.
Federal Trade Commission, 297
Fiber, in diet, 209, 213
Fibroid tumors, in pregnancy, 65
Fibroids, 180
Flouride, 312
Food and Drug Administration, 309
Food. *See* Nutrition.
Ford, Betty, 331
FORUM, 3
Freud, Sigmund, 145

Gallbladder disease, 174
  and nutrition, 220
Gestalt therapy, 146
Glaucoma, 304–305
Goddard-Cambridge Graduate Program
  in Social Change, 76
Gordon, Ruth, 191
Grandmothering, 21–24
  bond with grandchildren, 23
  burdens of, 22
  delay of, 24
  grandmother as role model, 22
  legal rights, 24–25
  nongrandmotherhood, 24
  positive aspects of, 22
  surrogate, 23–24
"Grandorphans," 23
Grandparents Anonymous, 24, 25
Gray Panthers, 195. *See also* Kuhn,
  Maggie.
Group therapy, 146
Gum disease. *See* Dental problems.

Hair, changes in, 310–311
  dyes and rinses, dangers of, 310–311
  electrolysis, 311
  facial hair, 311
  loss of hair, 311
  nutrition and, 310
Harris Poll, 129, 163
Harris, Dr. Ralph, 200

HDL, 200
Health insurance. *See* Medical insurance.
Hearing loss, 294–300
  causes, 294
  hearing aids, 298–299
  incidence, 294
  onset, 294
  prevention, 299–300
  rehabilitation, 297–298
  symptoms, 295
  types, 295
Heart disease
  and alcohol, 323
  angina, 238, 239
  bypass surgery, 239
  causes, 238
  cholesterol and, 238
  and cholesterol, 210
  coronary thrombosis, 238
  estrogen and, 238, 239
  and exercise, 200
  heart attack
    first aid for, 240–241
    symptoms, 240
  incidence, 238
  and nutrition, 221
  oral contraceptives and, 239
  prevention, 240
  risk factors, 239–240
  and sex, 188
  smoking and, 239
  and sodium, 211–212
  testosterone and, 238
  treatment, 241
    drugs, 241
    nitroglycerin, 241
    pacemakers, 241
    reperfusion therapy, 241
    transplant, 241
Helping Hands, 327
Hemorrhaging, in pregnancy or childbirth, 65
Hepburn, Katharine, 348
Herbal and natural remedies for menopausal symptoms, 176–177
High density lipoproteins. *See* HDL.
Holiday Dinner Group, 30
Holidays and singlehood, 30
Holmes Stress Test, 141
Holmes, Thomas H., 141
Homemakers Bill of Rights, 123
Homosexuality, 190, 192–193
  fear of, 194
HOT FLASH, 3, 154
Hot flashes, 169
House of Ruth, 92–93

Housing. *See also* Living alone; Elderly,
  caring for; Nursing homes.
  companionship, need for, 103
  Elder Cottage, 102
  "granny flats," 102
  intergenerational communities, 104
  mobile homes, 108
  outside help, 102
  own home, 100
    Home Equity Living Plan (HELP),
    102
    Lifetime Income Plan, 102
    reverse annuity mortgages, 102–103
  parents' apartment, 101
  retirement/leisure communities, 106–
  107
  sharing with offspring, 101
  sharing with others, 103–105
    agencies, 104–105
  subsidized housing, 108–109
  travel, Peace Corps, and other options, 109–111
Hunter, Alberta, 348
Hyman, Helen, 85
Hypertension, 242–244
  causes, 242
  and hypertensive retinopathy, 242
  incidence, 242
  and kidney failure, 242
  measurement of, 243
  and nutrition, 220
  obesity and, 242
  in pregnancy, 65
  prevention, 243
  salt and, 242
  smoking and, 242
  stress and, 242
  symptoms, 243
  treatment, 243–244
    biofeedback, 244
    diet, 244
    exercise, 244
    medication, 244, 335
Hypochondria, 163
Hysterectomy, 177–182
  cost, 181
  indications, 179
  oophorectomy, 178
  partial, 178
  prevalence, 178–179, 181
  risks, 180–181
  second opinions and, 181–182
  sexual effects, 182, 187
  simple, 178
  for sterilization, 179
  total or complete, 178
  unnecessary, 179–180

Illinois Council for Long Term Care, 89
Incontinence. *See* Urinary incontinence.
Infection, in pregnancy, 65
Infertility, 65
Insulin, 274, 275, 277
Intimacy, 193–196. *See also* Sexuality.
　collective living, 195
　divorce and, 193–194
　loneliness, 194
　widowhood and, 193–194
Iodine, 212
Iron, 212
Isolation, 140
　and hearing loss, 295

Jackins, Harvey, 148
Janeway, Elizabeth, 10
Job. *See* Work.
Job discrimination, 119–122
Job market, reentering, 75

Kanin, Garson, 191
Kegel exercises, 291
Kennedy, Joan, 327
Keyes, Paul, 313
Keyes technique, 313
Kilpatrick, Dr. Jeanne, 327
Klingman, Dr. Albert, 307
Kornhaber, Arthur, 23
Kuhn, Maggie, 163, 192, 195, 347, 348. *See also* Gray Panthers.
K-Y jelly, 176, 187

Lasers, in treating eye disorders, 303, 304
Lesbianism. *See* Homosexuality.
Le Shan, Edna, 3
Lessing, Doris, 10
Librium, 330, 332
Life expectancy, 9, 140
Lindbergh, Anne Morrow, 10, 16
Lindsay, Robert, 232
Liver disease, 174
Liver spots, 306
Living alone, 27–56
　statistics of, 99–100
Loneliness, 140, 194
　and friendship, 140
　and hearing loss, 295
Luce, Dr. Gay, 147
Lupus. *See* Arthritis.

Magnesium, 212
　and osteoporosis, 230, 233
Malignant melanoma, 270
Malnutrition, 207, 208

alcoholism and, 324
　signs of, 208
Marital satisfaction, 15, 18
Marital status
　changes in, 8, 10
Marriage
　age taboos, 29
　over 40, 29
Marriage counselors, 15
Marriages, long-term, 13–17
　successful, 13–14
　bases of, 14–15
　unsuccessful, 14
Mastectomy, and sex, 188
Masturbation, 41, 190–191
McKain, Walter, 60
McLaughlin, Dr. Charles, 180
Mead, Margaret, 177, 348
Meals on Wheels, 84
Medical insurance, 343–344. *See also* Medicare and Medicaid; Medi-Gap
　HMO's, 343
Medicare and Medicaid, 147, 298, 312, 313, 325, 340–342, 343
　disadvantages for women, 341
Medi-Gap, 342–343
Megavitamins, 213
　as cancer treatment, 272
Meir, Golda, 118, 348
Menopause
　alternative treatments, 175–177
　　herbal and other natural remedies, 176–177
　　vaginal lubricants, 176
　　vitamins E and B-complex, 175–176
　climacteric, 168, 171–172
　emotional changes, 170
　estrogen therapy
　　and cancer, 172–173, 187
　　and cardiovascular disease, 174
　　contraindications, 174
　　and gallbladder disease, 174
　　and hypertension, 174
　　and osteoporosis, 234
　　what it alleviates, 173
　　what it does not help, 173–174, 234
　hormone balance, 171–172
　myths about, 186
　stress and, 170–171
　symptoms, 168–170
　　hot flashes, 169
　　other physical symptoms, 170
　　vaginal changes, 169–170
Menstrual pain
　fibroids and, 180

Mental health, 139–155. *See also* Depression; Loneliness; Senility; Stress; Therapy.
Mentors, 75–76
Midlife crisis, 15, 16
Migraine, 174, 335
Minerals, 211–212
Miscarriage, 65
Moran, Barbara, 44
Motherhood, 60–67
　adoption, 66
　career and, 64–65
　danger to baby
　　amniocentesis, 65–66
　　birth defects, 65
　　cystic fibrosis, 65　66
　　Down's syndrome, 65
　　Tay-Sachs disease, 65
　health problems in pregnancy
　　cesarean birth, 65
　　diabetes, 65
　　endometriosis, 65
　　fibroid tumors, 65
　　hypertension, 65
　　infections, 65
　　miscarriage, 65
　　toxemia, 65
　infertility, 65
　negative aspects, 64, 66
　positive aspects, 64
Mutual support, 10. *See also* Support groups.

NAFOW, 154
National Action Forum for Midlife and Older Women. *See* NAFOW.
National Alliance of Homebased Working Women, 125
National Cancer Institute, 261
National Coalition of Older Women's Issues, 154
National Commission on Diabetes, 276
National Institute of Arthritis, Metabolism, and Digestive Diseases, 274–275
National Institute of Dental Research, 312
National Institute on Aging, 210
National Institute on Aging, 274
National Institute on Alcohol Abuse and Alcoholism, 320
National Institutes of Health, 274
National Organization for Women. *See* N.O.W.
National Women's Political Caucus, 154

Networking, 2, 125
Nin, Anaïs, 10
N.O.W., 2, 10, 123
Nursing homes
    for aging parents, 86
    for disabled spouse, 88–91
    questions to ask about, 89–90
Nutrition, 206–223
    changes in eating habits, 206–207
    guidelines and rules, 221–222
    needs for older people, 207
    solutions for medical problems, 215
        anemia, 221
        arthritis, 252
        cancer, 221
        cardiovascular disease, 221
        constipation, 221
        diabetes, 220
        gallbladder disease, 220
        hypertension, 220
        leg cramps, 221
        obesity, 214, 218–220
        osteoporosis, 220

Obesity, 214, 218–220
    and arthritis, 249
    and breast cancer, 255
    causes of, 218
    and diabetes, 274–275, 278
    dieting and, 218
    exercise and, 219
    health problems associated with,
        219–220
    and hypertension, 242
    mild to moderate, 218
    morbid, 218
    social attitudes toward, 218
    surgical solutions, 219
Occupation. *See* Work.
Ochsner, Altan, 222
Older Americans Act (1978), 74, 208
Older Women's Caucus, 154
Older Women's League. *See* OWL.
"One-step" vs. "two-step" procedure,
    260
Orgasm, 185, 187, 189
    faked, 189
Os-Cal, 232
Osteoarthritis. *See* Arthritis.
Osteoporosis, 162, 227–234
    among alcoholics, 230
    calcium and, 229–230
    causes of, 229
    defined, 228
    in diabetics, 230
    diagnosis, 230–231
    dieting and, 230

and exercise, 200, 231
and hip fracture, 228
    recurrence, 228
incidence of, 229
minerals and, 230, 232–233
and nutrition, 220
susceptibility, by race, 229
teeth, loss of, 230, 311, 312
total hip replacement, 233–234
vitamins and, 230, 232
Otosclerosis, 295
Overeaters Anonymous, 218
Overweight. *See* Obesity.
OWL, 110–111, 154

PABA, 306
Para-aminobenzoic acid, 306
Parathyroid hormone, 233, 234
Parents Without Partners, 40
Parkinson's disease, 290
Peace Corps, 110, 128
Pensions, 134
    ERISA, 134
    joint survivor option, 134
Phenobarbital, 176
Phosphorus, 212
    and osteoporosis, 232–233
Physical abuse. *See* Abuse.
Pituitary hormones, and menopause,
    169
Plaque, 311, 312
Polansky, Eleanor, 85
Porter, Sylvia, 46
Postparenting years, 17–21
    early vs. later years of, 17–18
    loneliness and, 21
    postponement of, 19
    preparation for, 18
    "revolving door," 19
    second honeymoon, 21
    single motherhood and, 21
Potassium, 212
Pottinger, Sam, 191
Poverty, 116
Premarin, 172, 255
Premarital contract
    remarriage and, 63
Presbycusis, 295
Progesterone, 171, 172, 175
Protein, 210
    and osteoporosis, 232
Psychodrama, 146

Queen Nursing Home and Treatment
    Center, 327
Quinn, Sally, 64

Racism, 116, 133
Ramey, Dr. Estelle, 238
Raynaud's Disease, 250
RDAs. *See* Vitamins.
Reentering the job market, 75
Reentry
    school. *See* Returning to school.
    work, 122, 124–129
Reevaluation counseling (R.C.), 148
Regional Bone Center, 232
Reitz, Rosetta, 176
Relaxation techniques, 142–143
Remarriage, 63–69, 194
    happy, factors of, 60
    legal aspects of, 63
    premarital contracts and, 63
    premarital counseling, 62
    questions about, 62
    resistance of children and friends,
        60, 62
    second divorce, 63
    statistics of, 60, 193
Remarried Association, The, 63
Retirement, 129–134
    husband's, 130
    income, 130–134. *See also* Social Se-
        curity; SSI; Pensions; ERISA.
    planning for, 129
    reactions to, 129
    widowhood, 131
Returning to school, 67–79
    support groups, 76–77
    age-segregated education, 78–79
    financing of, 72–73
        alimony or maintenance money,
            72
        loans, scholarships, work-study,
            73–74
    intergenerational schools, 78
    obstacles to, 69–73
        family, 70
        fellow students, 70–71
        friends and relatives, 71
        lack of money, 71–72
    reasons for, 68
    reentry programs, 77–78
    statistics of, 68
RE Years, 8
Rheumatic disease. *See* Arthritis.
Rogers, Carl, 146
Roosevelt, Eleanor, 348
Roth, Dr. Jesse, 274
Roughage. *See* Fiber.

SAGE, 147–148
Salt. *See* Sodium.
"Sandwich generation," 83

Sarton, May, 10, 347
School, *See* Returning to school.
Scott-Maxwell, Flora, 10
Secondary hypertension, 242
Second honeymoon, 21
Second opinion, 181–182
Sedatives, 330, 332
SEICUS, 191
Seizure disorders, 174
Self-help groups, 153–154
Self-Help for the Hard of Hearing. *See* Shhh.
Senile Macular Degeneration, 303
Senility, 148–150. *See also* Alzheimer's disease.
  misdiagnosis, 148
    causes of, 148
  treatability, 148–149
Senior Actualization and Growth Exploration. *See* SAGE.
Sex Information and Education Council of the United States. *See* SEICUS.
Sex roles, 20
Sexism, 115–122
  in health care, 162–163
  and Social Security, 131–132
Sexual activity
  and hysterectomy, 182, 187
  and menopause, 176
Sexuality. *See also* Intimacy.
  abstinence, 192
  alcohol and, 188
  arthritis and, 188
  attitudes toward, 188–190
  changes with age, 17, 186–187
  drugs and, 188
  dysfunction, 189–190
  fatigue and, 188
  fear of, 194
  heart disease and, 188
  homosexuality, 190, 192–193
  hysterectomy and, 187
  Kinsey, 185, 186
  lesbianism, 190, 192–193
  mastectomy and, 188
  Masters and Johnson, 185, 187
  masturbation, 190–191
  myths about, 186
  orgasm, 185, 187, 189
    faked, 189
  values, 188–190
  younger men, 191–192
Sharing, 10
Shhh, 298
Shields, Laurie, 122
Silverstone, Barbara, 85

Singlehood, 10–11
  conscious choice of, 28
  holidays and, 30
  income and, 29
  lifelong, 28–31
  motivation for, 30
  older women, 29
  younger women, 29
Sjogren's Syndrome, 251
Skin, changes in, 306–307
  dry skin, 308
  moisturizers, use of, 308
  sun
    and cancer, 307
    and premature aging, 307
  wrinkles, 308–309
Smeal, Eleanor, 123
Smoking
  and cancer, 255, 266, 315
  and fibrocystic disease, 255
  and gum disease, 314, 315
  and heart disease, 239
  and hypertension, 242
Social Security, 44, 49, 50, 131–133
  changes in, 132–133
  sexism, 131–133
Society of Nutrition Educators, 222
Sodium fluoride, for osteoporosis, 234
Sodium, 211
  and heart disease, 211–212
  and hypertension, 211, 242
Sommers, Tish, 2, 110, 122, 126
Splaver, Sarah, 265
SSI, 133, 341
Steinem, Gloria, 191
Stress, 140–143
  and anger, 141
  and cancer, 271–273
  exercise and hobbies to reduce, 143
  and gum disease, 312
  Holmes Stress Scale, 141
  and hypertension, 242
  and menopause, 170–171
  positive and negative, 141
  relaxation techniques, 142–143
Stroke, 244–248
  atherosclerosis and, 245
  depression following, 246
  diabetes and, 246
  heart disease and, 246
  hemorrhagic, 245
  hypertension and, 246
  ischemic, 245
  paralysis, 245
  risk factors, 246
  smoking and, 246

  stress and, 246
  thrombotic, 245
  treatment, 247
    aspirin, 247
    CAT scan, 247
    rehabilitation, 247
    surgery, 247
  warnings, 245
Sunscreens, 307–308
Supplemental Income Security Program. *See* SSI.
Support groups, 10, 40, 76–77
Support, mutual, 10
Swanson, Donna, 193
Swanson, Gloria, 191

Tay-Sachs disease, 65
Taylor, Dr. Robert, 174
Therapy, 145–148
  alternative programs, 147–148
  different kinds, 145–146
  expense of, 147
    Medicare and Medicaid, 147
    private insurance, 147
  therapist, how to select, 145–147
Thrombophlebitis, 174
Thrombosis, 239
Tinnitus, 295
Total hip replacement, 233–234
Toxemia, in pregnancy, 65
Transactional analysis, 146
Transition, 8, 8–11, 15
Truth, Sojourner, 348
Tubal ligation, 179
Tupperware, 126

United States Public Health Service, 266
Urinary incontinence, 289–292
  causes, 290–291, 292
  fixed, 291
  incidence, 290
  temporary, 290
  treatment, 291–292
Uterine tumors. *See* Cancer.
Uterus
  cancer. *See* under Cancer.
  prolapsed, 180

Vaginal bleeding, 174
Valium, 330, 332
Veterans' benefits, 50
Vision, loss of, 300–306
  age and, 300–301

Vision, loss of (*cont.*)
  cataracts, 302–303
  color sensitivity, 301
  compensating for, 305–306
  degrees of, 301–302
  detached retina, 304
  diabetic retinopathy, 303
  farsightedness, 300
  glaucoma, 304–305
    cause, 304
    incidence, 304
    symptoms, 304
    testing for, 304–305
  laser treatment for, 303, 304
  senile macular degeneration (SMD), 303
  visual field, changes in, 301
Visitation rights
  for grandparents, 24–25
VISTA, 110, 128
Vitamins, 213–214, 215–217
  B-complex, 176
  controversy between doctors and nutritionists, 213
  D, and osteoporosis, 230, 232. *See also* Parathyroid hormone.
  E, 175–176
  RDAs, chart of, 215–217
  supplements, 213–214
  in treating symptoms of menopause, 175–176
Volunteer work, 75

Water, in diet, 212–213
  and osteoporosis, 232
WEAL, 154

Weight Watchers, 218
Wetzel, Janice, 348
White House Conference on Aging (1981), 88
White, Dr. James, 201
Widowhood
  and divorce, contrasted, 27
  emotional aspects of
    adjustment to, 42
    anger, 48
    bereavement centers, 53
    grief, 47–48, 53
    guilt, 48
    support from family, 51
  financial aspects of, 44–46, 49
    employer benefits, 50
    life insurance, 45, 50
    medical insurance, 45
    pensions, 134
    Social Security, 44, 49, 50
    Veterans' benefits, 44, 50
  friends and, 52
  funerals, 44
  health aspects of, 51
  preparation for, 43–46
  probate, 45
  and singlehood, 49
  statistics of, 42
Wife abuse, 92–94
  divorce, 94
  incidence of, 92
WIT program, 76
Women for Sobriety, 327
Women in Transition. *See* WIT program.
Women Who Care, 87–88

Women's Equity Action League. *See* WEAL.
Work
  Peace Corps, 128
  VISTA, 128
  applying for, 119
  assertiveness training, 122
  creating one's own job, 126
  discrimination, 115–122
  displaced homemakers, 122
  flex-time, 128
  interviewing, 122
  legal aspects of, 119–122
  in midlife, 116
  networking, 125
  "overqualification" for, 118
  part-time, 128–129
  reentry, 116, 122
  résumé, 122, 124, 125
  statistics of, 115–117
  traditional, nontraditional, and entrepreneur fields, 126–128
  training programs, access to, 117
  "transferrable skills" concept, 122
  unemployment, hidden, 117
  work sharing, 128

X-rays
  dental, 315
  in diagnosing osteoporosis, 229, 230
  in diagnosing rectal and colon cancer, 267

Zinc, 212
Zyderm, 309